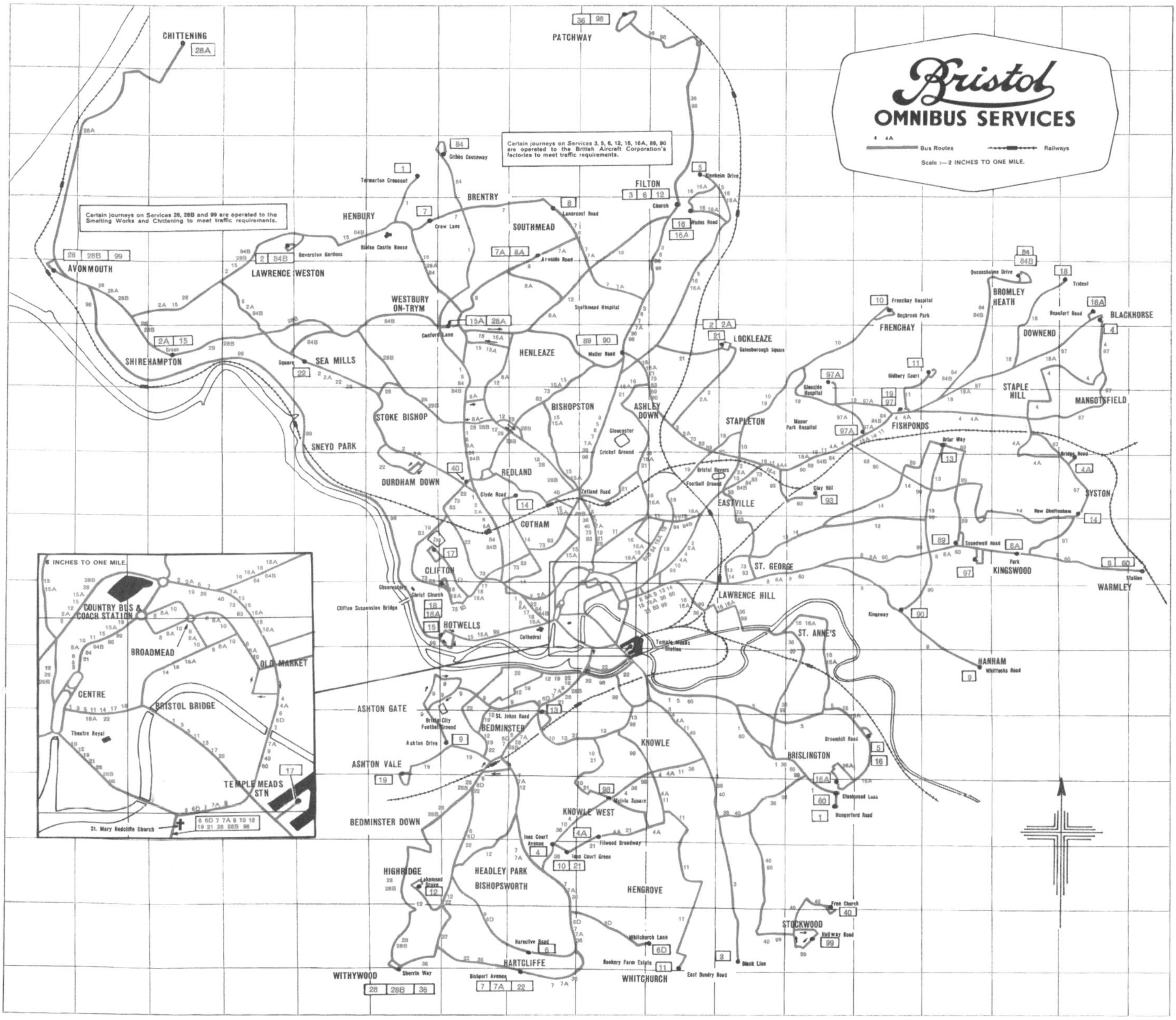
Bristol
OMNIBUS SERVICES
Bus Routes
Railways
Scale :— 2 INCHES TO ONE MILE.
Certain journeys on Services 3, 5, 6, 12, 18, 16A, 89, 90 are operated to the British Aircraft Corporation's factories to meet traffic requirements.
Certain journeys on Services 28, 28B and 99 are operated to the Smelting Works and Chittening to meet traffic requirements.
CHITTENING
PATCHWAY
FILTON
HENBURY
BRENTRY
SOUTHMEAD
AVONMOUTH
LAWRENCE WESTON
WESTBURY ON-TRYM
SHIREHAMPTON
SEA MILLS
HENLEAZE
LOCKLEAZE
FRENCHAY
BROMLEY HEATH
DOWNEND
BLACKHORSE
STAPLE HILL
MANGOTSFIELD
STOKE BISHOP
BISHOPSTON
ASHLEY DOWN
STAPLETON
FISHPONDS
SNEYD PARK
DURDHAM DOWN
REDLAND
COTHAM
EASTVILLE
SYSTON
CLIFTON
ST. GEORGE
KINGSWOOD
WARMLEY
HOTWELLS
LAWRENCE HILL
ST. ANNE'S
HANHAM
ASHTON GATE
BEDMINSTER
KNOWLE
BRISLINGTON
ASHTON VALE
KNOWLE WEST
BEDMINSTER DOWN
HIGHRIDGE
HEADLEY PARK
BISHOPSWORTH
HENGROVE
STOCKWOOD
WITHYWOOD
HARTCLIFFE
WHITCHURCH
2 INCHES TO ONE MILE.
COUNTRY BUS & COACH STATION
BROADMEAD
OLD MARKET
CENTRE
BRISTOL BRIDGE
Theatre Royal
TEMPLE MEADS STN
St. Mary Redcliffe Church

Bristol Omnibus Services
The Green Years

Open-top bus with open-top church. The Old Church of St Nicholas, Uphill, which dates back a thousand years and has lost much of its roof, stands on the hill above Bristol Lodekka FS 8577. The bus is destined for Sand Bay on service 100, in this July 1980 view. (*M.S.Curtis*)

Bristol Omnibus Services
The Green Years

Martin Curtis & Mike Walker

Millstream Books

About the Authors

Both authors were born and grew up in Bristol, and separately developed an interest in the Bristol Tramways/Bristol Omnibus company from an early age. They attended PSV Circle meetings from the late 1960s but became work colleagues at Bristol Omnibus during the 1970s, both in Bristol and later, at Weston-super-Mare.

Born in Clifton, Martin Curtis grew up in Brislington. He joined the Bristol Omnibus Company in 1972 in Bristol Division and later worked throughout the company's area. From 1978 he became Traffic Assistant, Weston-super-Mare but in 1982 left the company to become a Traffic Superintendent with Western National.

Following a period as District Manager with Southern National, he returned to the former Bristol Omnibus area to join the newly created Badgerline bus company and took over as Regional Director, Bath from 1987.

Later he became Managing Director of Bath Bus Company, formed with former colleagues in 1997, and currently works for Ensign Bus Company, based in Bath – and when required, in Sydney, Australia.

He has written a number of books covering aspects of Bristol Omnibus and Bristol Commercial Vehicles history and is a Chartered Fellow of the Institute of Logistics and Transport.

Mike Walker joined the bus industry at Southend-on-Sea straight from school, and after receiving an introduction to bus operations, returned to his home city to join Bristol Omnibus Company one year later. At the Bristol company he held a number of positions, culminating in that of Area Traffic Superintendent (South); when the company split in 1983 he became District Manager, Bristol Country Bus, before becoming Regional Director for Bristol with the management/staff buy-out of the Badgerline company in 1986.

In 1990 he was seconded first to consultants working on the Maltese Structure Plan, and then to the bus and coach industry trade association to work on a national scheme for government backed pro-bus initiatives: he went on to complete an M.Sc. and Ph.D. in Transport Studies at the University of Wales, Cardiff, before returning to the Trade Association as Regional Director for Wales, and, initially, the West Midlands.

He returned to live in Somerset in 1999 (in his old operating area) where for a while he was the Chairman of the East Somerset Railway: he is now retired, although takes an active interest in all aspects of the bus industry, and can occasionally be found behind the wheel, either of a bus or coach belonging to one of a number of local operators with whom he has a relationship, or one of the preserved vehicles of the Bristol Omnibus Vehicle Collection, of which he is a founder member.

The authors welcome any comment, information or personal recollections arising from the publication of this book: they may be contacted at info@thegreenyears.co.uk.

Front cover illustration: *Bristol Omnibus Services converge on Wedmore, Somerset, during May 1964, as they did in towns and villages throughout the company's territory. On the right, LS saloon 2843 (PHW 933) heads for Glastonbury from Weston-super-Mare on route 94, while sister vehicle 2844 (PHW 934) faces the opposite direction. In the distance, a new MW saloon waits at the service 37A bus stop, before continuing to Cheddar from Burnham-on-Sea. (Photobus)*

First published in 2007 by Millstream Books, 18 The Tyning, Bath BA2 6AL

Text set in 11 point Times New Roman

Printed in Great Britain by The Amadeus Press, Cleckheaton

© Martin Curtis & Mike Walker 2007

ISBN 978 0 948975 80 6

British Library Cataloguing-in-Publication Data: a catalogue record for this book is available from the British Library

All rights reserved. No part of this publication may be reproduced, stored in a retrieval system, or transmitted in any form or by any means electronic, mechanical, photocopying, recording or otherwise, without the prior permission of Millstream Books

Preface

Bristol Omnibus Services – the Green Years is not intended to be a complete history of the company from the end of the Second World War until the advent of deregulation and privatisation in 1986 and 1987; certainly green buses started to appear in the fleet before hostilities had ended and were still to be seen as the 1980s drew to a close. In addition, although a large variety of sources have been consulted in the preparation of this volume, we readily recognise that for the preparation of a complete history much more research would have been necessary, and although we believe that this could well have revealed an amount of additional, interesting information and would have enlarged this book considerably, the basis of the story of one of the largest bus companies in Great Britain would have remained substantially as revealed in this volume.

The history of the Bristol company is initially charted through the intake of their public service vehicles, and for that we are grateful for the very full and detailed records kept by the PSV Circle and The Omnibus Society in their published histories of the company's vehicles. This structure was chosen since not only are the variety and type of buses used by an organisation the backbone of their *raison d'être*, they reflect the trends in the marketplace that the company serves. Double-deckers replaced single-deckers so as to accommodate the postwar boom in traffic, with that pattern being reversed some 25 years later as passenger numbers declined, principally because of the growth in the ownership of private transport, and this decline, coupled with employment trends, necessitated the removal of conductors; single-deck vehicles were thought to be best suited to being operated by only one person. The trend was to reverse again some 15 years later as the company, along with many others, sought to re-plan its services to cater for as many of its existing passengers as possible with the minimum of resources, and again, double-deckers found favour.

Deliveries of coaches and semi-coaches again reflected the company's desire to serve as much of the marketplace as they felt they could profitably do, although even with its Bristol Greyhound coaching arm, the express, excursion and tours market was only ever considered to be a small element of their overall operation.

It was often suggested that many of the staff treated the company as a second family, and we have sought out a variety of former employees so that they can add their own interpretations to important events in the company's history. In addition they have recorded their personal memories of sad or amusing incidents that were part of the everyday life of working on the road, in the workshops or in the offices of such a major bus operation. In addition much use has been made of *Bristol Omnibus Magazine*, the wonderful staff magazine produced by the company from just after the war.

The Bristol company covered a large geographical area and we have tried to reflect this spread in the book. However, both the nature of the information available to us and the authors' own experiences have led to the final result concentrating on certain areas of the operation, and for this we apologise. We hope this does not detract from portraying the character of the company's operations as a whole.

Setting the Scene

On 9th August 1875, the Bristol Tramways Company commenced operations with the inauguration of its first horse-tram service from Upper Mauldlin Street to the bottom of Blackboy Hill. This was a significant landmark in Bristol's social and transport history.

With a fare of 2d, many Bristolians discovered for the first time that they had the means to travel other than by walking. What was more, individuals from different social classes could rub shoulders, riding side-by-side in a situation that had not occurred before. This represented a change that would ensure the world would never be quite the same again for the people of Bristol.

Some 35 years earlier, another great transport revolution had taken place with the introduction of railways across the country. For Bristol, this initially meant Brunel's broad-gauge line of the Great Western Railway opened from the newly built Temple Meads station in 1840 with connections all the way to London the following year. Journeying by horseback was previously the fastest method of transport, but this was not available to everyone, so only the most wealthy could travel far. Most ordinary folk journeyed no further than they could walk, and usually spent their entire lives in one location. That was, unless they travelled by sea. And Bristol was an important and thriving port, which not only created a centre for trade but allowed a few to journey far away, sailing for months or even years over established trade routes or newly discovered seas.

At home, horse-drawn carriages and carts were of course also in use, as were some coach services, but roads were poor and progress extremely slow. Apart from the highways, canals offered a means of transporting goods around the country, while many smaller vessels carried cargo on sailings around the British coast.

Railways changed everything. Not only did they provide a new means of transport, but additionally introduced the phenomenon of viewing a means of propulsion which was faster than a horse – a compelling spectacle in its own right. Various classes of accommodation were available on the trains, but railway travel was still beyond the means of many.

In many respects, the tramways repeated the railway revolution three and a half decades later, but on a smaller scale. They allowed travel more extensively within cities and towns which had previously been quite difficult, and most importantly, could be afforded by almost everyone.

In Bristol, the tramcars glided over their lines which were secured among stone sets, while the remainder of the city's roads were frequently not properly surfaced, dusty in summer and muddy in winter. The tram network grew rapidly with new lines opening across the city linking several of its suburbs. Within six years, 70 cars were in operation while horse buses had also been introduced, initially to act as feeders to the tramway network, while experiments with steam-hauled trams were also conducted, with limited success.

In 1887 the company was re-titled Bristol Tramways & Carriage Company Ltd when the tramways company was merged with the Bristol Cab Company Ltd, which

The Bristol Tramways Company commenced operations using horse power. Initially horse-drawn tram services were introduced but later horse buses appeared, often providing feeder services to the trams. Here an early bus prepares to link the Westbury, Henleaze and Redland areas of Bristol with the 'city cars'. (*M.J.Tozer collection*)

itself had been formed the previous year to consolidate many of the city's cab and carriage interests.

Fifteen million passenger journeys were being made annually by 1895, during which year the BT&CC pioneered the use of electric traction in Britain with the introduction of electric trams from Old Market to Kingswood. Fixed stopping places for trams were introduced at the same time, and conversion of the whole tramway system to electricity was complete five years later. The service to Clifton however remained horse-bus operated, as a result of opposition to trams from residents of this wealthy and fashionable area of the city. Horse-buses were considered superior as they more closely resembled private carriages! The company's total passenger numbers per annum had more than doubled to over 36 million during this five-year period.

Electrification of the tramway network clearly demonstrated that the company was at the forefront of modern thinking, and that process was to continue with the introduction of motor buses from 1906. A batch of Thornycroft vehicles was introduced, initially running on the Clifton bus route from January that year, followed by FIATs and Berliets. These vehicles allowed the company to inaugurate more new services into Bristol's countryside. The Bristol company was not satisfied with the performance of these vehicles, however, and famously brought legal action against FIAT for supplying defective equipment which did not meet the required specifications.

Believing it could substantially improve on these models, the company set about designing and building its own motor buses, the first of which was introduced on the Clifton route during May 1908. In doing so, the BT&CC had introduced a new manufacturer of motor buses which became a prominent vehicle producer for the following 75 years: 'Bristol' buses and coaches becoming familiar throughout the United Kingdom and abroad.

The company was committed to motor road vehicles, and motor taxi cabs, predominantly of French manufacture, were additionally introduced from 1908. This was a further period of rapid expansion with more motor vehicles being added to the fleet. In addition to the buses and cabs, the company introduced motor lorries, vans, and a variety of private touring cars and motor charabancs, all of which were available for hire.

Motor coach tours to locations further from Bristol became established while the company's territory expanded with the opening of new branches at Bath (1909), Weston-super-Mare (1910), Cheltenham (1912) and Gloucester (1913). In addition, the Clifton Rocks Railway was acquired in 1912, the BT&CC at this time becoming the largest passenger transport operator outside London.

The telephone system was widely promoted by the Tramways company which was a further indication of its modern approach. The company's chairman, Sir George White, Bt., was in no small way responsible for these advances and had simultaneously established a new aircraft building business which rapidly developed into a huge organisation to the north of the city at Filton, and later beyond into Patchway. Here 'Bristol' aeroplanes were built, many of them carrying the 'Bristol' scroll emblem, an insignia which was shared with the Tramways company for use in association with its bus and tram services, and bus manufacturing.

The company inaugurated its first motor bus service between the Victoria Rooms and the Clifton Suspension Bridge on Wednesday 17th January 1906, using Thornycroft vehicles, one of which stands here ready for the road. (*Authors' collection*)

Dissatisfied with the products of other manufacturers, Bristol Tramways started to build motor buses of its own design from 1908. With seats for 16 passengers, AE 770 was the first ever 'Bristol' which was introduced to the Clifton route on 12th May of that year. (*Bristol Vintage Bus Group*)

This progress was interrupted following the outbreak of war in 1914, many of the company's staff leaving for military service – some never to return. Bus building at the Brislington works was suspended the following year in order to concentrate on the production of aeroplane parts to assist output from Filton, a situation that was reversed after the Great War had ended, with the Filton aircraft factories temporarily building bus bodies following a reduced requirement for new aeroplanes.

Further new 'Bristol' bus chassis of improved design were developed in the 1920s at the company's Brislington Motor Constructional Works with bodywork usually constructed at the nearby Body Building Works at the Brislington Tram depot. Many of the chassis were actually bodied as goods vehicles, and increasingly production for operators other than Bristol Tramways itself was being undertaken.

Operationally, the company continued to expand its network of bus services and in 1921 a new branch opened at Swindon, the Wiltshire town established largely around the works of the Great Western Railway. At the end of the following year, yet another BT&CC branch was opened in Wells, Somerset.

The opening of each branch saw an extension of the bus service network, allowing new travel opportunities throughout the company's operating territory, which had grown to cover a far greater area than the city, which the title 'Bristol Tramways & Carriage Company' implied. As the fleet expanded, so too did the number of staff employed, a position of employment with the company commanding considerable respect and prestige.

Queen's Road, Clifton in March 1914 with electric tramcars, Bristol-built motor buses, taxis and vans. All belong to the Bristol Tramways & Carriage Company which was growing at an impressive rate.
(*M.J.Tozer collection*)

With bus building firmly established at Brislington, the company's Motor Constructional Works produced this A-type in 1925 (registered HU 4325) with seats for 32-passengers. (*Bristol Tramways*)

Company livery throughout this period was blue, usually relieved with white, and often with red wheels (the company's motor cabs actually advertised themselves as 'Blue Taxis'). Furthermore, the use of red, white and blue, the colours of the Union Jack, was encouraged and viewed as patriotic, reflecting a widespread pride in Britain and its Empire of a kind that may not be so readily understood today. Bristol's blue electric tramcars are still fondly remembered by many, with trams, buses, cabs and carriages all finished in this livery (although bottle green could be found on some motor cars and charabancs used for private touring, while motor charabancs were later painted light blue/grey).

The original horse trams of 1875 were painted in a rich lake colour (relieved by white). We know this from contemporary newspaper accounts which described such things in great detail, as photographs had still to make their appearance in newsprint. 25 years later, with electric trams firmly established on the Bristol network, livery was dark blue relieved with white, and these were to remain Bristol's tram colours throughout their existence. Exactly when the change to blue occurred is not certain but R. Edghill Coles, writing to the Bristol *Evening Post* during November 1940, recalled the company's early activities and described horse tram livery as walnut, crimson or blue, depending on the route being worked, while Clifton horse buses were red.

Nevertheless, blue and white was certainly still carried on buses and trams throughout the 1930s (the taxi and carriage side of the business having ceased by this time), although latterly the red areas were replaced by more blue, or black.

By the early 1930s the Bristol Tramways company had become a member of the Tilling group, in which it was to play a major role. This came about as a result of the Great Western Railway acquiring a controlling interest in the Bristol company in 1929, an interest which it transferred three years later to the Western National Omnibus Company Ltd.

During this period, railway companies were regularly establishing an interest in regional bus companies but the Great Western had some difficulty in holding Bristol Tramways & Carriage Co Ltd shares because of a potential conflict between railway and tramway activities. By transferring this interest to Western National, in which the railway also had an interest, these problems were overcome, but this arrangement was not completed until early 1932. By then, Tilling had gained a controlling interest in Western National, which in turn led to BT&CC becoming a Tilling associated company.

Western National was a neighbouring bus operator with services throughout the south-west, and to the north and east of Bristol's own main operating territory. Perhaps more significantly, Bristol's chassis building department went on to form a lasting and unique partnership with another member of the Tilling group, Eastern Coach Works of Lowestoft. Together, they not only became principal vehicle suppliers to the whole Tilling organisation, but also to many other operators, both at home and abroad.

The 1930s was also a period when much tighter regulation of bus services commenced, overseen by Area Traffic Commissioners, under the provisions of the Road Traffic Act 1930. This form of licensing control over bus and coach services, staff and fares remained little changed for the next half-century.

An activity which complemented local 'stage-carriage' bus services was long-distance express services, the

The Tramways Centre in 1936, with brand new G-type double-decker (DAE 372) nearest the camera. The company's famous offices supporting the Tramways clock stand to the right, while left, electric trams pull around the triangular island which formed the hub of the system. (*Authors' collection*)

first of which ever operated in Britain was introduced between Bristol and London in February 1925 by another Bristol company, Greyhound Motors Ltd.

Bristol Tramways gained a controlling interest in Greyhound during 1928, and Greyhound Motors Ltd was later wound up in 1936. However, the Greyhound identity was not lost, as it was retained by the BT&CC for the company's coaching activities. By this time a growing network of express services, provided by a range of companies, had been established with several operators in the Midlands and south-west (including Greyhound) having formed the Associated Motorways pool in 1934, which involved the co-ordination of many express services.

Expansion elsewhere during 1936 resulted in Bristol's take-over of Gloucester city services, which were initially operated on lease from Gloucester Corporation. In the city of Bath (Bristol's nearest neighbour), BT&CC acquired a controlling interest in the Bath Electric Tramways Ltd and its bus operating subsidiary, Bath Tramways Motor Company Ltd, followed by the rapid replacement of Bath's trams with motor buses. A similar situation occurred in Weston-super-Mare, where control was taken of the town's trams, to be replaced by more buses from April 1937.

Abandonment of Bristol's electric trams in favour of buses also began in 1938 but here a change of ownership of a different kind had taken place. Under the provisions of the Tramways Act 1870, Bristol Corporation had the power to purchase the Bristol tramway undertaking in 1915 or any seventh year thereafter. This option was never exercised, but it led instead to the Bristol Transport Act 1937. This resulted in the establishment of a Joint Transport Committee, comprising officials from both the Bristol Tramways company and the Corporation of the City and County of Bristol, with control of Bristol's city buses and trams shared equally between the two, and any profit or loss divided between them.

Effectively, this arrangement resulted in joint ownership of the city services with day-to-day operational control nevertheless remaining with BT&CC. Moreover, city services were protected as other routes running into Bristol from the country, which remained entirely in company hands, were required to charge higher fares.

A new fleetname of 'Bristol Transport' was considered for buses working under this arrangement, but not adopted. However, 1937 was also the year in which a new fleet numbering system was introduced across the Bristol Tramways fleet, and those buses belonging to Bristol Joint Services (BJS) were to be identified by a 'C' prefix to their fleet number.

In 1939 Britain again found itself at war with Germany. As in the Great War of 1914-18, many of the Bristol Tramways company staff were among those called-up for active service, although others were required to remain. Over 4,000 female conductors were recruited and a few women trained as drivers. The role of bus driver became a reserved occupation and took on a new importance in civilian life with the requirement to transport thousands of workers to and

With the establishment of Bristol Joint Services in 1937, G-type double-decker 3080 (EAE 289) was experimentally given a 'Bristol Transport' fleetname in addition to the city arms, while the small legal address carried the BJS title with BT&CC shown as 'managers'. None of this was adopted, however, as city buses were in future distinguished by a simple 'C' prefix to their fleet numbers. (*Bristol Vintage Bus Group*)

from munitions factories and for other essential war work. In Bristol's case, the aeroplane factories were again to play a vital role and the company's bus building works at Brislington assisted once more with aircraft production, while bus manufacture all but ceased.

Among other projects, Bristol's Motor Constructional Works also manufactured gas producer trailers, to be towed by vehicles in an effort to conserve precious petrol and oil supplies. The operation of gas producers was not without its problems; nevertheless, some 2,500 were built for use by over 90 bus and haulage companies, including London Transport (630), Pickfords (366), Scottish Motor Traction (19), South Wales Transport (10), Southern Vectis (3), Southern and Western National (90). Bristol Tramways itself placed 100 into service, with 11 more going to Bath Tramways.

While much attention focused on hostilities overseas, Bristolians rapidly discovered that (in contrast to World War I) the Second World War would come to them with devastating consequences. Intensive air raids started in 1940, Bristol being one of the most 'blitzed' cities outside London. Drivers had to negotiate debris and craters, often in blackout conditions, and one street after another was often closed as a result of bomb damage.

Assistance with troop movements, often at short notice and sometimes requiring over 100 vehicles, took place on several occasions. Over 20 single-deckers were converted to ambulances – an operation undertaken overnight! And the arrival of the American Army placed further pressures on the company's resources.

Civilian transport requirements also increased, not least with the arrival of many evacuees throughout the

The struggle to maintain services during the Second World War became most difficult during the period when the company's operating area suffered many air raid attacks. This is Lawrence Hill depot in 1941, following a direct hit during 'the blitz'. Despite all the problems, the services kept running. (*Bristol Vintage Bus Group*)

With so many of its male employees away in the armed forces, women were called upon more than ever to help keep Bristol's buses on the road. This posed photograph appears to emphasise the point, with a supervised crew change involving all female staff. (*Western Daily Press & Bristol Mirror*)

company's area. Industry also expanded, not just in Bristol but also in Gloucester, Cheltenham, Swindon, Weston-super-Mare and Bath. The latter itself suffering from several serious air attacks.

Indeed, it was the fierce bombing raids which continued over a period of several years that caused the greatest losses of passengers and staff, in addition to vehicles and buildings. Brislington depot was damaged in late 1940, followed in January 1941 by the destruction of Bedminster tram depot, and shortly afterwards by the loss or serious damage of 157 buses when the main depot at Lawrence Hill was hit. The Good Friday raid of April 1941 was particularly severe and caused the destruction of St Philip's Bridge which carried the main power supply to the remaining Bristol tramcars and brought them to a standstill. The trams never ran again, being substituted by buses the following morning.

Finally, a terrible incident occurred on 28th August 1942 at Broad Weir, when a lone raider dropped a single bomb in daylight, without warning. Three loaded double-deckers instantly burst into flames killing over 40 passengers and seriously injuring many more; seven company personnel were among the casualties.

The condition of the fleet in these circumstances was understandably reaching breaking point. Many hurried repairs were made to keep vehicles operating, a few extra buses being received on loan from London, Brighton, Devon, Essex and elsewhere in an attempt to ease the situation.

The blue livery had largely been lost as many vehicles appeared in wartime grey or khaki, and of those still in blue, the white roofs and in many cases white window surrounds had been painted in a dull colour to minimise identification from the air. White mudguards and edging was added however as part of the blackout procedures, to help pedestrians and waiting passengers.

The BT&CC title on vehicles had gradually been reduced in size so that it generally formed little more than that required to show legal ownership. Even the trams had the display of their company lettering drastically reduced in most cases, by the time of their withdrawal; a much smaller version replaced what had previously extended over the length of their rocker panels.

Seemingly always present, however, was the Bristol coat of arms. On trams and buses, on blue paint and grey, regardless of the poor or deteriorating condition during the war years, there it was proudly carried on the vehicle sides. This was unique among company-owned bus fleets which generally preferred to display geographical fleetnames. The Bristol fleet took the Bristol crest to locations many miles from the city itself.

Various versions of the Bristol arms were carried over the years, the company actually developing its own style since this avoided paying a royalty to the corporation. Indeed, the company's version became so well established that the Bristol fire brigade adopted the same design!

By 1944, a full year before the end of hostilities, which brought peace first to Europe, and then Japan, it was clear that the war was turning in favour of Britain and her Allies.

The local press carried a series of advertisements from the Tilling group, offering a reminder of the important role the 'Bristol Omnibus Services' were providing. Rationing was of course in force and would remain for some time after the war. Almost everyone who travelled locally did so by bus, and there are reports about ever increasing demands on the services, long queues and at times insufficient staff numbers to crew the vehicles available. Nevertheless, on Bristol city routes alone, 1,200,000 more passengers were carried during July 1944 compared with the same month in 1939, a situation even more significant when compared to mileage operated, down by 350,000 miles each month.

Two months earlier, in May 1944, just weeks before D-Day and the Normandy landings, the Bristol *Evening Post* reported with great anticipation that Bristol Tramways' buses had been spotted on the routes to Westbury, Eastville and Bath wearing green and cream livery. There was considerable speculation as to whether these colours were to be adopted by the whole fleet. The change was likened to springtime, and was warmly welcomed as a contrast to the drab appearance of the rest of the fleet.

In fact the colours were to become known as Tilling green and cream, and become standard for a number of the bus fleets within the Tilling Group of companies.

Meanwhile, the local services continued to struggle to cope with demand. Long queues, lengthy waiting times and full buses passing by bus stops were common but huge movements of passengers were nevertheless being achieved day after day. The public was soon being urged to assist by not abusing staff when buses were full to capacity (including large numbers of standing passengers) and could not accept more on board.

The long-awaited arrival of peace in May 1945 was immediately followed by a flood of cars on Bristol's roads. By the summer, motor coach tours had been re-instated to such locations as Wells, Cheddar, Burnham-on-Sea, Portishead, Clevedon and, of course, Weston-super-Mare. The bus fleet was rapidly converted to diesel, rather than petrol, and the *Evening Post* reported that the company's Motor Constructional Works at Brislington was gradually returning to bus chassis production, the supply of which remained under Government control, with many buses expected to be exported.

The Regional Transport Commissioner had approved an expansion of bus services but there remained a shortage of labour, with the return of many employees from the Services still awaited, while high levels of staff sickness were also being recorded.

Despite continuing Ministry of Supply controls, delivery resumed to Bristol Tramway's own operating department of brand new K-type double-deckers of its own design. From 1945, these too began to appear in the new Tilling green and cream livery.

And so the Bristol Tramways & Carriage Co Ltd entered its green years. It marked a new beginning and was synonymous with the air of great optimism that existed after the Second World War, even though a period of austerity was to remain in Britain a few years more. The Bristol Tramways company, and the passenger transport industry in general, was about to enter the busiest period of its entire history.

Although Bristol's trams remained on a few routes until 1941, they disappeared from the Centre itself during July 1939. Shorly after the change-over, buses can be seen driving over the rails on every service, still proudly wearing their blue and white livery. (*Western Daily Press & Bristol Mirror*)

1. The Postwar Years Of Reconstruction

1945

Having entered the Second World War as a blue company, Bristol Tramways emerged as a green one. 1945 saw the first deliveries of new green buses, following the green repaints that had started the previous year. Lifelong enthusiast and transport historian Peter Davey recalls that double-deckers C3134 and C3144 were the first two to emerge in green livery.

The new livery also made a lasting impression on Tony Peacey, aged three or four at the time, who remembers seeing a green bus (among the dull blue or grey ones) for the first time while with his parents in Old Market Street. They later caught up with the bus just so they could take a ride. Such was the significance of the new colours, as buses played an important role in almost everybody's daily lives.

Local press reports and readers' letters of the period reveal the enormous strain being placed on the service, with a shortage of staff and of suitable spare parts contributing to the constant struggle to reduce delays for the large numbers of waiting passengers. Suggestions and even complaints regularly appeared. In early 1945, with newspaper reports of the war continuing to rage over much of Europe (and elsewhere), a turn of the page would reveal two ladies complaining about how dreadful it was to queue outside a fish shop, not only due to the length of the queue itself, but also because 'the pavement was wet; and there was a strong smell of fish'!

Reports of long waits were however commonplace, with bus after bus loading to capacity to clear the waiting passengers from stops.

Following a period when new bus deliveries had been reduced to little more than a trickle, 1945 saw an upturn in the arrival of brand new vehicles. Thirty-two double-deckers were delivered that year, 12 being 13'6" high 'lowbridge' buses for country services while a further twenty were 14'6" tall 'highbridge' ones for Bristol city services. With the exception of one Gardner 5LW-engined example, all were 6-cylinder AEC-engined, Bristol K-types with utility style of bodywork either by Strachan (the lowbridge ones), Park Royal or Duple. Ten of these new buses were recorded as painted in 'standard Tilling green' with cream bands below the upper and lower deck windows, with a further note that this green livery was 'to be applied to all subsequent deliveries' marking the start of a new era for the Tramways, or 'Bristol Blues' as the company's buses had previously been widely known.

At the meeting of the Bristol Joint Services Committee on 13th September 1945 the policy with regards to the colour of the vehicles was mentioned and the committee 'agreed the adoption of the new green and cream colour scheme now coming into general use'.

In addition to the new vehicles, five double-deckers were acquired secondhand from Plymouth Corporation – an AEC Regent and four Leyland TD2s – along with

Midday in Old Market Street on Saturday 9th February 1946 and Bristol is beginning to recover from the effects of the Second World War. Buses represent an important means of transport for the majority of the population but of the six double-deckers in this picture, most are still in drab grey or khaki wartime livery. Only one bus (with two relief bands) is painted Tilling green. (*Bristol Tramways*)

(*left*) Initially the green livery for double-deckers was relieved by two cream bands, one below each line of windows. C3365 (JAE 257) was among the first vehicles delivered new in this livery, during 1945, and is seen at the Centre where there is no shortage of passengers. It is an AEC-powered Bristol K6A of the wartime W2 sanction, and carries Duple bodywork to austere Ministry of Supply specification. (*Bristol Vintage Bus Group*)

(*right*) Bristol Tramways made extensive photographic records of its activities. C3317 (GHT 135) a K5G with the company's own BBW bodywork, was among the vehicles used to replace the last Bristol trams during 1941. In this view, taken on 25th March 1946 in Haberfield Street (moving up to Careys Lane), it is wearing new green paintwork, while of the single-deckers behind, one continues to wear plain grey. (*Bristol Tramways*)

seven from Exeter – three AEC Regents and four Bristol GO5Gs (although in the event one of the AECs was not used). Of the Bristols, AHW 953 had originally been a Bristol demonstrator, passing to Exeter in 1935.

Plymouth Corporation, Brighton Hove & District and the Eastern National Omnibus Company each loaned a number of double-deck Leylands or Bristols to the company. Eastern National provided one bus which was particularly significant, since it was the second of two prototypes of the proposed Tilling Group postwar double-decker (on Bristol K chassis), both of which came to the company as visiting demonstrators.

Bristol's own chassis type designations were based on an alphabetical sequence (having reached K for double-deck chassis, and L for single-deckers) followed by a number and letter to denote engine cylinders and make. A *Bristol K5G* model was therefore a double-decker with *5-cylinder Gardner* engine.

1945 also saw the occupation of two major new depots in Bristol, at Muller Road and Winterstoke Road. The former had been used during the war for military production and the latter had been briefly occupied before hostilities until being given up for the war effort. It was reported to the June 1945 Joint Services Committee meeting that the Muller Road depot 'had now been re-instated to normal conditions'.

After the war, many vehicles in the fleet needed considerable or extensive rebuilding; new wartime deliveries had fluctuated wildly, totalling 153 in 1939, 15 in 1940, 78 in 1941, 42 in 1942, 35 in 1943 and only two in 1944. New vehicles were scarce and these deliveries, often of unfamiliar chassis and body makes, were allocated between operators on the basis of most need. They were supplemented by a variety of secondhand purchases and loans, often of equally unfamiliar vehicle makes and colours; and by extending the lives of many other buses in the fleet that in other circumstances would have gone to the scrapyard. In addition to the extra traffic generated by the various factories and military establishments around the company's operating area, a number of vehicles had been destroyed by enemy action.

By the time that peace came, therefore, the company – like many others around the country – had a mountain to climb in terms of achieving a reliable and modern fleet. Indeed, at the end of the war some 400 buses, over one third of the fleet, were ready for scrapping.

As the Motor Constructional Works returned fully to civilian production the intake of new vehicles increased sharply, allowing the scrapping or rebuilding of those buses in the worst condition and the return of hired vehicles, further standardising the fleet. It was during these early postwar years that the company embarked upon the series of chassis and body swaps that became its trademark. Many older chassis were re-bodied in the first instance so as to dispose of their substandard or rotten bodies, their new bodies subsequently being transferred to other, newer chassis when, in turn, the bodies of those vehicles were deemed to need replacing! Indeed, in co-author Mike Walker's own experience on a journey to school, the green leathercloth on which had been printed the bus fleet number had come unstuck from the rear body wall at the foot of the stairs, to reveal a much older number which seemed to bear no relation to the vehicle on which he was travelling!

Such rebuilding expertise also resulted in the proverbial case of the 'new hammer'. Twelve new L5G chassis were fitted with lengthened Ministry of Supply bodies built by Bence of Longwell Green, previously carried by Bristol B-types from the 1920s and 1930s: the L5G's construction counted as 'rebuilding' despite the fact that the chassis were new, so they retained their B-type chassis numbers (albeit suffixed 'L') and registration numbers. The ruse was completed when, between 1954 and 1957, the old bodies were removed and replaced with secondhand BBW or ECW bodies taken from withdrawn pre-war, re-bodied, J-types, resulting in a batch of 1949 Bristol Ls with standard 1949 era bodies but displaying registration numbers from much earlier B-types. The registration and chassis numbers were the only parts of the B-types left! Bristol chassis were built in 'blocks', known as sanctions, which varied in number but typically ranged from around 50 to 200.

Aside from the buses, other changes were also taking place on the roads in and around Bristol. On 1st June 1945 the Bristol *Evening Post* reported a 'Flood of cars on roads' as basic rations became available. Hundreds of applications for driving licences were made as cars, unused through the war years, returned to the streets. Many were soon seen at the roadside after being involved in accidents or having suffered mechanical failure! It was also suggested that additional capacity thus became available on buses, although the company's passenger numbers had still to reach their peak.

1946

Vehicle deliveries in 1946 comprised 47 Bristol K types (both K6A and K5G), including the first non-wartime sanction (the 62nd), and ten Bristol L types (two AEC-engined and eight Gardner 5s). Twenty-one of the double-deckers were for Bristol Joint Services (BJS), including five lowbridge ones, and most were fitted from new with the lower bonnet line and low PV2-type radiator that were to become the postwar standard. The livery of double-deckers was also altered involving the replacement of the lowest cream band with one in the more familiar position at the waist, above the lower deck windows. Increasingly, many of the buses were now finished to the new Tilling standard design. Six of the K6As were for the Bath Tramways Motor Company, taking up the fleet numbers 3830-3835 in the Bath series, to replace the London Transport ST buses that had been on loan since 1942.

The winter of 1946/1947 was not good for the Tramways Company. The whole country suffered from very severe weather conditions and much of the company's operating area was adversely affected, resulting in a loss of service coverage and reduced revenue, as well as damage to vehicles and the need to rescue buses from the deep snow drifts.

Fred Spencer, who started work as a conductor at Weston-super-Mare depot in 1946 and retired as a member of the Badgerline management team after 47 years service, recalls that in many places the snow was 'piled high'. On the route between Weston-super-Mare and Wells through the Mendip countryside, the farmers piled the snow on each side of the road and 'it was like going through a tunnel without a roof'.

On a lighter note, Fred recalls that whilst operating the Weston-super-Mare to Wells route as a conductor he had been

> chatting up the girls. That went all right until the three I'd been chatting up, one in Draycott, one from Rodney Stoke and one from Westbury, all got on the bus at the same time! You can tell – I didn't know what to do with myself!

There was a more serious side to life on the road however. On one occasion Fred was operating past Weston airport at Locking when a plane coming in to land hit the top of a double-decker on the road at the end of the runway, killing quite a few of the R.A.F. men on board.

> I asked to come off that route for the rest of the evening, and I was told that I would be better off going past the accident, and I went past five more times that night.

(*above*) Looking over the Centre from the CWS Building in April 1946. Almost half of the buses in this view are wearing green livery. The Centre itself has been extended, work on covering more of the river and docks area having started shortly before the outbreak of war. What would become the Centre Gardens is being used as a car park – an indication of growing car ownership. (*Bristol Tramways*)

(*right*) It was Bristol Tramways' practice to photograph locations such as the Centre at regular specified intervals on a given day, in order to assess passenger and bus movements. This picture, one of a series of many, was taken at 5.20pm on 2nd July 1946, at the side of the company's offices looking towards Colston Street. BBW-bodied double-deckers, and J-type saloon 2369 are in view, but what is of particular significance is the queues of waiting passengers. Whilst the company did its best to meet demand, this also reflects how almost everyone in society at the time relied on buses as their main means of transport.
(*M.J. Tozer collection*)

The 'BTCCL' lapel badge still worn by bus operating staff during the 1940s.

1947

The new year saw the delivery of 58 double-deckers and 32 single-deckers. Two of the double-deckers (lowbridge K-types L3900 and L3901) were for the Bath Electric Tramways fleet, and 24 were for Bristol Joint Services, including the first 15 of a batch of 50 Leyland PD1 'Titans' allocated to the Bristol company out of a Tilling Group order for 150 of such chassis. The bodywork order for Bristol's Titans was divided between Eastern Coach Works of Lowestoft; the company's own BBW workshops at Brislington; and Longwell Green Coachworks (to BBW designs). This body-building factory was based in the area of Longwell Green just outside Bristol, in south Gloucestershire and was all that remained of the Bence family business, whose bus operating arm had been absorbed by the Tramways before the war.

Of the single-deckers received, two were for the Gloucester City fleet whilst 20 were also for BJS, being 2-doorway Ls, a combination of chassis and body layout unique to the Bristol company.

For an operator that was trying to build up a standardised fleet of their own manufacture, the introduction of new Leylands seems somewhat odd and warrants further examination: secondhand Titans had previously been purchased to reduce the postwar vehicle shortage – and it was this very shortage that caused this exception to the pattern of vehicle orders. The slow rate at which the Motor Constructional Works was able to resume chassis production after the war and the continuing increase in the number of passengers offering themselves for travel led Tilling man Sir Frederick Heaton, the then chairman of the joint corporation/company BJS Committee, to suggest that, to overcome these difficulties, the Committee might like to consider placing orders for rolling stock with other manufacturers. Minutes for the meeting on 12th September 1946 record his words thus:

> If additional buses could be obtained in 1947 to supplement those on order it would place the Transport Committee in a more satisfactory position to meet transport demands. It was anticipated that the production of 'Bristol' buses would be stepped up in 1948 sufficiently to allow the Committee's requirements to be adequately supplied, so that it would be unnecessary to consider other sources of supply after 1947. It was generally recognised that 'Bristol' buses were superior to other makes, but delivery difficulties pointed to the necessity for breaking away temporarily from the policy of a standard 'Bristol' fleet.

And so it was agreed that 50 double-deck buses be purchased from 'leading manufacturers', if available.

At the next meeting on 6th December of that year Sir Frederick Heaton was able to report that 'the Company had been able to place an order for 50 Leyland chassis at £1500 each'. The chairman thought it might be appropriate to inform the Committee:

> that the 'Bristol' Companies' chassis was regarded by transport managers generally as being the best in the country. It was a very robust and soundly constructed vehicle and had the advantage of costing less than any other make of chassis. The bodies, which were constructed by the Eastern Coachworks Company, also cost less than those f other manufacturers and were of better construction. The complete vehicle cost about £300 less than would have to be paid elsewhere and was a considerably better product.

This was an extremely interesting move by the Tilling chairman of the BJS Committee. A shortage of new buses there most certainly was, and Bristol's own models were very highly regarded. However, in the bus industry generally, the Leyland Titan, together with the AEC Regent, were often regarded as the leading double-

(*left*) The decision to buy a batch of 50 Leyland PD1 double-deckers not only boosted Bristol's intake of new vehicles but also created an opportunity to compare this model alongside its own K-type design. Brand new C4017 (KHW 628) was among the first to be bodied by ECW and was photographed by them during October 1946. It entered service the following year. From the rear, the Leylands looked very like other ECW-bodied buses in the fleet. (*ECW*)

(*right*) The top-deck interior of an ECW-bodied Leyland, reflecting the layout of a standard height 'highbridge' bus. (*ECW*)

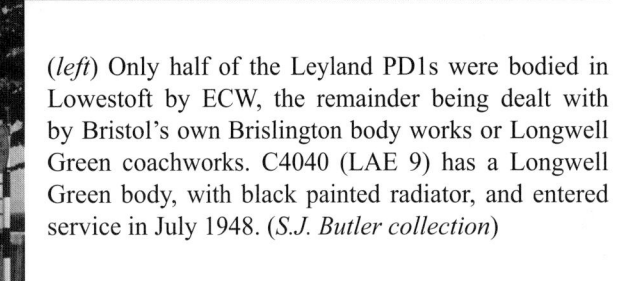

(*left*) Only half of the Leyland PD1s were bodied in Lowestoft by ECW, the remainder being dealt with by Bristol's own Brislington body works or Longwell Green coachworks. C4040 (LAE 9) has a Longwell Green body, with black painted radiator, and entered service in July 1948. (*S.J. Butler collection*)

(*right*) Deliveries of desperately needed, brand new vehicles began to increase during the late 1940s. One of Bristol's own products received during 1947 is this 55-seat 'lowbridge' bodied K5G, L4102 registered KHU 623. (*ECW*)

19

Seen from the front, the Leylands could easily be identified by their radiator (and engine sound). Another ECW-bodied example, C4044 (LAE 13) is resting here at Eastville. This bus is now preserved by the Bristol Vintage Bus Group. (*Bristol Tramways*)

decker bus chassis of their time, each achieving sales double that of the Bristol K model. One is therefore left to speculate whether Tilling were keen to place a large batch of Leylands in service with Bristol, in order to offer operator experience of the type with the Group's bus chassis builder! As these were to become BJS buses, the corporation even met half the cost of their purchase – but there was no hint of comparative trials to the civic representatives.

Despite being non-standard in a growing 'Bristol' fleet, the Leylands lived out a full life of between 13 and 15 years, mostly at the city's Eastville depot and operating busy cross-city routes, perhaps the closest to a 'municipal' bus to be operated in the city. Thankfully, two examples survive to this day, both of which carry ECW bodies, and one has been faithfully restored by the Bristol Vintage Bus Group to represent this interesting diversion in a fleet that was growing in standardisation.

Discussion about new buses at the December 1946 meeting was accompanied by an account of growing unrest amongst the staff following a report from the Transport and General Workers Union that there were 15 non-members amongst the platform staff and that it was 'undesirable that these men should remain in the Company's employ'. The Committee authorised the management to reach a 'reasonable settlement'!

1948

Deliveries this year included the balance of 35 Leyland double-deckers for BJS, and no fewer than 111 Bristol Ks powered by AEC 6-cylinders, Gardner 5-cylinders or Bristol's own AVW 6-cylinder diesel unit: 26 of these highbridge Ks were for the Joint Services fleet. Thirty-four of the new deliveries were L type single-deckers, 12 of which were ECW-bodied, dual-purpose 31-seaters with Bristol AVW 6-cylinder engines, the rest being 35-seat, ECW-bodied, rear-entrance buses. The delivery of the dual-purpose saloons was appropriate as in June 1946 the Bristol to London express service was reinstated after being withdrawn for four years because of hostilities, following the resumption of local motor coach trips the previous summer.

During September 1948 it was announced that the assets of the Thomas Tilling Company, including those of Bristol Tramways, were to be sold to the British Transport Commission. This was a result of the 1947 Transport Act, introduced by the first Labour Government with an overall majority, which had been elected two years earlier with a mandate to nationalise much of the country's transport, including railways, docks and inland waterways, road haulage and bus services.

The Tilling Group was composed of 23 operating companies across the country with some 8,000 vehicles. Unlike other sections of the road passenger transport industry, Tilling took the view that it would be better to sell voluntarily to the newly formed Government body, the British Transport Commission. As part of the Tilling Group, Bristol Tramways was included in the sale, which provoked mixed reactions and considerable uncertainty.

The Bristol Junior Chamber of Commerce produced an explanatory booklet about the Act and included this epitaph from a Bristol Tramways driver with over 40 years service:

> Good-bye to Bristol Tramways,
> You set your standard high;
> Another name may do the same.
> We wonder – you and I.

3043 (CHY 120), on route 154 at Weston-super-Mare, is a 1936 Bristol G-type, but fitted with a modern 1949 ECW body and new 'PV2' radiator, giving the appearance of a brand new bus. (*S.J. Butler collection*)

The bus-building activities of Bristol and Eastern Coach Works were also affected by nationalisation, as amendments insisted upon by the government's opposition henceforth restricted their sales, so in future only orders from other state-owned organisations could be accepted. While existing orders were nevertheless honoured, many loyal Bristol customers could no longer buy its vehicles and a promising export trade – which was valuable to the country – was short-lived. Future models such as the Lodekka, would also be out of reach for many bus operators.

1949
The 1949 intake redressed the single/double-deck balance somewhat with the delivery of 83 single-deckers, again including a batch of 12 dual-doorway buses for BJS. Apart from three bus-bodied Bedford OBs the rest were standard 35-seat Bristol Ls, together with two Beadle-bodied, lightweight, integral single-deckers (2500 and 2501) with Morris components and Saurer diesel engines – a significant delivery considering that the Motor Constructional Works were known to be working on their own design for a lightweight chassis-less single-deck bus at the time. Clive Norman (who grew up in Cheltenham and joined the company as a conductor, later becoming a driver, wages clerk and schedules clerk, retiring from that position with Stagecoach at Gloucester in early 2007) recalls that he occasionally saw one of the two integrals operating out of Gloucester bus station to Arlingham on service 113 – a service that was shared on alternate weeks with independent operator S.K. Silvey.

Double-deck arrivals consisted of only 16 K-types, five of which were for Joint Services (one, C3436, carrying an aluminium-framed, 4-bay body), and the first prototype Bristol 'Lodekka' bus, also for Bristol city services.

The Lodekka was a revolutionary Bristol design to overcome problems posed by existing highbridge and lowbridge-type double-deckers. The problem of bridges with low clearance had plagued bus operators for many years: although the operation of single-deckers was a necessity for some clearances, others could tantalisingly take the height of a double-decker, but only if it was of the lowbridge type where the upper deck gangway was displaced to the offside of the bus and sunk into the headroom above the seats in the lower saloon. This arrangement (referred to locally as 'skittle alleys' because of the obvious similarity between the sunken, upper deck gangway and the popular Somerset pub sport) caused many problems for passengers. Those on the upper deck had to sit four abreast and close together (making it difficult for the passengers close to the nearside to exit their seats) whilst those on the offside lower deck could easily bump their head when they got up. Bristol's Motor Constructional Works had been working on a specially designed chassis that would dispense with this arrangement by changing the alignment of the normally near centrally mounted prop-shaft and reducing the depth of the rear drive axle so as to allow for a central sunken lower deck gangway, thus producing a low-height bus that was also able to offer the passenger advantages of central gangways on both decks. Bodied by ECW, with

The internal arrangement of 'lowbridge' buses was far from satisfactory. The four abreast seating and offside gangway is illustrated in this internal view of L4102, looking towards the rear. (*ECW*)

whom the company worked closely, the result was Bristol Tramways' C5000 (later LC5000), LHY 949.

C5000 remained unique in Bristol until its withdrawal from service in 1963 and the appearance of its distinctive radiator heralded excitement amongst the early Bristol enthusiasts. It was initially allocated to Eastville depot, working on Bristol city routes 2/2A, and later moved to Easton Road (Lawrence Hill) depot where the bus often appeared on service 36, latterly alongside its more modern successors. (Service 36 is, incidentally, believed to be the oldest surviving route with its original number in the whole of Bristol).

As a very young boy, co-author Martin Curtis lived on the 36 route and was beginning to take a close interest in buses. He recalls noticing that some buses had narrow radiators while others were wide – not realising till much later that only C5000 had a wide radiator, the feature which distinguished it from the rest of the fleet.

The Lodekka's transmission was to be modified before production commenced a couple of years later, but the basic design was to become the standard Tilling fleet double-decker for over 15 years, and influenced double-decker bus design generally thereafter.

The population of the country was still suffering from postwar shortages at the end of the decade, and industry was in the same position, especially as the government was encouraging Britain's manufacturing companies to export their products to earn foreign currency. For the Bristol Tramways & Carriage Company, one of the shortages suffered was of the linen material used for the destination roller blinds, and John Batten comments that in Bath

> many postwar vehicles were fitted with a single aperture showing both terminal points ... the rear destination box was removed with the blind (fitted) against the glass. This necessitated the permanent allocation of buses to routes, a practice that continued after conversion to roller blinds.

Traffic conditions were such that buses were still the principal passenger-carrying vehicles on the roads and as such there were few other vehicles impeding their progress. An extract from the staff magazine *Omnibus* of October 1949 suitably illustrated this point:

> Driver of the second bus as yet a third arrived at the terminus: 'I'm six minutes sharp – thee's got time to go down to Weymouth!'

In this context, 'sharp' seems to be very much a Bristol term for early running and is still used in the city today, despite the more logical use of the word as 'sharp to time', i.e. exactly on time.

By the end of the 1940s, the company's operating fleet, which still included vehicles up to 20 years old, comprised over 1,360 vehicles, 564 of which were members of the BJS city fleet. Almost 1,200 were based on Bristol chassis while vehicles of AEC, Bedford, Dennis, Guy, Leyland and Thornycroft manufacture could also be found on company services.

Schoolboys and others whose interests included keeping track of the Bristol Tramways fleet found that Ian Allan publications would assist them from the late 1940s, with the first *Bristol Tramways ABC* published in August 1949, closely followed by the appearance of *Buses Illustrated* later that year. Already, however, more serious study of Bristol buses and coaches was developing with the Bristol Interest Circle who exchanged information about the company's vehicles – much of which continues to be referred to today.

The company's operating area by now extended well beyond the Bristol boundary to reach as far afield as the Bristol Channel coast to the west; Monmouth, Great Malvern and Tewkesbury to the north; Oxford and Hungerford to the east; and Salisbury and Bridgwater to the south.

Despite its name, the Bristol company had become a major, regional transport provider, as well as a highly respected vehicle manufacturer.

* * *

Spotlight on the Lodekka Prototype

In 1949 Bristol Tramways (in collaboration with Eastern Coach Works) produced one of the most revolutionary double-deck bus designs ever seen. This was the Lodekka (Low decker) which was built to the same overall height as a 'lowbridge' bus, which was then essential on many routes with high passenger loadings but where overhead obstructions such as low railway bridges were prevalent.

Of equal importance was the low saloon floor which allowed the vehicle's overall height to be reduced, but provided the additional benefit of having a step-less floor from the platform into the lower deck. This was of great assistance to the elderly and infirm. This arrangement was achieved by dividing the transmission to either side of a dropped-centre rear axle, which in turn allowed the lower saloon floor, and gangway, to be lowered.

The first experimental Lodekka (designated LDX) was registered LHY 949 and allocated fleet no C5000 (later LC5000). With its distinctive, wide radiator and chrome bumper bar it stood out from the Bristol Ks and other types and was used to test features of the design. A Bristol 6-cylinder engine provided power while its body seated 58 passengers.

This bus was loaned to a number of other BTC Tilling and Scottish companies for evaluation including Griffin Motors (associated with Red & White), Eastern National, Hants & Dorset, Scottish Motor Traction, Westcliff-on-Sea and Wilts & Dorset.

LHY 949 was followed by a second prototype (JWT 712) in 1950, which was allocated to the West Yorkshire Road Car Company.

Following its demonstration tours, C5000 settled down to work on Bristol city services where it undertook a full service life until withdrawn in 1963. It was then quickly sold to North's (a well-known bus dealer) in Yorkshire who subsequently sold it on again, to be scrapped. Nevertheless, over 5,200 production Lodekkas followed from the Bristol works for use by state-owned operators throughout the country.

LHY 949 when brand new in September 1949. It was finished in a non-standard livery layout of Tilling green with cream window surrounds which very successfully disguised its low height. In this view, its inner front wings are painted green, although they subsequently became black. (*ECW*)

(*above*) A view inside the lower saloon, looking forwards. Bristol and ECW cooperated closely in order to achieve the low build of the vehicle, which involved a slightly sunken lower saloon gangway and rear-facing seat for five passengers across the front bulkhead. (*ECW*)

(*right*) The open rear platform showing the step-less entry into the lower saloon. (*ECW*)

(*below left*) Viewed standing at the Carey's Lane terminus of route 36, on which service it spent a large proportion of its life, the prototype Lodekka prepares for a journey to Knowle, which involved passing under a low railway arch at West Town Lane. (*R.H.G. Simpson*)

(*below right*) By now re-designated 'LC5000' (from 1955), LHY 949 is here approaching St James Barton and Jones's department store. Although much photographed, this is the only known picture of the rear of this bus 'in service'. (*Geoff Bruce collection*)

(*right*) LHY 949 toured all over Britain to demonstrate its design to other BTC bus companies. Here it is at Southend, about to depart for Chelmsford while on loan to Eastern National. (*Bristol Vintage Bus Group*)

(*left*) Upon its return to Bristol, C5000, which here looks immaculate, spent a normal working life on Bristol Joint Services although it occasionally strayed into other parts of the Bristol operating territory. (*Roy Marshall*)

(*right*) A comparison of the LDX and standard K-type features can be made as LHY 949 overtakes C3416 (LHU 524). Whilst the differences of radiator and bonnet are obvious, it will be noticed that the upper deck windows and roof dome of both types are extremely similar. (*M. Mogridge*)

(*right*) Among the oldest buses of Bristol's own manufacture to survive into 'the green years' was this 1930 B-type. 378 (HW 8370) stands here on Bath's Grand Parade. (*M. Mogridge*)

(*left*) With so much of Britain's manufacturing capacity directed to the war effort, few new buses appeared during those years despite the immense pressure placed on bus services. The Ministry of Supply selected Bedford as the sole manufacturer of single-deckers during this period and 50 of its wartime, petrol-engined OWB model were allocated to Bristol. Delivered in khaki livery in 1942, and finished to austerity standards including wooden slatted seats, C234 (HHU 302) heads for Clifton Suspension Bridge after the war. (*M. Mogridge*)

(*right*) In addition to buses of its own make, Bristol Tramways also found itself operating a variety of other makes during the 1940s. FHT 77 (2089) was a 1938 Dennis Lancet supporting the company's own bodywork. (*Authors' collection*)

(*above*) Long-distance coach services were abandoned during the war but with their resumption from 1946, Marlborough once again became an important stopping point for Greyhound coaches to and from London. Here three 'FHT' registered 1939 L5Gs (2148/50/51) with Duple 32-seat bodies pause while their passengers take refreshment. (*Geoff Bruce collection*)

(*below*) Another 1939 coach was this 20-seat Duple-bodied Bedford WTB, which carried fleet number 200 (FHT 817). It saw little use on its intended tours and excursions programmes until after the war, and is here touting for customers to take a trip to Cheddar. (*Bristol Vintage Bus Group*)

(*left*) A side-on view of C3393 (JHT 809) taken at Lawrence Hill in September 1946 when still new. Based on a Bristol K5G chassis, the ECW 56-seat body has sliding ventilators of a design which was about to be superseded. In standard Tilling style, the arrangement of the two cream bands had been amended to that shown. (*Bristol Tramways*)

(*right*) The interior lower saloon of similar bus C3395 with seats covered in the Tilling pattern moquette of the period. (*ECW*)

(*left*) Guy was favoured by the Ministry of Supply as one of only two manufacturers permitted to build double-deck motor bus chassis during the darkest days of World War Two. Twelve Guy Arabs were therefore taken into stock by Bristol during 1942-43 as the only new double-deckers available. 3632 (HHU 354) is pictured at Weston-super-Mare, where the type was allocated, operating the seafront service. (*Roy Marshall*)

(*right*) Bodywork on the Guy utility buses was built by Park Royal with one exception: 3641 (HHW 16) received a Weymann body. Delivered in grey paintwork, 3641 stands here outside the Lawrence Hill workshops having been overhauled and repainted in the latest style of Tilling green and cream. (*Bristol Tramways*)

(*right*) 1939 Bristol L5G 2253 (GL 6618) was new to Bath Tramways Motor Company – hence its local 'GL' registration. It is seen at Devizes having completed a journey on that company's service from Chippenham. (*C.W. Routh*)

(*left*) Bus 2427 (HY 2396) is recorded as a 1931 Bristol B-type although after rebodying and rebuilding, including the fitting of a new radiator, it looks much more modern. In fact, the chassis is effectively a 1949 Bristol L-type which had been classified as a 'rebuilt-vehicle' and therefore retained the identity of the earlier chassis. (*P. Yeomans*)

(*right*) A handful of Leyland Titan TD1 double-deckers found their way into the Bristol fleet, including WH 3303 (3614) which was purchased from Wilts & Dorset, but was new to Bolton Corporation. It was one of a number of secondhand vehicles acquired during 1939. (*C.W. Routh*)

(*above*) AEC Regal 2228 (GL 5079) displays its destination as Trowbridge as its climbs Wellsway out of Bath during November 1949. This vehicle was new to Bath Tramways Motor Company in 1937, having been ordered before that concern was taken over by Bristol Tramways. (*R.R. Bowler*)

(*below*) Another November 1949 photograph in Bath, this time showing buses at Parade Gardens (Terrace Walk) operating on services 6 (to Bathampton), 11 (to Odd Down) and 15 (to 'GWR' Station and Whiteway). (*R.R. Bowler*)

(*above*) Bristol K5G 3678 (JHT 127) in Bloomfield Road, Bath. New in 1946 with Duple body to a relaxed utility design, this was another vehicle to be among the first delivered in Tilling green with both cream bands positioned between the windows. (*R.R. Bowler*)

(*below*) Bath in 1949 once more, with two buses on Wellsway. The one nearest the camera is 3826 (DKN 43), a former Maidstone & District Bristol GO5G-type new in 1936, which had been rehabilitated, and re-bodied by ECW. In contrast, behind is 3838 (KHY 389) a one-year-old Bristol/ECW K6B. (*R.R. Bowler*)

(*left*) Epitomising the role played by the Tramways Company during the postwar period, this scene in Careys Lane from February 1946 shows a line of K-types – the majority still grey – amid the hustle and bustle of people using buses in order to go about their business; three smart company staff in heavy uniforms approach the camera. (*Bristol Tramways*)

(*right*) A queue of waiting passengers, of various ages and from all walks of life, in Temple Way, Bristol, with a crew also in attendance – possibly waiting to take over an arriving bus. Cream painted shelters of this style were seen all over Bristol from this period onwards. (*Bristol Tramways*)

(*below*) The July 1948 city bus timetable, showing details for route 1, from Brislington to Westbury.

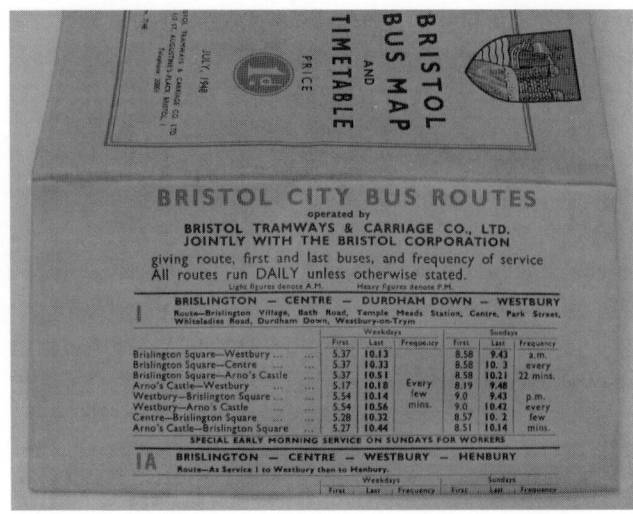

2. The 1950s

Now established as an operator of green buses, Bristol Tramways' activities continued to attract great interest – even to non-bus users – since the livery and appearance of bus fleets characterised individual towns and cities in a way largely lost today; the colour of buses helped identify a location. More importantly, buses continued to play a vital role in most people's lives as their principal means of travel – whether for work or pleasure – before widespread car ownership, and before television replaced cinemas as a major form of entertainment. Local buses mattered to almost everyone and the demands placed on the service were, at times, enormous.

New vehicle deliveries continued to improve fleet standards as did the necessary extensive rebodying and rebuilding of existing vehicles. The company's Central Repair Works at Lawrence Hill and Body Building Works at Brislington remained extremely busy as a result.

1950

New vehicle deliveries for 1950 reflected both the continuing standardisation of the Tilling fleet and the changes brought about as a result of acquisition by the British Transport Commission. Fifty-three single-deckers were received during that year, including the last of the L-types, 19 of which were to the now familiar two-doorway layout for BJS – a layout not thought necessary for service in the other towns and cities in the operating area, such as Gloucester and Bath. There were 18 small Bedford OBs, comprising bus versions for lightly trafficked routes and coach versions for excursions, tours and express services. The single-deck 'stars' however, were three L6Bs with the newly introduced ECW 'Queen Mary' 31-seat bodies for the 'Greyhound' coach fleet, one of which survives today.

(*left*) A 1950 Bedford OB supporting a Duple 27-seat coach body. 221 (MHU 993) is operating a private hire in this photograph, with a Bristol LL-type behind. (*Roy Marshall*)

(*right*) A welcome addition to Bristol's coach fleet in 1950 was a trio of 31-seat ECW-bodied L6Bs with 'full-front' coachwork. With registrations NAE 1-3, the second example, 2466, is shown here. (*P. Yeomans*)

Appropriately, along with the delivery of these new coaches, the company reported to the 15th December 1950 BJS Committee meeting that guided tours of Bristol operating on Sunday afternoons and Wednesday evenings between 9th July and 1st October and manned by conductors trained as guides, had carried 1,798 passengers and grossed £111. 9s. 6d!

The Bristol guided tour wasn't the only attempt by Bristol Tramways to satisfy the growing desire for postwar leisure travel, for in the same year open-top buses were introduced at Weston-super-Mare: three pre-war AEC Regent double-deckers acquired with the Cheltenham company (see below) had their roofs removed, were painted cream with green bands and sent to the seaside to operate service 152 between the Sanatorium, near Uphill, and the Old Pier. Fred Spencer recalls that they carried passengers on their delivery run from Bristol and those passengers arrived 'all wet through, because it had rained half way down and they couldn't get downstairs to shelter!' The Old Pier was the calling point of the famous Campbell's Steamers which connected the Welsh, Somerset and Devon coasts with their popular fleet of paddle steamers, and Fred further recalls that 'we would have six or seven buses at the Pier, waiting for the boats to come in' so that the passengers could be distributed about the town.

The Bristol to Weston-super-Mare service, route 24, was always busy during the summer and more so as the postwar travel boom progressed. Tony Peacey, who grew up in Bristol just after the war, recalls that on summer bank holidays there were always long queues of prospective passengers waiting at Bristol Centre near the Cenotaph, but that there were always plenty of buses and as soon as one was full it would leave, to be replaced by another that had been waiting elsewhere. It seemed however that there was a separate queue for

(*right*) Inside Weston-super-Mare bus station and garage with a fascinating collection of vehicles. Nearest the camera are 2112 (BHU 970), a much rebuilt Bristol J-type, next to Dennis Mace 654 (DHY 650), new in 1937. Behind can be seen the top of a Bristol-bodied double-decker and an L-type, while three brand new Bedford OBs are at the rear. (*M. Mogridge*)

(*left*) 1950 saw the introduction of Weston's open-top seafront service. Also tucked away at the rear of Weston garage is former Cheltenham District AEC Regent 3612 (BAD 28) one of three similar vehicles used to inaugurate the service, alongside two later Bristol Ks. (*L.B. Lapper*)

those commuters working on a Bank Holiday to ensure that they had priority. He remembers that:

> conductors had an easy time as passengers were in a holiday mood and once the fares had been collected the conductor often spent the journey sat on the stairs. At Weston-super-Mare the return queues often went up and down the waiting area as many as 14 times but the queue was continually moving as when one bus filled up another appeared.

He recalls of Weston that it was an interesting place in those early postwar years:

> There were a few different buses around from those normally seen in Bristol; I remember in particular the Guy Arab double-deckers used on the 154 route and the small Dennis Mace single-deckers used on the route to Kewstoke and Sand Bay, and some small Bedford single-deckers. I also remember buses with wooden slatted seats.

During this year general fuel rationing was relaxed, but there was an increase in taxation of at least 9d per gallon on motor fuel which, by the end of 1950, had increased operating costs by £171,900: this represented 17% of the amount reported to the Board as being 'on deposit with the British Transport Commission' earlier that year. This was a double blow to the company, increasing the tax on the motor fuel it used for providing its services, while allowing this fuel to be more easily available to its customers which would encourage them to make greater use of private transport. Of necessity this resulted in a general fares increase early in 1951 designed to yield £180,000.

The double-decker deliveries consisted of a further 19 K-types which, along with the Ls, were the last of their type since the balance of the Bristol-built double-deck chassis were to the recently introduced KS design, being an updated and longer (and, in the case of the KSW, wider) K-type. The newly revised 4¼-bay ECW 60-seat highbridge body on the KSW chassis became the new standard for BJS and both Bristol city and country examples were soon to be seen over the entire operating area. Nine of the KS double-deckers and 15 of the wider KSWs were for the Joint Services fleet.

Despite the ending of hostilities some years previously, and the return to full time employment with Bristol Tramways of many demobbed ex-servicemen, all was not well with the staffing levels within the city of Bristol: the subject of non-collection of fares was raised at the 29th September 1950 BJS Committee meeting and the company's response was that 'there was a large wastage among male conducting staff and, as the Committee was aware, there was prejudice against the employment of females and the recruitment of additional females was therefore restricted'. Despite this wastage, the Tramways Company at the time had a reputation for military-style discipline. Fred Spencer recalls that at Weston-super-Mare, before he trained as a driver in 1948, he was called to see the manager, J.D. Howell (who himself completed 30 years as Weston Branch Manager, retiring in September 1951 only to die in the following February) because he had paid in 10d 'over' – i.e. more than he should have done.

Six small, 26-seat petrol-engined Dennis Mace buses, built in 1937 with Duple bodywork, continued to operate from Weston-super-Mare depot in the early fifties. 654 appears with a 'standing load' while working to and from Kewstoke. All of this batch had been withdrawn by 1955. (*Roy Marshall*)

I had to try and explain to him where the 10d had come from, as no way should I be 10d over at any time. It used to be said that when Mr Howell came out of his back door into the garage (he lived in a company house next to the depot) even the buses stood to attention!

Although the Tramway staff were supplied with an outer uniform at that time they were expected to report for duty 'properly' dressed with a white shirt, black tie and black shoes.

> I remember one driver reporting for work in a coloured shirt and brown shoes and he was sent home and told to try again tomorrow!

The remaining delivery of four double-deckers came to Bristol Tramways directly as a consequence of operating boundary changes made by the British Transport Commission (BTC). These buses were Duple-bodied, highbridge Guy Arab double-deckers ordered by the Cheltenham District Traction Company, and delivered in dark red and cream, a livery that would single Cheltenham out as an oasis of different colour in an otherwise green fleet for many years to come.

The operation and assets of the 33-vehicle strong Cheltenham fleet were transferred to Bristol Tramways as a result of territorial changes implemented following the BTC's acquisition of another transport group, the previously privately owned Red & White Group, which included the neighbouring Red & White Services Ltd as well as Cheltenham District Traction. This was not the only change, however, as the opportunity was taken to exchange Bristol Tramways' Coleford operation (deep in the Forest of Dean on the other side of the River Severn) with Red & White's Stroud operation which covered much of Gloucestershire – adding over 30 further vehicles, including just one 'Bristol'.

(*right*) Cheltenham District Traction Company became a Bristol subsidiary during 1950. During that year, CDT Guy Arab II 49 (FAD 250) loads in Clarence Street. Cheltenham's distinctive dark red and cream livery was to be retained for over 20 years after the takeover. (*L.B. Lapper*)

(*left*) Territorial changes in 1950 resulted in the services and vehicles of Red & White's Gloucestershire operations passing to Bristol Tramways. Included in this arrangement was Albion CX19 (EAX 637) with Duple 'lowbridge' 56-seat body, which became L4143. Here it has reversed onto the loading platform at Gloucester bus station. (*Roy Marshall*)

The Stroud area operations of another Tilling company – Western National – were also transferred to Bristol, bringing 46 more buses into the fleet, but this time including a large proportion of Bristol-made vehicles. For people in the Stroud area this of course meant a change in the colour of some of their local route buses from red to green. The staff magazine *Omnibus* for August 1950 illustrated the point:

Heard in Stroud:
George: That's the Gloucester bus.
Bill: No it's not, the red bus goes to Gloucester.
George: Don't you know, the green buses run anywhere now?

Clive Norman, growing up in Cheltenham, recalls family outings,

when we would travel from Tuffley to Edge taking a picnic into the country. The service was operated by Red and White Albions, until one day, to my surprise, the Albion turned up but it was now painted green with the Bristol coat of arms on the side.

Although this tidied up the operational areas under BTC control, inexplicably it left the Trowbridge and Chippenham areas of Western National as isolated outposts – cut off from the rest of the Western National company by the huge area covered by Bristol Tramways' services.

The British Transport Commission had also acquired the passenger services of Bristol haulier, H. Russett, during 1950, and his ten coaches and services passed to the Tramways. Finally, the small business of Dundry Pioneer, based on the outskirts of Bristol was bought for £1,850.

This series of swaps and acquisitions brought many unfamiliar vehicles to a fleet which the Tramways was trying hard to standardise, and whilst this position was gradually rectified, the new operating boundaries of the company were to stay for over 20 years.

(*left*) Nationalisation of large parts of the transport industry resulted in some hauliers whose fleet also included buses and coaches passing their passenger vehicles to the local BTC operator. One such vehicle to enter the Bristol fleet is this rare Foden PVSC5 with Plaxton body, LAE 906, which came from H. Russett. It took Bristol Tramways fleet number 2200. (*P. Yeomans*)

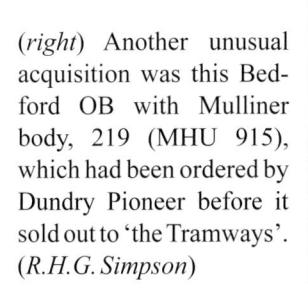

(*right*) Another unusual acquisition was this Bedford OB with Mulliner body, 219 (MHU 915), which had been ordered by Dundry Pioneer before it sold out to 'the Tramways'. (*R.H.G. Simpson*)

Spotlight on the Light Saloon Prototype

Only a year after the Lodekka prototype had been unveiled, Bristol Tramways revealed a second vehicle of entirely new design. This was the Light Saloon prototype which appeared at the end of 1950, and with experimental designation LSX, was allocated fleet number 2800 (registration NHU 2).

The Light Saloon (or LS-type) was an underfloor-engined single-deck model which was integrally constructed in order to reduce weight (and accordingly fuel consumption). By placing the engine amidships, below the floor, the floor area could be increased to accommodate more seating, which was a layout being adopted by a number of major bus manufacturers at this time. This however, increased the floor height and therefore had the opposite effect to the Lodekka in terms of improving ease of boarding for passengers.

Bus No.2800 was fitted with an experimental XWA horizontal Bristol engine (which would be replaced by a Gardner unit later in its life) while both front and rear, power-operated passenger doors were incorporated into the design. Most production LS types had only one door, alongside the driver. Seating for 42 passengers was nevertheless achieved, increased further to 44 during 1956 when the rear passenger door was removed.

The design formed the basis for future Tilling group single-deck buses and coaches, while NHU 2 remained in Bristol's own service until 1967, at which point it was stored by the company in the hope that it might be placed in a proposed transport museum. Unfortunately, this project came to nothing, so after ten years the bus was sold to North's dealership. It was retained by them, however, until acquired for possible preservation in the early 1980s, and later still passed into the hands of the authors. It is now fully restored and forms part of the Bristol Omnibus Vehicle Collection.

(*above*) In original condition with small wheels and narrow axles, 2800's appearance heralded the way forward for single-deck bus design. For Bristol Tramways' passengers, the layout was radically different to anything they had seen before. (*M. Mogridge*)

(*right*) NHU 2 was first seen in service on route 85 from Bristol to Portishead. With the lack of a radiator grille, there was no longer any reason to arch the windscreen over the centre, but the temptation to break with this tradition was too great when the LSX was designed. Production LS types had straight, deeper windscreens. (*M.J. Tozer*)

(*above left*) A nearside view of NHU 2, illustrating the dual-door arrangement. At this stage, there was no thought of operating this type of bus without a conductor. The half cream/half green livery style helped identify this vehicle from a distance. (*ECW*)

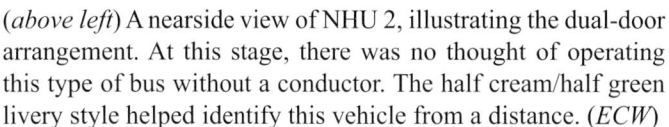

(*above right*) The front of the interior. For the first time, the driver was no longer separated from the passengers – or his conductor. The side-facing seats over the wheel arches were eliminated on production LSs by further raising the floor level. (*ECW*)

(*right*) Reaching the summit of the notorious Rownham Hill, which climbs steeply away from Bristol into Somerset, 2800 demonstrates that it can continue the Bristol tradition of slowly but surely tackling the most severe gradients. (*M. Mogridge*)

(*below left*) While still retaining its rear door, this mid-1950s photograph illustrates that larger wheels and wider axles have been fitted, and of course, standard bus livery applied. (*Peter Davey*)

(*below right*) Departing from Weston bus station for Wells (where it spent much of its later life), in the early 1960s, this view clearly shows that the second, rear door has been removed. Bristol Tramways' standard indicator box has also replaced the Tilling group's preferred three-piece destination display. (*S.J. Butler collection*)

(*above*) With the transfer of Western National's Stroud-based services to Bristol Tramways in 1950, came this 17-year old Bristol H-type (FJ 8959). It is depicted immediately after its transfer, displaying Bristol fleet number 2490 but otherwise still in full Western National livery. (*C.W. Routh*)

(*below*) Stroud Bus Station following the takeover of services from Western National. On the left is former Western National K6B L4132 (KUO 945); in the centre is L4121 (LHU 517), a K5G model new to Bristol Tramways in 1948; and on the right is 215 (MHU 57), a 1950 Duple-bodied Bedford OB. (*S.J. Butler collection*)

1951

Vehicle deliveries in 1951 were virtually all of the Tramways' own manufacture. The new KS double-deck chassis, which became the basis of what was the standard type for the next four years, formed the bulk of the new buses, with no fewer than 37 of the narrow 7'6" wide examples being delivered, alongside 18 of the newly permitted eight-foot wide variant, the KSW: all of the deliveries were powered by Bristol's own AVW engine and carried Eastern Coach Works' new standard 4¼-bay, aluminium-framed body.

The Bristol Joint Services fleet benefited from 14 buses, only one of which was eight feet wide, although all were to the new 60-seat standard seating layout. A further six of the KS-types joined the Gloucester city fleet (whose buses, incidentally, carried the Gloucester rather than Bristol coat of arms and carried fleet numbers in a separate series), where they joined one of the previous years' deliveries in the conversion of city service 9 from single to double-deck. Clive Norman recalls the occasion:

> I took up a position at the junction of Tuffley Avenue and Tuffley Crescent and stopped there until I had 'spotted' every one of them!

Eighteen vehicles were for country services (including five for the Bath Tramways Motor Company and one for the Bath Electric Tramways fleet), although these were hybrids that supported a full eight-foot wide body on their narrow chassis. These could easily be identified by the gap between the edge of the mudguards and the tyre, and were apt to roll noticeably when corners were taken at speed! Fifteen of the wider KSW chassis were also allocated to country services, including the nominal prototype, chassis 80.101, and a new numbering series was introduced for all of the wider buses from 8000 onwards (1800 onwards for the Gloucester city fleet), with the driver's cab sporting a nice white steering wheel to remind him of the extra width of his charge! In addition, the duty cardholder in the cab carried the warning 'AVOID PRINCE STREET BRIDGE WITH THIS VEHICLE' in red on a white background. Prince Street Bridge was (and indeed still is) a very narrow swing bridge in the centre of Bristol allowing boat access to Bristol's inner harbour. The bridge, complete with its 7'6" width limit, is still there, although it now also carries a weight limit and is no longer used by local buses.

One of this early batch of hybrid buses, 8008 (NAE 40), was kept back by the company when withdrawn in 1967 with the intention of displaying the bus in their proposed museum, but after ten years of languishing (mostly behind Winterstoke Road depot) and deterioration, it was sold, along with other prospective preservation prospects, and scrapped.

An exception to the fleet numbering series was allowed for the recently acquired Cheltenham fleet where three Bristol-engined KSWs received by this subsidiary company, continued the existing CDT number series below 100.

The BJS deliveries saw the withdrawal of the first of the wartime K-types that had survived the hostilities and which were by that time only 10-12 years old.

Single-deck deliveries were, with one exception, for the coach fleet, comprising 17 eight-foot wide 'Queen Mary' bodied 35-seaters, this time featuring radiators concealed behind ornamental grilles. They were the first vehicles for the company built to the newly permitted length of 30 feet, seven being on the narrower LL chassis and the remaining ten on LWL chassis, all again with AVW engines. These new stylish coaches saw the demise of the last pre-war AEC Regal coaches.

The new 35-seat coach with LL chassis, 2803 (NAE 6), stands outside the company's booking and enquiry office in Prince Street, Bristol, a location from where many country bus and coach services departed before the opening of the Marlborough Street bus station. (*Roy Marshall*)

The remaining single-deck arrival of 1951 was very special indeed. Chassis number LSX.001 was one of two prototype underfloor-engined, integrally constructed, single-deck, lightweight buses to be built by the company's Motor Constructional Works and was delivered to the Tramways' operating department fitted out as a 42-seat, dual-door (front and rear) bus. Interestingly, however, the Works' records indicate that in 1949, under chassis number XC101, units were ordered for a chassis-less vehicle, but the project was closed on 5th September of that year and marked as 'not likely to be completed'.

The engine for LSX.001 was Bristol's first attempt at turning its Bristol AVW unit on its side and was referred to as the LSW. It was fitted under the floor, between the 7'6" wide axles (despite its body being a full eight feet wide) with the road wheels attached by only eight stud fixings, as befits a lighter vehicle. The complete bus weighed only 5 tons 12 cwt, almost a ton lighter than a contemporary 35-seat Bristol L which was typically 6 tons 11 cwt. Painted in a brighter version of the standard Tilling green and cream, 2800 entered service on 10th February 1951, initially on the busy Bristol to Portishead route which included Rownham Hill with its maximum gradient of 1 in 6. Later in the year it was loaned to Bath Tramways Motor Company for operation in and around Bath.

After two years' operation the Bristol engine was replaced by a Gardner 5HLW (which became the standard power unit for Bristol's own underfloor-engined fleet), while the axles were modified to suit an eight foot wide bus. Later still, the rear door was removed, thereby bringing this vehicle into line with the production LS buses delivered later, and thus modified, 2800 settled down to an uneventful and normal service life, principally at Weston-super-Mare and Wells (latterly as a one-man bus). When withdrawn in 1967 this unique bus was saved by the company for exhibiting in their proposed museum; the museum, of course, never materialised, but almost 40 years after withdrawal from service, and with her rear door restored, this remarkable survivor again carried passengers, fully renovated and under the ownership of the authors.

The second of the two prototype LSX buses, which also survives today, was sent to ECW's local operator, Eastern Counties, but was fitted with one door from new and a Gardner 4-cylinder underfloor engine. There is some speculation that construction of the body for this bus was started first and that it was to be produced to the then maximum length of 27 feet 6 inches, but was put aside to allow the building of the longer, 30 foot long, two-door version when the regulations changed, and indeed, during the restoration of 2800, certain body markings found on the interior panel work would seem to add weight to this theory. After 2800 was delivered the Bristol Tramways received no more new vertical-engined, single-deck service buses.

Delivery was taken of one more double-deck bus that year and this was non-standard, although the last of the 'traditional' Cheltenham buses to be delivered to that fleet, being a Duple-bodied Guy Arab III.

The takeover of the Cheltenham District fleet allowed for some rationalisation in the town, since early in 1951 the Bristol Tramways' board approved the use of the coach parking area at Cheltenham District's St Marks depot, while by early 1955, following alterations and extensions, the green service buses at Cheltenham had vacated their Montpellier depot to join the CDT vehicles at St Marks. This followed the merger of the two companies' offices in the town, which had occurred a few months earlier.

Following the creation of the British Transport Commission, which effectively employed up to a million people, it was decided to form a film unit to record and promote the Commission's activities. This resulted in the establishment of British Transport Films, whose work soon represented the benchmark by which other documentary films would be judged. Among its earliest productions was *Work in Progress*, released in 1951, which sought to explain the role of the Commission through coordination of each transport mode. The Bristol Tramways operation was among those featured, to explain how careful coordination attempted to match service levels with passenger demands. This suddenly thrust the city's bus services before a wider audience, with the film appearing around the country in cinemas, schools, church halls and within the transport industry itself.

At Bristol's Motor Constructional Works pressure was building on the Design and Drawing Office because of the simultaneous development work required to get both the LS chassis into production and a newly authorised goods chassis for use by the road haulage sector of the BTC, British Road Services. The result was that operators which had ordered Lodekkas for 1952 delivery were asked to continue to accept K-types as there was insufficient capacity available to bring the Lodekka design up to a workable production model. Among the reasons it had been decided to progress the design and production of a heavy goods chassis was that, with restricted sales, the British Transport Commission foresaw future slack capacity on the bus production lines and was looking to ensure that the Works was kept busy.

Two different transmission designs had been tried on the Lodekka prototypes, Bristol's own C5000 (chassis no.LDX.001) and a second one for West Yorkshire (chassis no.LDX.002), but neither was satisfactory and the resultant production vehicle eventually had a much-simplified driveline. Records from the Constructional Works reveal that four Lodekka prototypes were envisaged, but one can speculate that the cancellation of two of them (the project is marked as 'closed 22/8/50') was due to insufficient capacity in the drawing office to design alternatives. In addition the MCW records indicate an order for miscellaneous parts for Lodekka chassis numbers LX005 to LX014, agreement for their construction having been authorised 'for trials' at a Board meeting the previous September, although in the event these projects were also closed on the same day.

The Lodekka was such an advance in bus design that the West Yorkshire example was exhibited at the Festival of Britain during 1951, which, it so happened, was the term that came to be used when referring to a revised livery introduced to the Tramway's double-deck buses during the previous year. The new brighter 'Festival of Britain' livery had the cream relief around both lower and upper deck window surrounds, and, in some cases, a darker Brunswick green for the wheel centres and mudguards. This was a very attractive livery and followed experiments which included both a single and double-deck bus repainted with no cream relief at all. Repaints into the new, brighter style did not last more than a couple of years however, and certainly failed to encompass the whole double-deck fleet before repainting reverted to the old style.

(*left*) The brighter 'Festival of Britain' livery with cream window surrounds was generally considered attractive, but failed to disguise the severe austerity bodywork fitted to K5G 3623 (HHT 144) when built in 1942. It is operating to Glastonbury from Wells. (*Roy Marshall*)

(*right*) Climbing Wells Road, away from Bath city centre for Combe Down, is 3839 (KHY 741) wearing 'Festival of Britain' livery. This is a Bristol-engined K-type with ECW body, built in 1948. (*R.R. Bowler*)

(*left*) NAE 38 (1525) formed part of a batch of six Bristol/ECW KS6Bs for Gloucester city services in 1951. Displaying the Gloucester arms, the 'Festival of Britain' layout was extremely well-suited to new vehicles such as this. (*Roy Marshall*)

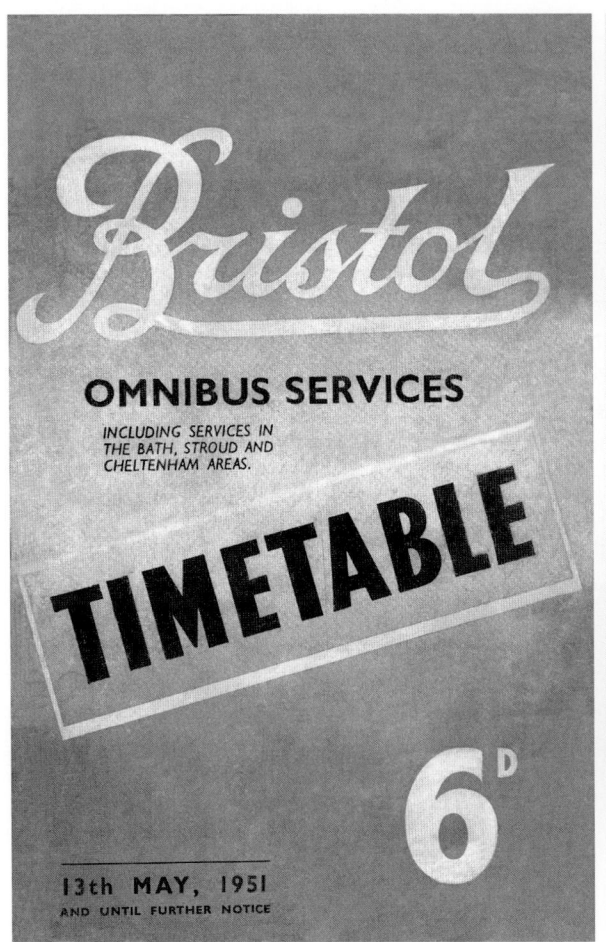

1952

Vehicle deliveries for stage carriage services this year were all of the now standard KSW double-deck bus. Joint Services received no fewer than 49, all to the standard H32/28R layout, and all but three with that favourite AVW power unit. The specification for these city buses included a four-speed gearbox and a gearing that allowed them to peak at just over 30mph – no problem when their operational life was expected to be almost entirely within the urban area – and sufficiently low geared to enable them to pull away from rest with a full load on Bristol's notorious hills, such as the steep Park Street which climbs out of Bristol city centre and had been considered too steep for electric trams. Passenger heaters were still not specified, and were never fitted to city KSW buses – a point that co-author Mike Walker remembers only too well when journeying to school or work on those cold winter mornings in the sixties when the inside of the windows were iced up, the leather seats were freezing and the crew were wrapped up in heavy overcoats, scarves and gloves (often 'fingerless' for the conductor to allow the handling of change)!

Country services took 11 similar vehicles (two with Gardner engines) including seven open-platform versions for Bath Tramways Motor Company. The remaining four had a new innovation for the company, that of platform doors and heaters! This was such a novel idea locally that the Bristol *Evening Post* carried a photograph of the rear of one of these buses in July 1952, describing it as 'a new type of double-deck bus' and a company spokesman commented that this arrangement would be reserved for country services. It was reported to the Tramway's Board in October 1952 that these additions cost £230 per bus at a time when the chassis of the bus was priced £30 short of £2,000, and the body a similar amount.

1952's delivery of green buses also included ten more KSWs, which were to remain unique within the main fleet. They were built to the lowbridge layout, and one can speculate whether, in view of the request by the Motor Constructional Works for the 1952 Lodekka orders to be switched to K-types, it was ever intended that the Tramways company should have had any lowbridge KSWs, despite the fact that a large fleet of lowbridge K-types was operated. These buses also featured platform doors and heaters and the familiar upstairs sunken gangway, and were split equally between the Bristol and Gardner power units, and

Cheltenham retained its traditional fleet numbering throughout the 1950s. With the crews wearing 'summer uniform' jackets and coats in this busy town centre scene, 1952 ECW-bodied 'lowbridge' KSW L80 overtakes 78, a Duple-bodied Guy Arab III of 1951. (*S.J. Butler collection*)

divided again between the main operating company and the Bath Tramways Motor Company – the latter's vehicles carrying the 'Bath Services' fleetname which had just been introduced. In the lower saloon the sunken offside gangway was matched by a nearside overhead luggage rack, a non-standard feature also seen on Thames Valley double-deck coaches and Southern Vectis buses.

When these buses became life-expired, seven of them were sent to the Central Repair Works at Lawrence Hill in Bristol to be converted to driver training buses, their low height making them far more flexible in this role than their highbridge siblings.

Two further KSWs completed that year's double-deck deliveries, but these were painted in the attractive Cheltenham red livery. One was otherwise virtually a standard Bristol 'city' bus with an AVW engine and an open-platform, 60-seat body, whilst the second, also with an AVW engine, was an open-platform lowbridge bus, which was to remain unique in the Cheltenham fleet.

Finally, the 1952 deliveries also included ten 'Queen Mary' style, AVW-engined LWL 37-seat coaches, whilst a link with the pre-war Bath fleet was ended during the year with the withdrawal from service of 20 ECW-bodied AEC Regal saloons.

New coaches for 1952 were similar in appearance to those of the previous year, but were based on the wider LWL chassis and had seating for 37. Two examples, Nos. 2820 and 2822, are seen on Associated Motorways work in the Midlands. (*S.J. Butler collection*)

Major Chapple, the chairman of the company, was the President of The Omnibus Society for 1952, and the Presidential Weekend was held at Bristol on the 17th and 18th of May: Mike Tozer of the Bristol Interest Circle compiled a commemorative brochure for the event with contributions from a number of the company's managers. J.P. Martin, then Head of Staff Administration at Central Repair Works and later to become the Engineering Training Manager, wrote that

> we now have in production the 'LS' and 'HG' types for underfloor engines and lorries respectively. Mention must also be made of the two 'M' types which were built but not put into production and the 'LD' which is at present dormant.

In the same publication it was stated that

> the fleet comprised 1,345 vehicles operating 3,779 daily route miles on stage services, carrying 325,000,000 passengers annually.

Major Chapple continued in his capacity of chairman of the company for two more years, after which he retired at the age of 74!

1953
This was Queen Elizabeth's Coronation year and the whole country joined in the celebrations. KSW deliveries for the year were 54 for Bristol Joint Services, 41 being AVW-engined and 13 Gardner-engined; and 5 for Cheltenham with AVW engines, all built to the open-platform, 60-seat standard. The country services allocation was one solitary bus, but a rather special one. Taking fleet number L8133, chassis 100.001 was the first of half a dozen pre-production Lodekkas, the Design and Drawing Office presumably having completed its work on the LS bus and lorry chassis. The Lodekka went on loan to neighbouring Red & White and then to Bath Services before settling down to a normal service life. Remarkably it kept its 'pre-production' bonnet and grille assembly until only a few months before being withdrawn in 1968. Despite initially being kept back for the company's intended museum, like LC5000, the prototype Lodekka, L8133 finally disappeared forever.

This year also saw the first production deliveries of the integral LS single-decker, Bristol taking

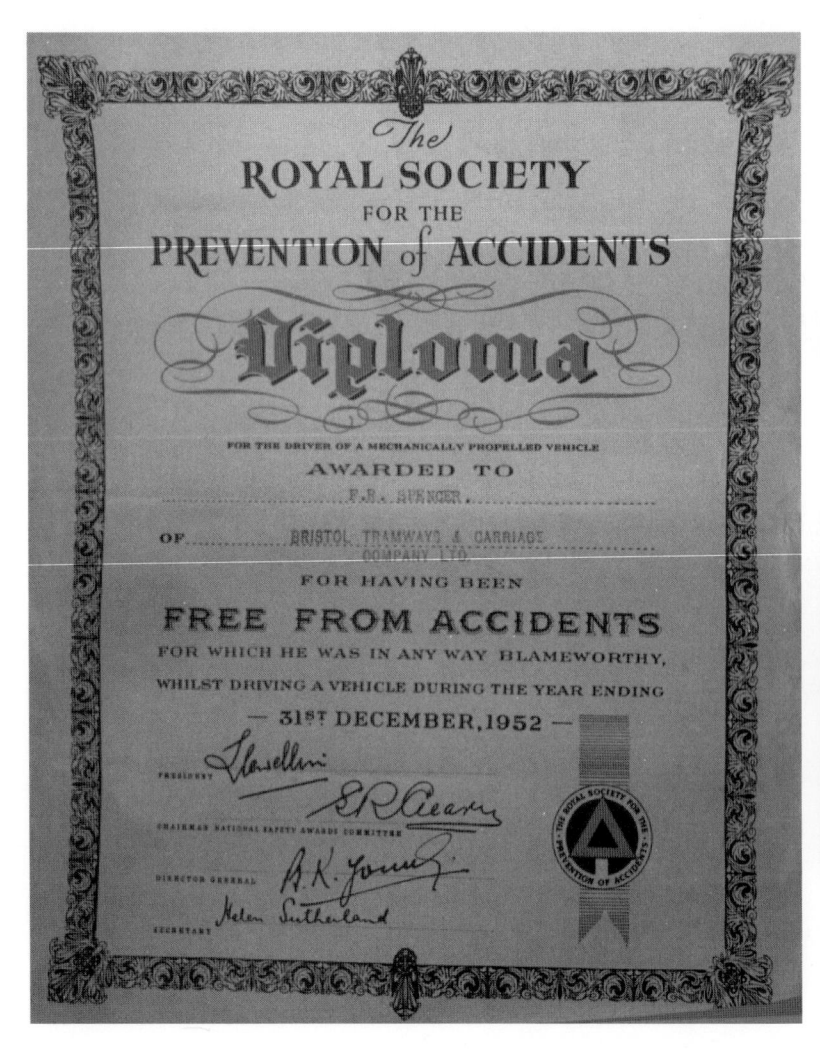

Fred Spencer, pictured outside Weston bus station early in his career, and the Safe Driving certificate that was awarded to him for 1952. (*Fred Spencer collection*)

delivery of six with Gardner 5HLW engines and 45-seat bus bodywork along with ten 39-seat coaches with 6-cylinder horizontal Bristol engines. The first of these buses, with fleet number 2828, arrived with a non-standard destination screen (front and rear) and in a distinctly unusual green livery, that of London Transport's Green Line fleet. It was soon sent to work in London, running comparison trials alongside two other lightweight single-deckers, an AEC 'Monocoach' and a Leyland 'Olympic' – although not before it had briefly operated in Bath wearing full London livery! The other five were actually intended for the Bath Tramways Motor Company.

Dave Clarke, who joined the Bath Tramways Motor Company as a conductor direct from his National Service in 1950/1, and went on to complete 45 years of service as conductor, driver, Inspector and Senior Inspector before his retirement, recalls that the arrival of the underfloor-engined, single-deck buses required a change of attitude for some drivers. Descending the hill into Radstock whilst working one such bus, Dave remembers that the level-crossing gates ahead began to close for road traffic, heralding the possibility of a long wait whilst the Somerset and Dorset railway train passed, and the prospects of dropping behind the scheduled time. As the gates closed the road the driver exclaimed 'You rotten xxx!', forgetting of course that unlike the separate cabs of the L-types that he was used to driving he was now in the bus with his passengers. 'Somebody upset you, driver?' asked a lady passenger sat at the back!

Dave went on to bus driving, but the rules were such at the time that a prospective driver had to be 23 years old – despite the fact that, like Dave, they had completed their National Service and been fighting for their country – and had to undertake driver training at first on single-deck buses and in their own time, it being quite normal for the driver to allow the conductor to drive the bus to and from the terminal points when running empty.

Six pre-production Lodekka buses were built in 1953, the first of which, L8133 (PHW 958), was allocated to the company's own fleet. The Lodekka's styling had been extensively modernised while new regulations governing maximum vehicle size meant that the Lodekka was now wider and longer than the prototypes. The revised styling with concealed radiator is displayed by L8133 as it enters Queen Square, Bristol, on the Street service. (*M.J. Tozer*)

Spotlight on the London Transport LS

The operating department of Bristol Tramways took delivery of production LS saloons from 1953, but the first of these was unlike any of the others.

PHW 918 (with fleet number 2828) was fitted with a three-piece destination display (similar to that fitted to 2800) and arrived in full London Transport Green Line livery. It went into service, wearing dark 'Lincoln green' London paintwork, at Bath from February 1953, but by the end of March had been sent on loan to London Transport.

It was to be used for comparative trials alongside two other lightweight single-deckers, an AEC-Park Royal Monocoach and a Leyland Tiger Cub. All three were set to work from LT's Reigate garage on country area service 447 and Green Line coach route 711. Later in the year, 2828 received a Hobbs semi-automatic gearbox.

By the end of 1953, this bus had been transferred to Dalston garage in London Transport's Central (red bus) area for further trials. However, by April 1954, its semi-automatic transmission had been removed, and PHW 918 returned to Bristol, where the company's standard destination equipment was fitted and it re-entered service in Tilling green livery. During 1957 it was modified for one-man operation and in this form remained in service until 1967.

(*right*) On arrival at London Transport's Chiswick works on 20th March 1953, still carrying its Bristol trade plates, PHW 918 finds itself surrounded by standard London bus types. Although finished in full Green Line livery with LT bulls-eye symbol below the windscreen, this bus was unlike any other in the LT fleet.
(*J.C. Gillham*)

(*left*) The interior of 2828 looking towards the rear, with seats covered in standard Tilling-style moquette of the period.
(*J.C. Gillham*)

(*left*) March 1954, and although still painted in London Transport dark green livery, gold underlined 'London Transport' fleetnames have replaced the 'Green Line' transfers initially displayed. Just visible, is the control lever for the semi-automatic gearbox. (*J.C. Gillham*)

(*right*) During its period working for London Transport, PHW 918 nevertheless returned briefly to the Bristol works on several occasions. Although very discreet, Bristol scroll badges were fitted below the windows front and rear for 2828's London role, the only LS so adorned. (*Peter Davey collection*)

(*left*) When back home, standard one-piece destination screens were fitted and the bus was repainted in Bristol livery. The small scrolls survived, however. 2828 disgorges passengers at Glastonbury, while operating service 159 to Bridgwater. (*R.H.G. Simpson*)

(*right*) Less than a year before withdrawal, PHW 918 rests inside Weston-super-Mare bus station before its next turn of duty, during November 1966. (*Peter Davey*)

Returning to the LS in London colours, the Tramways Board minutes of 25th September 1953 record that

> after three months operating on various routes with standard transmission [the bus is] now fitted with a Hobbs [automatic] transmission unit, [and] is returned to service with other light weights.

The minute continues to record that 'then trials would be undertaken with a 6-cylinder engine'. No record exists of that second trial actually taking place, but one can speculate that, had it done so, London's newly introduced RF fleet could well have been joined by further automatic LS buses! At the end of its life, vehicle 2828 was also kept back as a preservation prospect but was not so lucky as the prototype 2800 and ended its days at a breaker's yard.

The same Board minutes record that 'preliminary investigations are being carried out with a view to the development of a small capacity lightweight single-deck' which was eventually to become the SC model. Although the operating department tested the first such vehicle built in 1954 (registration 724 APU, which became Eastern National 395) on routes at the edge of the Bristol conurbation, none were taken into stock – the only Bristol-built passenger model never actually purchased by the Bristol operating section of the organisation. Presumably it was content to soldier on with its fleet of small-capacity Bedford buses, many of which were only a few years old.

A steady increase in patronage in the early 1950s saw a proposal come before the Board to purchase additional premises at Wells because of the increase in the number of vehicles allocated there, the intention being to build a new garage and bus station, with improved offices and customer services. However, in one of those strange events that seemed to militate against the work that the Bristol Tramways company was doing to encourage and cater for increased growth, the Ministry of Transport proposed that the number of standing passengers that could legally be carried on public service vehicles should be reduced from eight to five: as a result the employers' representatives at the National Wages Council proposed that the platform staff's wages should suffer a commensurate cut! The employees' side of the Wages Council was obviously set against this and made their feelings known to Government, with the result that the Ministry of Transport quietly dropped its proposals!

1954

Double-deck deliveries this year were again all KSW types, by now the Tramways' standard double-deck bus. The Joint Services order came in at 27 buses (three of which were to be Gardner-engined) and a further open-platform, Bristol-engined bus went to the Cheltenham fleet. Of the Bristol city deliveries, bus C8205 (SHW375) was the first open-platform bus to be fitted with two rear lights, following recent changes in legislation. The remaining 15 of the delivery were country buses with heaters and platform doors, three of which were for the Bath Tramways Motor Company, all powered by Gardner 6-cylinder engines with a 5-speed over-drive gearbox allowing a top speed of over 40mph.

In Bristol, the postwar boom was well advanced and the Joint Services Committee meetings continued to plan for service changes and extensions to cater for the construction of new housing estates and the resultant passenger growth. One such postwar estate, Hartcliffe, in the south of Bristol, benefited from an increase in frequency of service 138 'from every 19 minutes to every 14 minutes off-peak', a frequency that would hardly make it easy to commit the bus times to memory! Of course, at this time few people had access to private cars and would just have waited at the bus stop out of necessity for the next bus to arrive. The September 1954 BJS meeting considered the new vehicle programme for 1956 and agreed that 25% of the intake would be Lodekkas, because 'an advantage would accrue to the Joint Services from the use of Lodekka buses as they could be used on routes where standard double-deckers could not', even though at £4,295 each, the price premium over the standard BJS KSW type was 6%. A particular reference was later made to access for the new Stockwood Lane estate which would then be possible via the more direct West Town Lane route (which passed under a low railway bridge unsuitable for highbridge buses) instead of the proposal to access the estate via Whitchurch.

Some of this new development was taking place on land that had been added to the city of Bristol

A 10-year Safe Driving medal issued in 1953.

from neighbouring Somerset in 1951 and the Council representatives on the BJS Committee strongly felt that these city service extensions should be considered, along with other routes, as part of the Joint Services. The company however disagreed and insisted that the extensions should be considered as 'B' mileage, i.e. entirely company-operated since it encroached upon the company's traditional operating area, necessitating the company to specify as part of the accounting process how much of the city services consisted of B, or company, mileage. As this was operated by Joint Services buses, some form of balancing had to take place, resulting in country buses occasionally operating on city services. The position was exacerbated, however, when, quite naturally, unused Joint Services buses and crews were used for duplication on the particularly busy service from Bristol to Weston-super-Mare during summer weekends and holidays, with the result that more than one councillor was moved to raise the matter at Joint Services meetings and required convincing that the mileage balance had been reconciled! It is believed one member of the Corporation even positioned himself at Ashton Gate on summer Saturdays to record which 'city' vehicles were being used as 'extras' to Clevedon or Weston!

It should not be forgotten, however, that for all legal purposes the Corporation's 50% share in the operation of the Joint Services meant that they were a municipal bus operator with all of the constraints that this implied. At the September 1951 Joint Services meeting it was reported that, because of the proposed extension of Joint Services routes from Kingswood (within the City and County of Bristol) to Warmley (outside of the boundary):

an application had been made by Bristol Corporation for consent under part V of the 1930 Road Traffic Act to operate public service vehicles on roads outside of the City and County of Bristol. These applications were published in the *London Gazette* and the local press ... as well as in the Traffic Commissioner's publication *Notices and Proceedings*.

By the end of 1954 no fewer than 230 buses of the KS/KSW type were in service, representing over 15% of the operational fleet.

Single-deck deliveries for 1954 consisted entirely of the LS-type, with 24 5-cylinder, 45-seat buses (five for Bath Tramways Motor Company) and ten 6-cylinder, Gardner-engined, 39-seat coaches; no more horizontal Bristol engines were taken into stock yet the vertical AVW engine still featured prominently in double-deck deliveries.

The Joint Services fleet was also increased by one secondhand single-deck bus during the year, but by the time the transfer to the fleet was confirmed the bus was 6,000 miles away and had never turned a wheel in the city for Joint Services! The company had received a request to send 'a bus from the City of Bristol' to the military authorities in Japan for the purpose of 'carrying troops on leave from Korea'. As the Joint Services had none to spare, a country bus was sent out 'after being put in a good state of repair' and in order that the bus should be regarded as a gift from the Joint Services, it was agreed at the September meeting that the bus should be transferred to the Joint Services for the consideration of £200, a figure below that which similar buses had reached at sale. It was also reported that appreciative letters had been received by both the company and the corporation from H.M. Forces in Korea.

2470 (CFH 608), a Bristol L-type, having been shipped from Portsmouth, is hosted ashore on arrival in Japan in 1954 as a gift from the City of Bristol to the W.V.S., to assist in transporting H.M. Forces on leave from Korea. (*Geoff Bruce collection*)

The Small Capacity Bristol SC model was the only Bristol-built chassis type never to be purchased by the company's own operating department. Nevertheless, the first SCX prototype of 1954, 724 APU, was tested on the Frampton Cotterell service and is seen here in very wet conditions. This vehicle carried the Tilling green livery of Eastern National, so looked perfectly 'at home' working in the Bristol fleet. (*Bristol Vintage Bus Group*)

This year also saw the first withdrawal of the 1942/1943 Guy Arab double-deckers, which, although often fitted with Bristol PV2 radiators and secondhand Brislington-built bodies – making them virtually indistinguishable from the pre-war Bristol K-types – were recalled by Tony Peacey as being very much part of the Weston-super-Mare bus scene at the time of his visits. Proposals were also laid before the Board for a bus station at Cheltenham, whilst in Cirencester the operation of local independent G.J. Miller and Sons was acquired although no vehicles were taken into stock.

1955

The bus manufacturing business, despite restricted sales, had produced some exciting designs which would set standards the rest of the industry were compelled to follow. Nevertheless, and whilst remaining under BTC control, it was decided to separate bus (and lorry) manufacturing from the operational company with effect from 1st January 1955 – henceforth to be performed by a separate company, Bristol Commercial Vehicles Ltd, which had actually been formed 12 years earlier. Body building at the company's Brislington depot also ceased around this time with all future bus bodying being concentrated on ECW at Lowestoft.

Brislington Body Works had been engaged on work for Bristol lorries while bus bodywork had become increasingly difficult to distinguish from that of ECW, as the BBW works adopted Tilling group standard designs. In fact, coach building on the site was to continue for some years beyond this, as bodies for railway and parcels vehicles (also under BTC control but managed independently) continued to be built there, sharing the Brislington depot premises (originally built for electric tramcars) with the operational buses that remained.

Bristol Commercial Vehicles nevertheless continued to have close links with the operating Bristol company. Both continued to use the 'Bristol' scroll as their emblem and early examples of new or trial chassis frequently went to the local operator.

Certain bus services passing the works were scheduled to stop specifically for BCV staff, and social and welfare facilities also continued to be shared. However, bus manufacturing matters were no longer reported to the Bristol Tramways & Carriage Co. board from this time.

Whilst production versions of the Lodekka (with type designation 'LD') appeared in the Bristol fleet during 1955, the KSW was still popular, with 75 taken into stock: 49 were standard Joint Services buses with AVW engines, whilst two similar vehicles (although Gardner-powered) joined the Cheltenham fleet. The 24 country service examples with rear doors and heaters again had Gardner engines, and six of them were directed to the Bath Tramways Motor Company fleet. Bus No.8187 (SHW 357) was notable in being the first bus with platform doors to be fitted with two rear lights.

In comparison, a modest intake of 37 Lodekkas came during the year: open-platform buses were for Joint Services (7) and Cheltenham (1), with AVW engines; whilst Bath Tramways Motor Company received eight (two with Gardner engines). A mixture of Bristol and Gardner engines were fitted to the 21 buses that entered service in the country services fleet, fitted with the now familiar platform doors. At a Joint Services Committee meeting early in March 1954 this modest number of low-height buses was proposed because of the development of housing estates that might require operation under low bridges, but the cost difference was crucial to the Corporation and their renewals fund, the standard KSW costing £3,990 against the Lodekka at £4,210.

During 1955, two experimental Bristol LS saloons which were no longer required for development work were acquired by the company. The first of these was 2883 (UHT 493), previously used as an unfinished shell with a Commer engine. After being brought up to service standards it received a Gardner power unit but for some time retained a second, rear entrance doorway (similar to the prototype LSX 2800). (*C.W. Routh*)

All Bristol's LD Lodekkas were delivered with a 58-seat layout, the lower saloon having only two-person, inward-facing bench seats over the rear wheel arches as the remaining space was occupied by built-in luggage shelves. Passengers also had to get used to a rear-facing front seat across the lower saloon bulkhead, whose occupants were forced to look into the eyes of the people sitting opposite, not really in keeping with English reserve! Travellers also had to get used to the absence of a step into the lower saloon from the platform, resulting in the apocryphal tale of passengers, so used to the arrangement of the K and KSW, stamping heavily or tripping up over the step that wasn't there! Many of these deliveries also offered less passenger information as a result of the Tramways' change in destination display sizes, with a 36 by 12 inch aperture replacing the 36 by 18 inch display that had been standard since just after the war, the intention being to reduce the quantity of linen necessary for the destination displays, many of which were produced in the Tramways' own Central Repair Works. At this time certain peak-hour bus workings still had their own individual linen because of the unique sequence of routes and destinations served during the duty.

Two former Bristol-ECW test rigs were also taken into stock in 1955. Although these vehicles were among the earlier LSs built they had been used for development work (one with bodywork developed for the lightweight SC), but were no longer thus required. Bus 2883 (UHT 493) had the unusual two-doorway layout (which, by this time, had been removed from the prototype LS 2800) and an unmistakeable Commer TS3 two-stroke, horizontally opposed engine (which must really have resonated from the buildings around the city), whilst 2884 (UHT 494) had the standard 45-seat body, but with a 'side by side' destination display (as on the SC) and an

The second of the two acquired LS types had been used for body development by ECW, and was powered by an AEC engine. It became Bristol Tramways 2884 (UHT 494). (*P. Yeomans*)

AEC engine. 2883 soon lost its unusual power unit in favour of the traditional Gardner 5HLW and by 1962 the rear door had disappeared too, when, along with others of the single-deck fleet, it was converted to a one-man bus. Despite being experimental both buses saw out a normal service life, and 2883 then continued to provide a public service for many years to come on the Portuguese colony of Macau. However, not to be outdone, 2884 didn't go quietly, being fitted with an MW-style grille as late as 1967!

As part of the Tramways' policy of improving passenger facilities a programme of establishing new bus stations commenced. Previously, Weston-super-Mare had been the only location where Bristol offered this facility. A new combined depot and bus station was opened in the small city of Wells, in Somerset, during 1955, the capital expenditure for which had been voted at a Board meeting some time earlier. Incidentally, the local service in Wells must have been one of the shortest city routes in the country, with a ten-minute journey time from The Horringtons into Wells city centre and a 9-minute journey time from Wookey Hole into the city.

1956

For 1956, KSW deliveries continued to exceed those of the new Lodekka, principally because there was little requirement for a low-height bus within the city of Bristol, and the Joint Services fleet continued to comprise approximately one third of the entire Tramways' operation.

The Bristol AVW engine was still regarded as ideal for the Joint Services' operation with its hilly terrain, and 32 of the Joint Services' delivery of 42 KSWs were so fitted. In addition to the balance of ten Joint Services buses for that year, the Gardner 6LW engine was also specified for the remaining 13 KSWs, 11 of which were for country services and fitted with doors, heaters and five-speed gearboxes, whilst two open-platform buses were again for the Cheltenham fleet. Cheltenham also took delivery of two LD6G Lodekka models with open platforms, and open platforms were also specified for two Lodekkas for Bath Tramways Motor Company, four for the Bath Electric Tramways fleet and four for country services, whilst the balance of 31 LD models were delivered with platform doors. Ten of the Lodekkas were fitted with the AVW engine.

Back in 1954 the Joint Services Committee had certainly foreseen the requirement for some low-height buses for city services, but at the May 1956 Committee meeting it was reported that the Stockwood Lane Estate had not yet been developed and so the ten Lodekkas on order would be cancelled, and 13 would be substituted for 13 KSWs in the 1957 programme. This would relieve the City Council's renewals fund of a £40,000 liability in 1956 and obviate the necessity to borrow for the foreseeable future. However, by the meeting of December 1956 the Lodekka had been embraced by the Joint Services Committee with an order for 35 being placed for the 1958 vehicle replacement programme, costing £159,250.

Bristol KSWs continued to be added to the fleet until 1957. C8126 (OHY 983) was among a batch to enter service in 1953, and by the end of the decade had begun to receive 'T' type destination indicators. (*P. Yeomans*)

1955 at last saw the introduction of production Lodekkas. Brand new and gleaming L8252 (THW 742), which has still to receive a destination blind, awaits departure from Royal Well bus station, Cheltenham, on 16th April 1955. (*L.B. Lapper*)

Single-deck buses for the 1956 delivery comprised only eight 45-seat LS buses.

Looking ahead, at a time when the Lodekka was making a faltering start to its dominance within the fleet, the company under BTC control was in its heyday, and future MW and FLF Lodekka models had yet to appear, who could foretell that four of the 1956 deliveries, one KSW and three Lodekkas, would survive long enough to acquire a new National green livery, 20 years later?

It was with some foresight that the Bristol Trades Council suggested to the Joint Services Committee that they acquire the old Whitchurch aerodrome as the site of a garage – Bristol having moved its airport some miles south of the city to Lulsgate. The Committee thought this would be a useful site but that it was not essential and not therefore appropriate for the allocation of capital expenditure. However, over 40 years later, successor company FirstGroup decided its operation in south Bristol should move to a purpose-built garage on the other side of the road from the old aerodrome, and during the intervening years the old airport itself became the home of the Bristol bus rally for a number of years!

As far back as 1953 the company had started to replace the Bell Punch ticket machine, which had been in operation for probably 30 years, with the new Setright Speed machine, and during that year had 150 in commission in Stroud and Cheltenham, with Swindon and Bath to follow (78 being authorised for Bath in February 1954 at a cost of £3,549). In 1956, at a Joint Services meeting in June, it was agreed that Bristol city services would benefit from 550 machines at a cost of £27,500; the Committee was told that they would effect a saving of £5,800 per annum, even after depreciation. The new machines enabled better accounting detail to be obtained and all aspects of the conductor's job of fare collecting and cash accounting to be streamlined.

Another of the same batch, L8259, at Gloucester on a hot day – judging by the windscreen position. Passengers in Lodekkas sat at a lower level than on earlier K-series buses, as can be seen when comparing the window-line with the bus alongside. (*Roy Marshall*)

An example of previous practice when the Bell Punch machine was in use, requiring the conductor to carry a rack of pre-priced tickets, is provided by Dave Clarke who was a conductor on the 2½-hour journey from Bath to Salisbury. He started to collect fares as the bus left Bath whilst carrying two separate double-decker racks of tickets to cater for the wide variety of individual fares available on such a long journey.

> When you got to Box, you could take out one row of tickets and put it to one side, and by the time you got to Devizes you could manage with only one rack.

Although the use of the Setright Speed machine varied across the company, in most areas of the company's operation the machine was allocated to the bus working and may have been used by as many as five or six different conductors during the working day, a system that enabled the maximum use to be achieved from the minimum number of machines whilst not allowing any particular conductor to form an 'unhealthy' relationship with a particular machine! However, a number of depots did adopt a one-man-one-machine policy, and this arrangement became more widespread as one-man operation progressed, so as to minimise the time taken at driver changeovers. With both systems, of course, some form of 'changeover' information would be left by the driver/conductor leaving the bus at the relief point, primarily to allow for continuity of accounting, but also to allow Inspectors to check properly for the payment of the correct fare.

After peaking in the country generally during the early 1950s, Bristol (like other operators) saw the highest levels of patronage during the early and mid 1950s. 167 million passenger journeys were made during 1953 in the Bristol area alone, with this figure almost doubled when the rest of the company's area was included. However, with an end to petrol rationing at the start of the decade, it seemed the boom in travel was at an end.

In the latter half of 1956, the Government became embroiled in the Suez Crisis which threatened to disrupt oil supplies severely. As the troubles worsened, and both British and French troops became involved in the region – only later to be replaced by a UN peacekeeping force – an increase of 1/- per gallon in the tax on fuel took effect from the end of December. The Government passed a Bill authorising an immediate surcharge on fares to cover the additional fuel tax – for the duration only – and in addition, an instruction was issued to cut the mileage operated by approximately 10%.

While the Suez Crisis occupied the national headlines, a major story for Bristol's local newspapers was the completely revised traffic arrangements introduced on the Centre (the former Tramways Centre) in September. The aim was to assist the flow of traffic movements which were steadily growing, while continuing to be the focal point for a great many city and country bus services. Almost every Centre bus stop was repositioned as part of the revised arrangements with squads of workmen making the changes overnight from the evening of Saturday 8th September, to ensure everything was in place by 5.00am the next morning.

1957

This was the first year since its introduction that deliveries of the KSW were surpassed by the Lodekka; the KSWs were all for Joint Services, and were not only the last delivered to the company, but also included the last ever KSW built (although a batch of eight of

Bristol Lodekka L8286 (UHY 415) represents the company's standard double-decker of the late 1950s. The shorter, more attractive grille became standard on the vast majority of LD-types. (*P. Yeomans*)

Bristol Tramways' standard single-decker of the fifties became the 45-seat Bristol LS. With destination blind set for Frome, 2909 (XHW 425) was among 1957's new deliveries. (*S.J. Butler collection*)

the narrower KS type were built for Brighton Hove & District after this chassis). Seventeen of this intake were once again powered by the AVW engine, with the balance of eight being fitted with Gardner units. The last ever KSW-type, C8431, YHT 927, chassis number 118.037, was delivered in time to be operated alongside the first ever K-type, chassis 42.1, EAE 280, C3082 (formerly C3063) which, although withdrawn during that year, was still on the company's books at the time: by early in 1958 C3082 was in the breaker's yard.

With the delivery of C8431, the company had received over 380 of the KS and KSW-type buses, most with Bristol's own engine, and this type of bus represented over 25% of the fleet. YHT 927 was also to prove itself a survivor, going on to serve the public of Macao for many years after its service in Bristol was no longer required, an especially interesting development as earlier attempts by the Tramways Company to offer the KS and KSW type for export had been stillborn.

Lodekka deliveries consisted of 13 for the Joint Services (with, of course, the AVW engine) and 11 for country services, four of which also had the Bristol power unit, and including two Gardner-engined buses for the Bath Tramways Motor Company fleet. Only three of the 1957 LD buses benefited from platform doors.

Single-deck deliveries were 31 LS-type, 25 being standard 45-seat buses and six being 41-seat, dual-purpose semi-coaches, one of which was for the Bath Tramways Motor Company fleet. The dual-purpose vehicles were later painted in a brighter version of the standard livery, with a cream roof and rear corner panels to complement the cream waist band. Some of these LS buses were to have an extended life when, on withdrawal in the early seventies, they were rebuilt with six-cylinder engines, modern (RE-style) interior and flat windscreen, and renumbered in the 3000 series.

The one final delivery that year was one of only six experimental, 30-foot long LDL Lodekkas built, taking advantage of the recently changed regulations on public service vehicle length and axle weight limits. As L8450, Gardner-engined chassis 134.153, carrying a 70-seat, rear-entrance body with platform doors, lasted until 1975, but was to remain unique in the fleet. For some time this bus operated from Bath depot, where its extra capacity was useful on the service to and from the troop camps at nearby Colerne.

Harold Ottway, who was the first black bus driver in the company, joined in Bath during 1956 and went on to complete 40 years of service; he remembers Colerne well. The RAF airfield was often shrouded in fog. He went up there on such a day and once past the Guard Room at the main entrance he had to follow the airfield perimeter road around.

> Of course, because of the fog my conductor should have been walking in front of me, but I was following the kerb and apparently I turned left off the runway I was on, without realising it, and these planes were parked up, and all of a sudden I heard a bang! I'd hit the wing of a plane with my bus!

Just before the arrival of L8450, the first 70-seater bus in the fleet, the company had taken another step towards modernisation by changing its name to the Bristol Omnibus Company Limited, as the BT&CC title had long become outdated, yet to many, the firm would remain known as 'The Tramway'. This change took place on 1st May 1957, although it had been discussed

In 1957, following a further relaxation of maximum permitted vehicle dimensions, Bristol built a trial batch of six extended, 30ft-long Lodekkas, designated LDLs. They were distributed among BTC operators, with one naturally allocated to the 'home' fleet. With seats for 70 pasengers, Bristol's local example became L8450 (YHT 962). (*Bristol Vintage Bus Group*)

at Board level as far back as November 1941, and a decision had been set aside for a future meeting! It was agreed at the same time that the assets of the two Bath companies should be purchased and merged with the Bristol company, although the Bath companies' names remained as subsidiaries for a further decade.

In the year when the first ever K-type was withdrawn, so too was the last G-type, which, although having been rebodied and rehabilitated, had seen a creditable 19 years' service.

In keeping with the new order the first of the extensive conversion of some country services to one-man operation took place during this year, using the small Bedford OB single-deckers, the underfloor engined LS buses and rebuilt J and L-types where the rear door had been replaced by one at the front, or, in the case of Joint Services vehicles that were transferred to country service, the rear door was removed; in each case the bulkhead on the vertical-engined saloons was altered to allow the driver to communicate with his passengers, albeit by rather awkwardly turning through almost 180 degrees.

In an effort to ease the driver's burden, however, at a Board meeting in September authorisation was given for the company to purchase its first batch of motor units to power the Setright machine, and, apart from

The arrival of coach versions of the LS, featuring underfloor engines, instantly led to the remainder of the coach fleet being considered old-fashioned. This official view of 2880 (THY 954), in delightful cream with green trim, was used to promote private hire work. (*Bristol Tramways*)

some flirtation with a small number of Almex machines, this was to become the company's standard one-man ticket issuing equipment until wholesale replacement by electronic Wayfarer machines some 30 years later.

Production of the reliable 8.14-litre AVW engine was coming to the end of its life, to be replaced by the larger, but seemingly less reliable, 8.9-litre BVW unit, designed to provide sufficient power for the up and coming generation of heavier, 70-seater buses: however, the remaining AVW engines continued to be supplied to the company for its rear-entrance Lodekka fleet.

Despite the attention that the Joint Services Committee had given to improving and extending the city services, it was reported to a Special Committee meeting in August 1957 that there had been a downward trend in passenger numbers since 1954 and that this had not been arrested in 1957, requiring yet another application to be submitted to the Traffic Commissioners for an increase in fare levels, whilst at the October 1957 meeting Mr Patey for the company pointed out that a platform staff strike in July involved the Joint Services in a substantial loss in revenue both during the strike and subsequently; it seemed inevitable that by early in 1958 the Joint Services would be involved in a continuing cycle of increased fares and reduced services in order to make up this loss.

Inevitably, any strike by transport workers tends to accelerate passenger losses as it encourages travellers to find alternatives, especially if coupled to subsequent fare rises. However, as part of the press coverage during the dispute, one interesting social observation was the appearance of a picture in the *Bristol Evening World*, taken outside a strike meeting, showing lines of bicycles as far as the eye could see. This, at the time, represented the usual form of personal transport for bus workers, as was the case generally for many personnel employed in industry, whose only alternative was the bus.

At a subsequent BJS meeting in December, agreement was reached to hold over the delivery of 14 of the 35 double-deck buses on order for the 1958 programme in order to help the Joint Services' financial situation, saving £61,000 in capital expenditure; this was to be accompanied by a major revision in services during 1958.

On a more mundane matter, time was taken at these meetings to agree that the words 'Bus Garage' should be added to the name displayed on each of the Joint Services' depots in Bristol!

1958

The demise of the K-type meant that for the first time since its introduction, none of this type was taken into the fleet in 1958. Double-deck requirements were fulfilled by the delivery of 33 standard-length, 58-seat, LD Lodekkas, the ten open-platform BJS buses featuring the AVW engine, whilst two similar ones for the Cheltenham fleet and four for Bath Electric Tramways were Gardner-powered. Of 17 closed-platform examples all but two were also Gardner-powered, and one of these also went to the Bath Electric Tramways fleet.

Single-deck deliveries were the last of the LS buses to be delivered (six with 41-seat, dual-purpose bodies) and the first of the new LS replacement – the MW (Medium Weight saloon). This was a 45-seat, 5-cylinder, Gardner-engined model, 19 of which were for country services while two went to Bath Tramways Motor Company, with the initial style of 'upright flat back' body, followed by two of the next (and new standard) variant of the body with 41 dual-purpose seats, also for the Bath Tramways Motor Company.

From 1958, the Bristol MW Medium Weight saloon took over from the LS as the standard single-deck model for Bristol Omnibus, as the company was now known, and indeed for all Tilling group operators. The first example of this type for Bristol was 2930 (920 AHY) which entered service early in the year, and is seen at Oxford, about to leave for Swindon with a full complement of passengers. Early ECW-bodied MWs reverted to having cream window surrounds, rather than a waistband. (*R.H.G. Simpson*)

In another attempt to improve the fleet's flexibility and reduce ancillary operating costs, deliveries during this year changed from being fitted with the 36 by 12 inch destination aperture to a new standard, the 'T' type destination box, complete with an ultimate destination and a four track number display, both front and rear: MW number 2935 and LD number L8466 were the first buses to be delivered with this new arrangement.

During the previous year it had been continually reported at the BJS Committee that traffic congestion in Bristol was hampering the operation of both the city network and the country services from Bristol, which terminated at various stops around the Tramways Centre (a name that is still in common use amongst older Bristolians today, over 60 years since the demise of the trams!). As a result, a major upheaval of city services took place in September 1958, with a view to making necessary economies and restoring reliability, together with the introduction of a system of Compulsory (white) and Request (yellow) bus stops.

This system of stops also found its way to other towns and cities within the company's operating area: Clive Norman recalls that the theory was all very well, but in practice many crews would agree between them a system of 'bells for all stops', meaning that every stop would be treated as a request stop. One driver, working a late shift, took exception to this and wished to work by the book, whilst his mate wanted the more unofficial practice. Their route was a very quiet one with few passengers, and the conductor might have expected to spend much of the evening relaxing in a seat in the lower saloon. However, the driver pulled up at each compulsory stop, requiring the conductor to get up and ring the bell. Rumour has it, says Clive, that after a while the conductor got fed up with this and refused to ring the bell. Passengers were then treated to the unusual sight of the driver getting down from his cab and walking around the bus to mount the platform and ring the bell. Having given himself the start signal he then went back to his cab to resume the journey!

In addition to the city service changes, a new Bus and Coach Station opened at Marlborough Street, on the edge of the shopping centre in Bristol, on the site of the company's old Whitson Street premises. Previously, many country services (together with express departures) had started from the Prince Street area, but the new covered bus station, which had been planned as far back as 1953 and was allocated a capital budget of £142,000 in September 1954, brought all of the country services from Bristol and the Express Coach services together on two platforms connected by a passenger subway, along with garaging and maintenance facilities. As a result, city depots lost their allocation of country service buses and crews, a move that created a further divide between the two types of operation which would eventually result in the formation of two completely separate and competing companies, at privatisation and deregulation some 30 years later.

For the immediate future, however, as transfer to the country rosters at the city depots was usually a matter of seniority, the average age of Marlborough Street staff was particularly high, and Trade Union agreements meant that up until the late 1970s direct entry recruits to the depot were positively discouraged; as Marlborough Street staff either retired or left the company's service, therefore, replacements continued to be drawn from those staff at the city depots who wished to transfer. This resulted in the prevailing staff shortage of the company being equally distributed throughout Bristol, the downside of which was that as the country operation from Marlborough Street had fewer of the frequent services that could cope with one or two buses missing, irregular rural services were occasionally withdrawn or the burden fell heavily onto those frequent services that it did operate, both of which scenarios caused major inconvenience for country service passengers.

Although the new facility was ideally sited for access to the new Broadmead shopping centre and the city's central business district, for many years, even until and beyond its redevelopment in 2006, there were many calls from transport lobbyists (who did not understand the passenger dynamics of the country services) to have the bus station relocated to Bristol's main Temple Meads railway station, a mile and a half away, to encourage integration. However, in the opinion of local transport professionals, it was really the legendary I.K. Brunel who had placed his railway station in an inconvenient location, not the Omnibus Company!

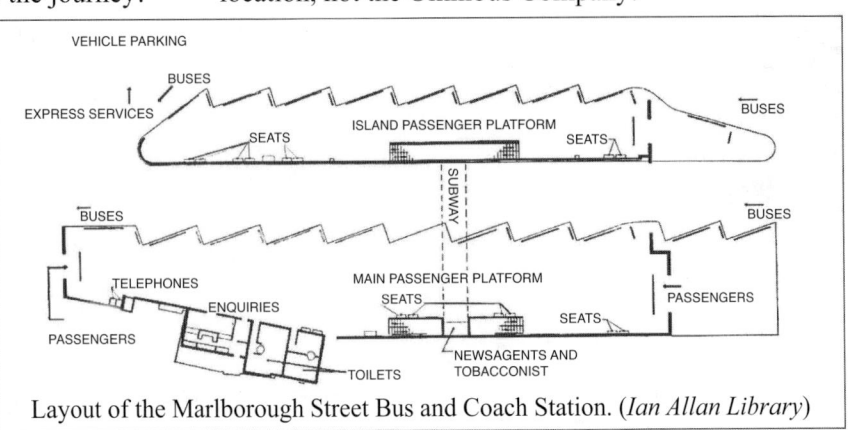

Layout of the Marlborough Street Bus and Coach Station. (*Ian Allan Library*)

Major changes to services resulted from the opening of the new bus and coach station at Marlborough Street. *On the left*, the building is nearing completion. *Below*, the spacious main platform shortly after it was brought into use in September 1958. The bays were of a saw-tooth design which allowed safe boarding for passengers alongside the kerb onto both front and rear entrance vehicles. (*Both photos, Bristol Evening Post*)

(*right*) This shows the second, island platform at Marlborough Street, immediately following the opening. In this view there seems to be more staff than public present, at what appears to be a quiet time of day. Express services also departed from this platform, to the left and behind the camera position. (*Bristol Evening Post*)

With an eye to passenger comfort and convenience, 1958 also saw the opening of a new bus and coach station in central Bath, which just happened to be next to the railway station, although the depot remained at Kensington, a couple of miles away. Bath's bus station, too, had been planned for many years, with a cost estimate of £74,950 being submitted in 1952.

Bath's long-established Kensington depot on the London Road was acquired with the takeover of the Bath subsidiaries, Bristol's own premises in Bath having previously been in the Kingsmead area.

(*right*) A plan of Bath Bus Station, which was of a completely different design to the station in Bristol. The passenger area was open, not covered (other than the platform) while buses reversed onto each bay, as they did at Gloucester, Stroud and Wells. As more forward entrance buses were introduced, this was later changed to a 'nose-first' arrangement. (*Ian Allan Library*)

(*right*) The opening of Bath's new bus station preceded Bristol's by five months. This view was probably taken on 31st March 1958, the day the station was opened. Two Greyhound LSs wait in Railway Street, that nearest the camera being 2882 which still displays 'Bristol Tramways' on its boot lid. (*Fox Photos Ltd*)

(*left*) Staff at Bath Bus Station enjoy their new canteen facilities on what appears to be the first day, with plenty of tea available though the only food visible is from a conductor's packed lunch! High standards of appearance and smartness among the crews are again in evidence. (*Fox Photos Ltd*)

(*left*) Royal visits always cause a certain amount of disruption: an advance notice leaflet issued by the company giving the alterations to services for the event.

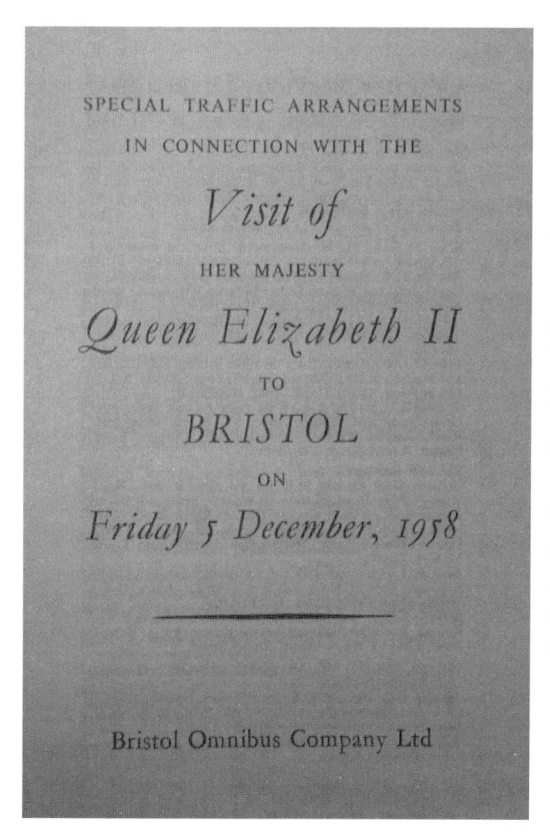

(*right*) A ticket for the Bath City Tour purchased by John Batten in 1958. Written by hand and carbonated, copies were kept by the office for charting the passenger numbers and reconciling the revenue. (*John Batten collection*)

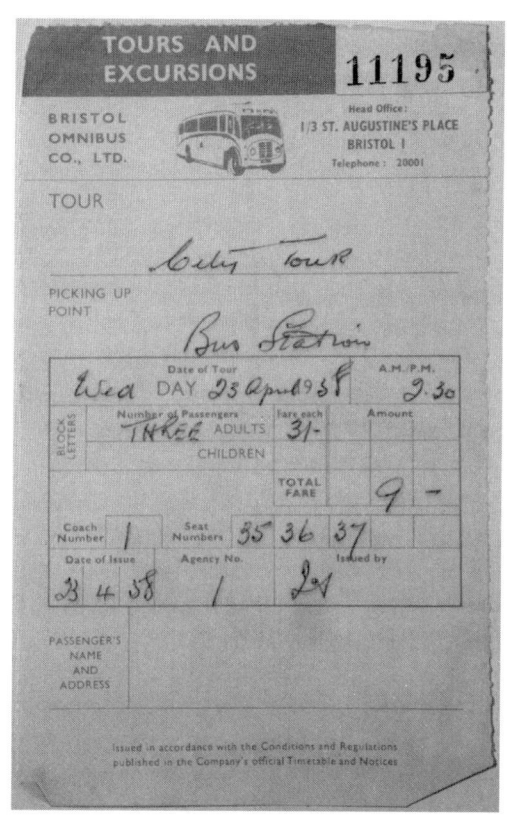

1959

Once again the LD Lodekka dominated vehicle deliveries, with 60 entering service during the year. Of the 30 for Joint Services, two-thirds were delivered with Bristol engines; the remainder, of course, were fitted with Gardner's 6LW unit. All had open platforms. Four other open-platform LDs were also delivered, three for Gloucester city services fitted with Gardner engines, and one for Cheltenham with a Bristol unit. Twenty-six country service LDs completed the batch, all with platform doors, five of which were for the Bath Electric Tramways fleet and five for the Bath Tramways Motor Company; the latter ones displaced the unique lowbridge KSWs of 1952 from some of the more prestigious country routes from Bath, such as the 2½-hour Bath to Salisbury service. All but two of the country services deliveries came with the Gardner engine, and it is believed that the changeover from the Bristol AVW to the new and larger BVW unit was made during the 1959 deliveries.

From Gloucester city bus GL8507 onwards, the double-deck delivery of LDs came with what was to become the new standard Cave-Browne-Cave heating and venti-lation system, a development that saw the radiator of the bus split into two units and mounted at the front above the cab, either side of the destination display. From his cab, the driver was able to direct the airflow at the front of the bus either through the radiators, to provide warm air into the saloons, or around them, to provide fresh air. Unfortunately for the citizens in the company's area these buses were also delivered with the less effective hopper vents to the front and just some of the side windows, rather than the familiar push out or sliding ones, and the buses entered service during a heat wave with the drivers unfamiliar with the new heating technology! After a number of complaints, and worse, the offending buses were quickly recalled to Central Repair Works or their depots, where more adequate opening window vents were fitted by means of a window swap with some of the older LDs.

Single-deck deliveries were all 5-cylinder MW types and of the 27, five went to Bath Tramways Motor Company and three to Gloucester city services. Most were 45-seat buses, but four were equipped with dual-purpose seating for 41 passengers.

Also in 1959, and partly as a result of the 1958 service changes, the Joint Services Committee had agreed to review the BJS fleet profile. The result of this review was that 28 single-deckers would be replaced by extending the life of double-deckers, and 12 dual-entrance L-types would be transferred to country services in exchange for 35-seat, rear-entrance country services buses: the company could, of course, more easily convert the dual-door buses to one-man operation, which was still not envisaged for the city services. Some city single-deckers were still required, however, not

One of the last new vehicles received during the fifties was Bristol/ECW MW5G 2974 (986 EHY), with 45 seats. It was photographed (with trade plates) on its delivery run from Lowestoft, with ECW window stickers prominently displayed. (*R.H.G. Simpson*)

only because of a small number of routes that operated under a low overhead obstruction, but because it was company practice in the 1950s to allow a small number of conductors to work only on single-deckers, as they were not considered fit enough to conduct on double-deckers! At the December Joint Services Committee meeting of that year, it was reported that single-deck L-type buses which had been sold realised between £79 and £240 each, the majority of the batch being sold for £150. Interestingly, at the same time it was revealed that some of the Leylands were similarly sold, and realised £188 each.

The final vehicle delivery for the year was another 'first' – an FLF 70-seat double-decker, registered 995 EHW and allocated fleet number LC8540. The F series, replacing the LD, was the latest, and last, reincarnation of the now popular Lodekka, the chassis having been redesigned to allow a completely flat floor throughout the bus, without the slightly sunken lower-deck gangway of the LD. FLF indicated a Long (30 feet), Forward entrance version of the F-series. 995 EHW was initially built with a sliding front door and was demonstrated to W. Alexander & Sons, Falkirk, Scottish Omnibuses and Crosville Motor Services, being later modified to folding jacknife doors, which, with the exception of a few coaches for Thames Valley, was to become standard on the FLF and shorter FSF types. Fitted with the Bristol BVW engine, the bus entered service on Bristol's busy cross city route 11, from Oldbury Court in the north-east of the city to Hengrove in the south-west. 995 EHW,

In 1959 Bristol and ECW produced this 30ft-long, forward-entrance Lodekka, the prototype FLF. It was powered by a Bristol engine and was the first Lodekka in the fleet to incorporate several other improvements, including a completely flat, lower saloon floor – with no sunken gangway. Registered 995 EHW, it was demonstrated to a number of other operators around Britain. This vehicle was initially allocated fleet number LC8540 (just to confuse everyone, as the only other Lodekka of this length was the LDL, L8450). It was later re-numbered LC7000 – by which time it had also lost its sliding entrance door, to be replaced by jack-knife doors, which became standard for the type. (*Bristol Vintage Bus Group*)

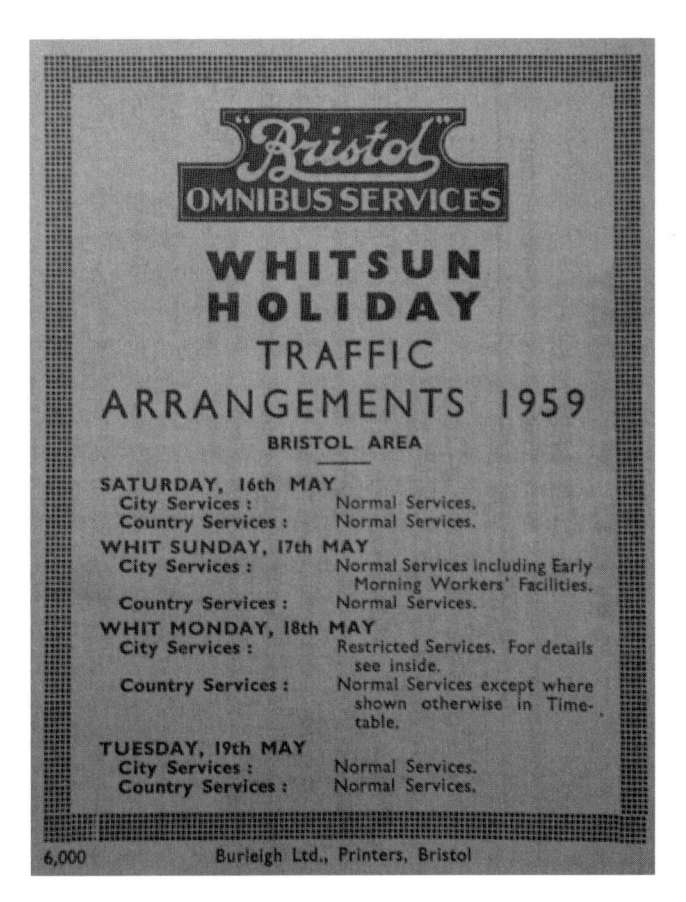

```
╔══════════════════════════════════╗
║         Bristol                  ║
║      OMNIBUS SERVICES            ║
║                                  ║
║         WHITSUN                  ║
║         HOLIDAY                  ║
║         TRAFFIC                  ║
║    ARRANGEMENTS 1959             ║
║         BRISTOL AREA             ║
║                                  ║
║   SATURDAY, 16th MAY             ║
║     City Services:    Normal Services. ║
║     Country Services: Normal Services. ║
║   WHIT SUNDAY, 17th MAY          ║
║     City Services:    Normal Services including Early ║
║                       Morning Workers' Facilities. ║
║     Country Services: Normal Services. ║
║   WHIT MONDAY, 18th MAY          ║
║     City Services:    Restricted Services. For details ║
║                       see inside. ║
║     Country Services: Normal Services except where ║
║                       shown otherwise in Time- ║
║                       table. ║
║   TUESDAY, 19th MAY              ║
║     City Services:    Normal Services. ║
║     Country Services: Normal Services. ║
║                                  ║
║  6,000    Burleigh Ltd., Printers, Bristol ║
╚══════════════════════════════════╝
```

together with later sister vehicles, was the cause of much fascination and many a diversion by co-author Mike Walker, who found that, on his way home from school, he could catch a number 11 for three stops to central Bristol before catching the old order, a Leyland PD1, for the remaining 30-minute journey home. One of the results of this regular diversion was achieving full marks for his science homework, drawing a diagram of the use of a mirror, when he faithfully reproduced that fascinating view from the upper-deck seats which enabled passengers to sit and watch the opening and closing of the platform doors in the staircase mirror!

The bus was renumbered LC7000 (later C7000) in 1961 in what was to become the start of a numbering series that would last until the Bristol city FLFs became the last conventional, vertical front-engined double-deckers in service with their original owners within what was to become the National Bus Company. At the time of writing this remarkable survivor is still in existence, although now non-operational, and rests in the delightful climate on the islands of Hawaii, having served tourists there for many years.

1959 also saw the last of the J-type single-deck buses bow out from regular service, although they had been much rebuilt since entering service in 1938 and many were indistinguishable from the L-types still in the fleet.

In an experiment that was to be a foretaste of things to come Joint Services KSW C8234 was fitted with an off-side illuminated advertisement panel; it was, of course, only lit by tungsten bulbs and was removed one year later, but the idea was to resurface on later deliveries of FLF buses with offside fluorescently-lit advertisement panels.

Continuing its attempts to encourage passenger growth, during 1959 the company completed an extensive refit of its bus station waiting-room facilities and travel office at Weston-super-Mare, and, during the summer, introduced 'Day-Out' tickets to encourage greater use of the services on offer, with the tickets initially being bought, pre-dated, from any company office. These tickets (which were later available on buses) proved to be a great incentive for many young enthusiasts – including the authors – to explore the extremities of the company's operating area, often leaving home on the first bus and not returning until late in the evening having covered many miles on all varieties of the Bristol-built product!

One of the facilities that the holder of a 'Day-Out' ticket could use, albeit briefly, was one of the six extra buses provided by the company over the Bristol-Radstock-Frome route following the withdrawal of the local railway service. However, the February 1965 issue of *Modern Transport* reported that this produced an average of only six extra passengers per bus – causing the service to be reduced to a peak-hour-only operation by a single vehicle. Clearly most of the railway traffic was lost to public transport for good, a pattern that was to follow with most of the rail replacement services. This was regardless of the level of service that the company was able to provide to replace those rail services subject to withdrawal under the proposals put forward by Dr Beeching.

Geoff Lusher, who joined the company in 1959 as a traffic trainee, recalls that the company set up a special department to deal with rail replacement services ('two of us under the stairs at the Centre offices'). The department was provided with station to station loading figures by British Railways and from this information produced the best possible service to replace the rail service scheduled for withdrawal. Of course, as with the Bristol to Frome service, the railway traffic did not usually transfer to the replacement bus service and was lost to public transport for ever.

Geoff also recalls that when the Rail Motor service between Chalford and Gloucester through Brimscombe, Stroud and Stonehouse, was proposed for withdrawal, the parallel bus service linking Chalford with Stroud was doubled in frequency. In the event, however, despite some Saturday rail journeys carrying 200 plus passengers, the traffic just did not transfer to the bus, almost certainly because the bus connections onwards to Gloucester introduced an uncertainty and delay to the journey that the passengers wished to make. Geoff also recalls that at the Public Inquiry arranged to hear the evidence for the rail closure, the bus company officers got the distinct impression that the public blamed them for their loss of train service, and, he recalls, the railway officers did not even turn up!

Nevertheless, with the redevelopment and modernisation of its passenger facilities, the introduction of one-man operation on country services, the arrival of the first 70-seat FLF bus and the recasting of its Bristol city services with a view to reducing the effects of congestion and ongoing financial losses, the company entered the 1960s with a positive outlook.

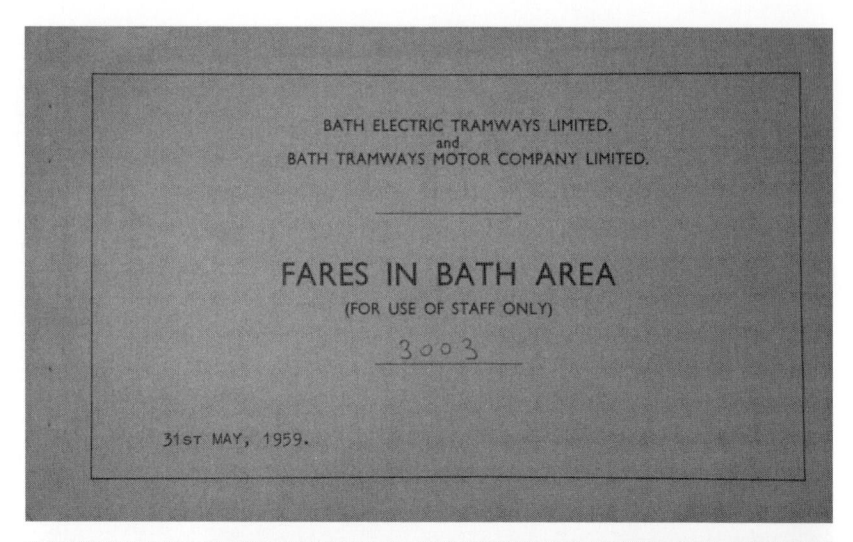

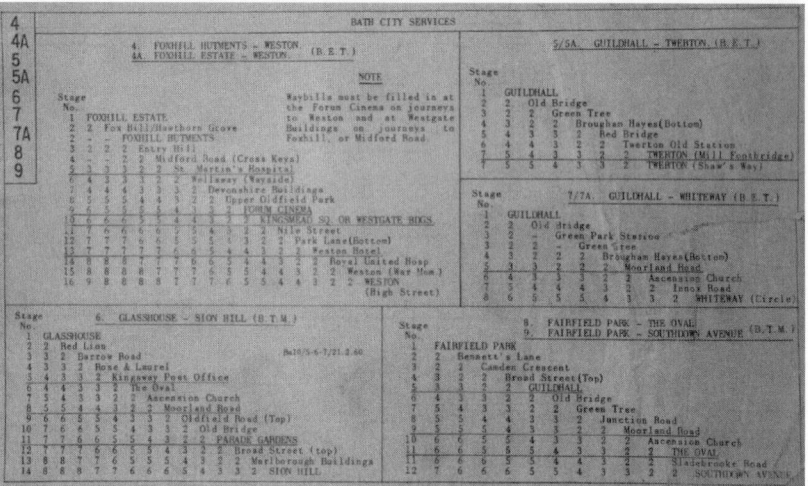

* * *

A selection of bus company items from the period, including, clockwise from above: a conductor's schedule of fares for Bath routes 4 to 9; a BTCCL uniform button; an Inspector's ticket punch; a conductor's paying-in cash bag; and a Bath uniform badge.

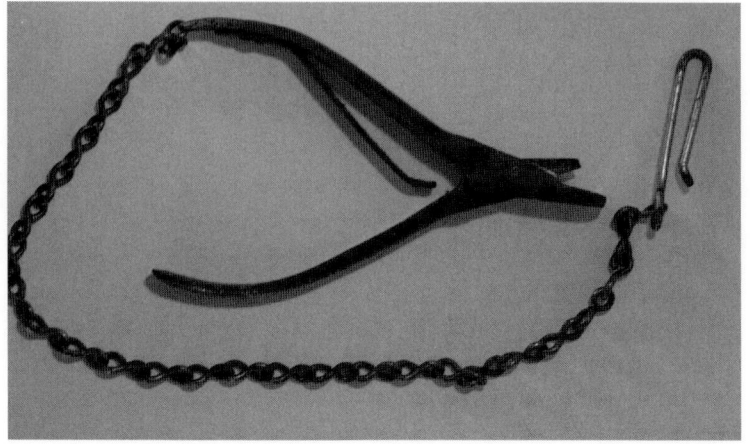

(*above*) The northern end of the Centre (officially named Colston Avenue) during the early 1950s. Traffic flowed in an anti-clockwise direction in this area, with bus shelters positioned along both sides of the island. The company offices are in the distance to the right. (*Reece Winstone Archive*)

(*right*) The exit from Bristol bus and coach station into Whitson Street, with short grille (L8401) and long grille (L8261) LD Lodekkas in view. During the fifties and early sixties there was a very distinctive, but not unpleasant, aroma in this building (and at Weston bus station) caused by trapped engine fumes. This changed however as both engine and fuel types developed, to become, at times, quite objectionable during later years. (*S.J. Butler collection*)

67

(*above*) Bath in 1950, and Bristol K5G 3803 (GL 6603) swings out of Manvers Street into Dorchester Street, destined for Whiteway Cemetery. This bus, built in 1939, carries Bristol's own BBW 56-seat bodywork. (*R.R. Bowler*)

(*above*) A 1955 photo of Bristol/ECW K6B 3867 (LHU 989) negotiating the top of Wells Road, Bath, on service 11. Vehicles in 'Festival of Britain' livery appeared with wheels and wings finished in either black, Brunswick green or Tilling green, each of which considerably changed the appearance of the bus. (*R.R. Bowler*)

(*above*) The mid-1950s at The Bear Flat, Bath, with Bristol KS-type 8019 (displaying 'Bath Services' names) operating towards Larkhall, while 3868, still in 'Festival of Britain' livery heads the other way for Combe Down. (*R.R. Bowler*)

(*below*) Bristol vehicles with BBW and ECW bodywork gather in the High Street, Bath, in the shadow of its vast Abbey, during the early 1950s. Before the opening of Bath bus station, many crew changes took place here. (*R.R. Bowler*)

(*left*) Two 'lowbridge' Bristol K6As with Strachans bodywork squeeze past each other on Bristol city service 36. On the left is LC3377 (JAE 765), while operating in the opposite direction is country services L3642 (HHY 586). (*Peter Davey*)

(*right*) Waiting to depart on the 2 hour 40 mins-long journey from Bristol to Swindon, 8021 (NAE 53) is a Bristol KS model fitted with an 8ft-wide body, which is clearly visible by the wheel-arch overhang (*Roy Marshall*)

(*left*) Vehicle 3641 is not at all that it appears at first sight. This is wartime Guy Arab HHW 16 as illustrated in the previous chapter, but by 1951 it had been fitted with a secondhand BBW body and PV2 radiator, giving the appearance (at first glance) of a Bristol-built vehicle. Several of the Guy Arabs were treated in this fashion, causing some confusion! (*Bristol Vintage Bus Group*)

(*right*) Cheltenham District L89 (THW 731) was another of the 'THW' registered LD-type Lodekkas which, like its sisters, originally featured a long grille and front wings. All LD front mudguards were rapidly shortened and many also received this later style of short grille, offering a less overwhelming appearance. (*A.J. Douglas*)

(*left*) 2364 (AHW 537), a 1934 Bristol JO5G with the company's own 35-seat bodywork, departs here fully loaded from Weston-super-Mare. When withdrawn in 1957, this bus was converted into a mobile electricians' workshop for use during the construction of Marlborough Street bus station, Bristol. The house behind the rear of the bus was the Weston manager's residence.
(*Roy Marshall*)

(*right*) 2501 (MHU 247) was one of two lightweight Beadle-Morris buses of integral construction, introduced during 1949. They were powered by Saurer diesel engines. Both could be found for a time working service 31 (Bristol-Malmesbury-Swindon) and lasted until 1958. (*Authors' collection*)

(*left*) A number of coach services were operated by modernised Bristol JO6As with BBW-bodies finished in bright cream and green colours. 2202 (DHY 654) was among them, originally having carried a Duple coach body when it entered service in 1937. It is pictured at Victoria Coach Station, London during the early fifties. (*C.W. Routh*)

(*right*) G1297 (MHW 993), a 1950 Bristol/ECW L-type 35-seater, was new as 2458 but was transferred to Gloucester in the late fifties and accordingly acquired that city's coat of arms and a new fleet number. (*C.W. Routh*)

(*left*) Towing vehicles formed an important part of the service vehicle fleet, especially when things went wrong. With trade plate 075 AE, this B-type-based vehicle has a Gardner 6LW engine and is assisting C3066, a GO5G type. (*Bristol Vintage Bus Group*)

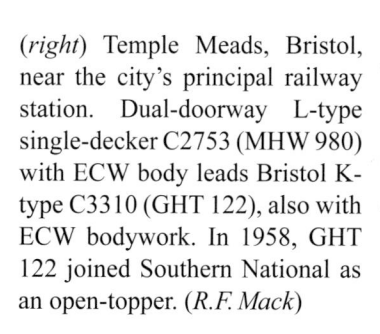

(*right*) Temple Meads, Bristol, near the city's principal railway station. Dual-doorway L-type single-decker C2753 (MHW 980) with ECW body leads Bristol K-type C3310 (GHT 122), also with ECW bodywork. In 1958, GHT 122 joined Southern National as an open-topper. (*R.F. Mack*)

(*left*) LHW 907 was another bus to become a member of the 'service vehicle' fleet, numbered W96 in the works series. This L5G started life as 35-seater 2284 in 1949, but became a stores van – involving a body swap – after withdrawal from the passenger fleet. (*C.W. Routh*)

(*right*) YHY 80 was a 1957 Bristol LS5G equipped with dual-purpose seating, and originally numbered 2922. When new, it wore green bus livery with a cream waistband, but in 1959 it received an additional cream roof to denote its dual-purpose status. Later still it was re-numbered 2004. (*R.H.G. Simpson*)

(*left*) A scene in rural Gloucestershire, with the crews of two typically 1950s vehicles exchanging gossip as they meet, although the block letter fleetname indicates that this is actually the very early sixties. Lodekka L8260 is travelling from Stonehouse towards Stroud, when it encounters Light Saloon 2837 on a working to Leonard Stanley from Gloucester. (*C.W. Routh*)

72

With Weston's seafront services in the hands of Bristol K-types throughout most of the 1950s, they grew in popularity as more and more visitors made the journey to the coast. 3614 (GL 6612) is a former Bath vehicle, looking resplendent in cream livery at the Old Pier. (*R.R. Bowler*)

3. The Swinging Sixties

The arrival of the 1960s – soon to be dubbed 'the swinging sixties' during which all sorts of social conventions began to be questioned and challenged by, in particular, younger members of society – initially made little impact on the Bristol Omnibus Company.

The Bristol passenger fleet at the time totalled 1,267 vehicles, with main depots located at Bristol (Avonmouth, Brislington, Eastville, Lawrence Hill, Marlborough Street, Staple Hill and Winterstoke Road), Bath, Cheltenham, Cirencester, Devizes, Gloucester, Hanham, Highbridge, Stroud, Swindon, Wells, Weston-super-Mare and Wotton-under-Edge.

1960
Despite the entry into service of production versions of the forward entrance Lodekka during 1960, a small number of rear-entrance buses were also taken into stock, comprising four FS versions of the Lodekka which were effectively updated versions of the earlier LD model. These were Gardner-engined 60-seat buses with enclosed rear platform doors for country services and although joined the following year by four rather different FSs, remained unique in the fleet. Further double-decker deliveries comprised forward-entrance Lodekkas of the 70-seat FLF type, similar to LC8540, and an even greater number of the shorter FSF type – with rumours abounding that the crews, especially in Bristol city, were reluctant to accept the 70-seater because of its greater seating capacity.

Eleven 70-seaters were delivered to the Joint Services fleet, continuing the Lodekka numbering series from LC8551 to LC8561, with LC8556 onwards being delivered with fluorescent lighting and an illuminated offside advertisement panel. All featured Bristol's

Bristol Joint Services 1960 ECW-bodied Bristol FLF LC7008 (ex- LC8558) at the bottom of Bristol's steep Park Street en route for the Centre and Warmley. The University of Bristol's Wills Tower is in the background at the top of the hill. The illuminated off-side advertisement panel can be seen standing proud of the body side panels between the decks in this May 1964 view. (*S.J. Butler collection*)

This bodybuilders' photograph of the rear offside of Bristol FLF, 509 OHU, which was to become country services bus 7064, shows that buses other than those for the Joint Services fleet were still being built with an ultimate destination display at the rear in addition to the four-track number display in 1962. (*ECW*)

revised 8.9 litre BVW engine, and the arrival of these buses heralded a further reduction in the amount of information on display for services in the city as they were delivered with only a number display at the rear, a display option that was to become standard on BJS buses, despite the fact that country services FLFs were to continue to be built with rear destination displays as well as the number tracks. The latter part of this batch of FLFs entered service on route 11 towards the second half of the year, initially without advertisements occupying those illuminated panels, which, with the addition of their ultra bright interior fluorescent tubes, singled them out as an impressive and distinctive glowing beacon illuminating the gloom and rain of the early autumn evenings in the city.

The delivery of the FLF Lodekkas was accompanied by a batch of no fewer than 19 of the shorter, 60-seat front entrance FSF types, 11 of which were BVW-engined for Joint Services and the remaining eight were Gardner-engined, three of which were for Gloucester

BJS received only 16 of the short Bristol FSF double-deckers. LC6015 (714 JHY), formerly LC8573, of 1960, is seen here parked at the service 36 bus stop in Lower Maudlin Street, close to Bristol's Marlborough Street bus and coach station, early in its life. (*P. Yeomans*)

ECW-bodied 60-seater 6037, the last of Cheltenham District's FSF buses, new in 1961 and sold to Western National in 1967. It has an off-side illuminated advertisement panel. (*S.J. Butler collection*)

city services, two for the Bath Tramways Motor Company and two for Cheltenham District, the latter being delivered in that delightful dark red and cream livery and numbered L99 and L100: this was to be the highest number reached in the Cheltenham series. The number series for the main fleet buses simply carried on with the existing sequence (which, having been started with eight-feet wide KSW types, continued through the LD Lodekka [plus one LDL], the FS Lodekka and the front entrance FLFs and FSFs), but in January 1961, the FLF series of 70-seaters were renumbered into the 7000 series and the FSF 60-seaters into the 6000 series. There were, however, buses already carrying 6000-series numbers, because the 1960 single-deck arrivals had consisted of 24 MWs, which, having been numbered in the existing series up to 2999 went on to be numbered

1960 45-seat Bristol MW 2998 (520 JHU) sets down passengers at Painswick, between Gloucester and Stroud, in August 1961. This batch of MW buses had hopper ventilators instead of the more usual sliders. On the right of the picture is one of the churchyard's 99 yew trees – legend has it that the 100th will never grow! (*S.J. Butler collection*)

6000 to 6003, the 3000 series being already occupied by the remaining K-types. When the FSFs were renumbered, therefore, it was felt to be less complicated for the continuity of engineering records to start the series at 6004, whilst 6000-6003 were renumbered in order to start a new series as 2500-2503.

Of the MW saloons delivered during 1960, 19 were standard 45-seat, 5-cylinder Gardner-engined buses, whilst five (numbers 2984 to 2988) were 39-seat, 6-cylinder coaches equipped with air suspension. These coaches were themselves renumbered early in 1961 when it was felt desirable to establish a separate numbering series for the entire coaching stock and this encompassed the total postwar coaching fleet, with the first postwar coach, 'Queen Mary' L-type NAE 1, being renumbered from the bus series to become 2050, and the rest of the fleet following on in sequence. At the same time, one coach, LWL number 2073 (formerly 2821) received a prototype revised livery with the green trim on the wings, wheels and within the aluminium mouldings being replaced by maroon, with 'Bristol Greyhound' in script lettering, surrounding the raised aluminium 'dog in wheel' Greyhound device that had been borne by Greyhound coaches since before the Second World War. (This followed trials during the 1950s when some of the company's earliest LS coaches carried cream with either dark red or black relief, instead of green).

The renumbering was not confined to the coaches, single-decks and F-types, since it was also felt desirable to introduce a separate series for dual-purpose vehicles, with the LS semi-coaches being renumbered 2000 onwards. As more new dual-purpose vehicles were delivered, earlier ones were released to be downgraded to buses, reverting to their original numbers.

Of the MW buses received that year, four were directed to the Bath Tramways Motor Company, whilst one further bus was loaned to them from new.

The company continued its policy of encouraging better passenger facilities, with the opening of Stroud bus station and the refurbishment of refreshment facilities at Marlborough, the latter being used for the London service. It should be remembered that in this time before motorways, the Bristol to London express

39-seat ECW-bodied 1955 Bristol Greyhound Bristol LS coach 2102 (THY 954) – originally numbered 2880 – pictured in the later Greyhound livery, introduced in the early 1960s. The outward opening door militated against downgrading these coaches to stage carriage work at the end of their coaching days. (*C.W. Routh*)

77

service operated along the A4 with a typical journey time of about six hours, calling en route at Bath, Chippenham, Marlborough, Hungerford and Reading. Through passengers – and the driver – naturally required a refreshment break, which the company provided at Marlborough, and which was also a crew relief point.

Co-author Mike Walker was once shown an express driver's duty from the early 1960s, which consisted of two return journeys to Marlborough from Bristol, with the driver exchanging his Greyhound coach at Marlborough for a Royal Blue one that had worked from London Victoria, returning it to Bristol, having a break and then doing the same again. He then returned once more to Bristol, with the coach he had started with in the morning – a duty time of over ten hours. The joint tenure of the Bristol to London corridor with Royal Blue ceased at the end of the summer timetable in 1965, and as the M4 motorway was opened in stages, the stopping service along the A4 reduced.

A cap badge, sported by Greyhound drivers throughout the 1960s.

For the engineering and platform staff, the year started well, since the May 1960 Board meeting reported that the working week had been reduced from 44 hours to 42, although not without a cost to the company of around £400,000 per annum. Within Bristol Joint Services particularly, this was still accomplished within a six-day working week for the platform staff, resulting in very short shifts (of around seven hours per day) and the ability to work 'before duty' and 'after duty' overtime to boost the weekly pay-packet.

There were quite often journeys within the city network that were expected to be covered by overtime. Geoff Lusher, along with a number of his traffic office colleagues, regularly performed 'auxiliary' conducting duties, and recalls that during his first weeks he was called to go from the Centre offices to the Bus Station and conduct a bus to the Bristol City football ground at Ashton Gate to take supporters to a home match. 'Being a City supporter I thought that was a new twist – being paid to watch the match!'

However, his first piece of work as a conductor was on a two-door Joint Services Bristol L shuttling the short distance between the Centre and Temple Meads railway station. He recalls that the driver-operated front door was seldom used, and then only at the terminus to allow the bus to be emptied, whilst the conductor-operated back door usually remained open.

1961

Deliveries in 1961 continued the previous year's format, with 26 MW5G service buses, five MW6G coaches, 22 FSF and 13 FLF double-deckers, with the last rear-entrance Lodekkas for the company, a quartet of the FS type that were very special indeed, as we will see later.

Of the 26 MW service buses, seven were for Bath Tramways Motor Company while five were for the Joint Services fleet (a little surprising considering the review of the BJS fleet profile only two years earlier had considerably reduced the single-deck requirements in the city fleet). The Bristol city vehicles were to be reduced to 43-seaters with a luggage rack during 1968 and 1969 when they were eventually operated without a conductor on Joint Services routes.

The MW6G coaches were to the usual 39-seat standard with luxurious green leather seating and were delivered in the new coach colours of cream with maroon trim. In an article in *Passenger Transport* for March 1961 the Bristol to London Express service, which became the 'home' for these coaches, was reported as the first express service route authorised to operate into London Airport.

Of the 22 shorter FSF double-deckers only five were for the Joint Services fleet and these were fitted with BVW engines; BJS were now to standardise on the longer 70-seat model and these were the last of the short versions to join the fleet. The remaining FSF buses were fitted with Gardner 6LW engines; the Cheltenham District fleet received two of these (now numbered into the main fleet series as 6036/7), Gloucester city services added three and Bath Electric Tramways received numerically the last bus, 6041.

All of them were equipped with illuminated offside advertisement panels.

It was a lean year for the Joint Services fleet, with only four of the FLF buses coming to them, surprisingly all powered by Gardner engines, whilst the Bristol BVW-engined ones entered service with the country fleet. The batch introduced cream window rubbers, and offside illuminated advertisement panels to the country services.

Dave Clarke, by then a driver in Bath, remembers those illuminated advertisement panels well. He was driving across Salisbury Plain (a well-known army training area) at night, en route from Bath to Salisbury in a new FLF recently delivered with this feature, when he experienced a strange noise and flash just yards from his bus; he continued his journey only to be overtaken and waved down by an army officer in a jeep. The officer asked 'what the ****' he was driving, illuminating the skyline so brightly, and Dave explained that this was a new type of bus recently delivered to Bath for service on country routes. The officer considered the matter and thanked Dave for the information; in the future, he said, their gun crews would have to be advised that such bright lights on a moving vehicle might affect the aiming mechanism! Dave continued to Salisbury thanking his lucky stars that this was a near miss!

To complete the double-deck deliveries, four rather special FS rear-entrance buses arrived towards the end of the year in an all-over cream livery, with black wings – and detachable roofs! They had been ordered to replace the ageing K-type open-toppers which had soldiered on providing the seafront service at Weston-super-Mare for some nine years and were now over 20 years old.

Unlike these, the FS convertibles had no green relief. Downstairs they were trimmed in the normal Tilling-style seating moquette of the period with green leathercloth side panels, whilst upstairs the seating was in green leathercloth, and internal lights were built into the sidewalls for use when the roof was removed. With the roofs in position, however, during the winter months, these buses were often to be found working Weston-super-Mare town services between the town centre and the Bournville Estate. Apart from the obvious differences, they were standard 60-seat, open-platform, Gardner-engined buses. They had a very long life at Weston-super-Mare (the last one being 20 years old when it was finally replaced by one-man-operated, rear-engined, open-toppers) and subsequently provided open-top services for other operators in such diverse locations as Newport, Poole, Scarborough and Edinburgh. As this book is being written, three of the four remain extant with two of them still licenced to carry fare-paying passengers – not bad for buses celebrating their 45th birthday!

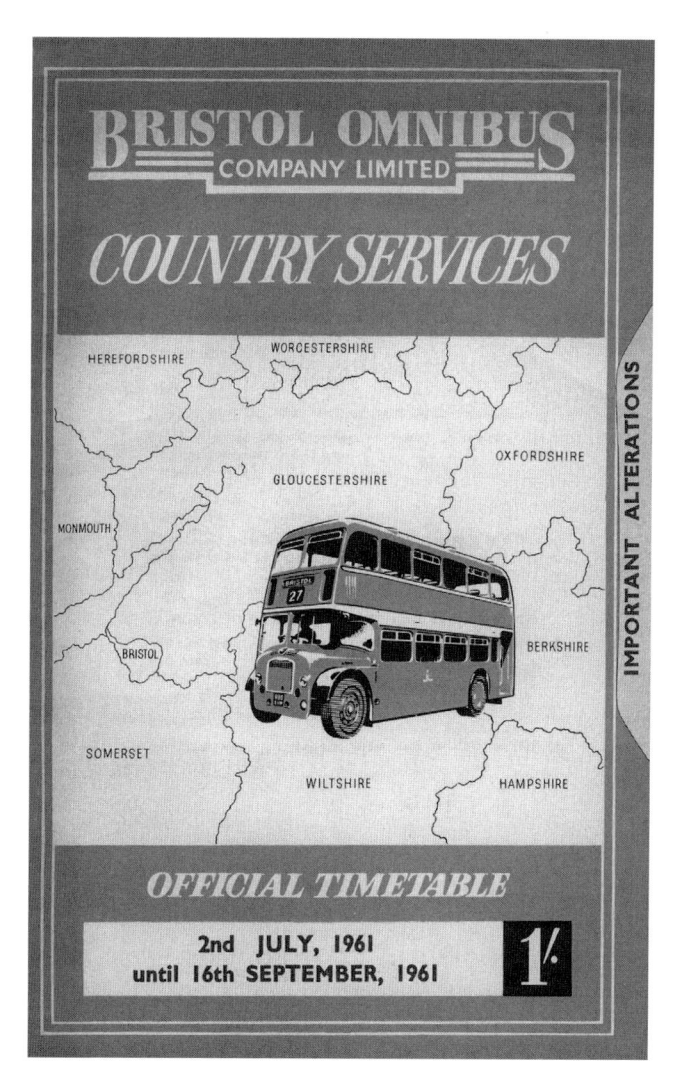

1961 also saw the withdrawal from service of the earliest Bristol L-type bus, chassis number 43.1, registered FAE 56, which, because it had been refurbished and re-bodied, had lasted for 23 years.

In the same year the company's public image began to change ... just a little. The Bristol coat of arms, so long a feature of the side panels of the company's buses regardless of their area of operation, was replaced by a simple yet dignified BRISTOL name, initially in gold block although this was soon changed to yellow as the original version was not prominent on a Tilling green background. This move seemed appropriate since the Joint Services fleet formed only one third of the operation. However, although this change could be accommodated on the vehicles entirely owned by them, and to carry a 'fleetname' was far more in keeping with general Tilling group practice, changing the insignia on the Bristol Joint Services fleet was not so easy.

Spotlight on the FS Open-toppers

Bristol Tramways instituted open top services at Weston-super-Mare during 1950, and continued to employ older vehicles converted to permanent open-top configuration throughout the following decade.

It was decided to renew the open-top fleet at the beginning of the 1960s, when four brand new Bristol Lodekkas of the recently introduced FS type were purchased. These received fleet numbers 8576-9 (866-9 NHT), and carried 60-seat bodywork incorporating open rear platforms (despite forward entrances being preferred for the remainder of the fleet). However, their ECW bodywork featured detachable roof sections which enabled them to run as open-toppers in the summer, or as ordinary covered buses in winter.

These vehicles were finished in all-over cream livery (relieved only by black wheels and wings) so were very conspicuous – even with their 'lids' on.

In open-top form the FS convertibles maintained the seafront service (152, later 103 and later still 100) from Uphill to the Old Pier, which in later years was extended. With roofs on however, they could appear on any town service, or country services from Weston. In addition, they were regularly employed for a range of special events and, together with open-top buses from around the country, would make the annual journey to Epsom racecourse for the Derby, where traditionally, open-top buses provide grandstand and hospitality facilities.

In 1965, when the main Bristol fleet changed from the gold block Bristol name to the scroll, it was decided that the Weston opentop fleet should carry the local Borough arms instead, which obviously met with the approval of the local council as they supplied the transfers!

In due course, black wings and wheels became Brunswick green, in line with the rest of the fleet but a drastic livery change occurred in 1976, by which time the open-top fleet had been expanded to include convertible LDs from Crosville, when Weston's open top Lodekkas each received a pseudo tram livery and name intended to represent towns and cities around the company's operating area. Unfortunately, the subtlety of this was lost on most potential passengers, and more importantly the new liveries acted as camouflage on the seafront, unlike cream which could clearly be seen from a distance as these buses progressed towards waiting passengers.

Nevertheless, the FS open-toppers remained at Weston for some 20 years, the last being withdrawn in 1982. Three are known to survive, one of which is now in the authors' ownership as part of the Bristol Omnibus Vehicle Collection.

(*right*) 8579 in as new condition, operating towards the Grand Pier with roof in position, and displaying gold Bristol block lettering. (*Roy Marshall*)

(*left*) 8578 (868 NHT) on Weston seafront on a chilly day, with more passengers downstairs than on top. The Weston coat of arms has replaced the Bristol fleetname. (*M.S. Curtis*)

(*right*) L8577, with top on, inside Weston bus station where one of these buses could frequently be found, waiting between services. There was some uncertainty concerning the 'L' prefix to the fleet numbers of these buses, since at various times in their lives they displayed plates with or without the 'L' included! (*M.S. Curtis*)

(*left*) The delightful area of Uphill village is the setting for L8576 (876 NHT) as it begins its journey towards the town and seafront, via Old Church Road – part of which was too narrow to allow two buses to pass. (*M.S. Curtis*)

(*left*) When NBC liveries were introduced generally, the open-top fleet initially retained cream, although a block letter Bristol name returned in NBC style, alongside the Borough arms. 8576 stands in the High Street, about to depart on a town service in February 1975. (*M.S. Curtis*)

(*right*) Demonstrating that the tops of convertible buses really do come off, 8577, wearing maroon and white 'tram' livery to represent Swindon, has its roof removed for the 1979 summer season. (*M.S. Curtis*)

At a meeting of the BJS committee in March 1961, Ian Patey, the then general manager of the company, brought the matter of this proposed change to the council members of the Committee, stating that the change was necessitated because the practice of using the city coat of arms on both country and BJS vehicles was misleading, especially as the vehicles were interchanged between Joint and country services for economy of operation, and it was agreed that the matter should be submitted in writing to the Town Clerk for consideration by the Finance and General Purposes Committee of the City Council.

At the subsequent meeting on 30th May it was reported that the Finance and General Purposes Committee had been unwilling for the coat of arms to be removed from BJS vehicles, although they had no objection to the company name being added! Mr Patey would not let the matter drop, however, and requested that the Finance Committee meet him and hear a further submission from the company.

An examination of the 8th May minutes of the Finance and General Purposes Committee reveals that the council members of the Joint Transport Committee had been asked for their views and four out of five had raised no objections! Alderman Hennessy, however, had written to the Committee that:

> It does appear to me most extraordinary that the Bristol Omnibus Company, after sixteen years of administration of the Joint undertaking, sees the existence of the Bristol coat of arms on buses operating in Bristol is particularly confusing to people living in Bristol, Tewkesbury, Swindon and other areas is not true. The Company is responsible for the change in colour of the buses from royal blue without the authority of Bristol Corporation [councillors have a long memory!] ... if it is particularly confusing for the public then the Company is responsible for it.

He continued: 'I am of the opinion that the Bristol coat of arms was painted on the buses without the consent of the corporation', and maintained that changing the name on the side would make no difference since the passengers were more concerned about where the bus was going! Unfortunately the minutes of the remainder of the meeting do not appear to be available, but one can be forgiven for wondering what all the fuss was about since at the 14th September BJS Committee meeting it was recorded that it had been agreed that the new fleetname would be adopted, and the coat of arms was gradually replaced by the simple word 'BRISTOL'.

1962

New vehicles for 1962 were more standardised than the previous year's deliveries, consisting mainly of MW single-deck and FLF double-deck types. No fewer than 32 standard 45-seat MW5G service buses entered service, all initially for country services, whilst of the 70-seat FLF double-deckers, 25 were for Joint Services – 18 with the BVW engine. Of the remainder, three with Gardner engines were sent to operate Gloucester city services and two to the Cheltenham fleet, whilst country service FLF buses were powered by both the BVW engine (11) and the Gardner 6LW (10). One of the city buses, C7073, incorporated illuminated advertisement panels into the lower-deck saloon lighting.

Finally, three buses of a new design entered the fleet in 1962. These were the delightful little 30-seat Bristol SUS buses, a Small-capacity, Underfloor-engined, Short-wheelbase bus developed by Bristol Commercial Vehicles but incorporating a number of proprietary parts – such as the Albion 4-cylinder engine that powered Albion's own Nimbus small bus chassis. This resulted in the full type designation SUS4A. BCV also built a Longer SUL model which, although employed extensively by the neighbouring Western and Southern National concerns, was not purchased by the Bristol Omnibus Company.

These attractive little buses were directed to Stroud, where they replaced the last of the Bedford OB single-deckers that had been so prevalent during the early 1950s, and allowed that type to bow out from the fleet. A small bus replacement was necessary as some of Stroud's services operated along very narrow roads with tight turnings, in order to serve a number of villages – particularly in the valleys surrounding the town and in Nailsworth.

Brian Ede joined the company at Stroud in 1962, direct from the forces. He was just in time to drive a Bedford OB on one trip from Stroud to Nailsworth before its withdrawal. He recalls that it seemed to him to be narrower at the front than at the back and he preferred a bus that was 'in a straight line, so that you can poke your nose through and the rest of it can come through!'

Brian also recalls that discipline was still quite strong when he joined: 'The District Traffic Superintendent, Mr Sollars, addressed me as 'Ede''. (Hubert Sollars had been appointed by Red & White at Stroud to oversee the transition in 1950.) Of the SUS buses, Brian comments that:

> They were very good for where we used them. One SUS bus spent all day in Nailsworth going to Newmarket, Shortwood, Windsor Edge, Tiltups End and Nympsfield; there were two drivers, one on early and one late. The other two were in Stroud doing Randwick, Ruscombe, Uplands, Summer Street and Kilminster Road.

This first batch of SUS buses were not so long-lived as their predecessors and remained in the fleet for only a decade, although some of their duties at Stroud were taken up by later deliveries of the same type, transferred from other depots where service revisions rendered them surplus to requirements. Geoff Lusher, spending some time at Bath, remembers preparing a scheme to re-route the Upper Westwood service so as to take an MW bus and release one of the later SUS buses from Bath depot, but was stopped from doing so by the 'powers that be'!

In addition to the withdrawal of the last Bedford OB from the fleet, 1962 also saw the demise of the last of the Joint Services Leyland PD1s along with the LL 'Queen Mary' coaches, and one of the L-type coaches (the remaining two of this type lasting until the following year).

On the positive side, the company continued to improve passenger amenities with the opening of new bus station facilities at Gloucester; and in a continuing process of improving passenger comfort, at a May 1962 Board meeting approval was given for the additional capital expenditure of £4,400 during that year, and

£4,200 for 1963, in respect of additional air suspension and air brakes for 22 and 21 MWs respectively.

During 1962 there was a drastic reduction in the level of service provided on the Bristol to Portishead railway line, with only a peak-hour service remaining. An article entitled 'Rail Replacement Around Bristol' in the February 1965 issue of *Modern Transport* commented that:

> The combination of a frequent bus service (every 20 minutes at off-peak times) and lower fares than the trains was sufficient to offset for most people the considerably shorter journey time by train, though even at the ultimate closure Bristol had to draft in seven extra double-deckers to augment the peak hour service.

The Bristol to Portishead service remained a busy and profitable route until beyond deregulation and into the 1990s.

1963

The winter of 1962/3 was particularly severe, not only within the company's operating territory but throughout the country. Geoff Lusher took bus driving lessons during the bad weather and recalls driving over ice-rutted roads in elderly training bus W97, a Bristol K5G double-decker. He also undertook some conducting duties from Marlborough Street, being sent once on the 2½-hour trip to Gloucester on service 26 in a dual-purpose Bristol MW. On the way back, just past Leyhill open prison, the bus descended into a dip, only to plough into a snowdrift whilst climbing out the other side. Wearing his company Wellington boots, he retrieved his company shovel from the boot, and began to dig the front of the bus out of the drift, assisted by some of the passengers. The driver, a senior man at the depot (the Bristol to Gloucester service 26 was one of the senior rosters) remained seated behind his steering wheel, puffing on his pipe, until the drift was clear and he was able to restart the journey!

Brian Ede recalls one day when he was en route from Minchinhampton to Avening, on the top of the Cotswold hills, that 'the snowdrifts were higher than the bus.' He also drove on the service from Stroud to Cheltenham, despite protestations from his conductress that he would never be able to complete the journey because of the snow. By the time he had reached Slad:

> the bus was spinning. There was a policeman at the side of the road holding something in his right hand, and he put his left hand on the bus and helped push. Anyway, I couldn't get beyond Birdlip and so I made my way carefully back to Stroud. When I got to Slad I saw what the policeman had been holding in his other hand – a road closed sign!

Harold Ottway, whilst driving from Bath, got stuck in the middle of Salisbury Plain for two days! He was rescued from his bus by a farmer in his tractor and stayed in the farmhouse until the company recovered him and his bus.

From 1st January 1963 control of the Bristol company, and indeed the whole of the state-owned Tilling group, was transferred from the British Transport Commission to the newly formed Transport Holding Company. There were no outward changes to the company or its operations however and, continuing under state control, things remained much as before.

Regrettably, this period was also the time that brought an unfortunate series of events within the company to the notice of citizens of the whole country; events that would come to portray the company, and some of its staff, in a very bad light indeed.

At the March 1962 Joint Services meeting Mr Patey referred to a request from the Town Clerk to discuss the employment (or rather lack of employment) of coloured bus crews, following questions raised in the February Council meeting. He stated:

> Based on factual experience in other cities, the employment of coloured bus crews could reduce the number of staff available. It was common experience that the effect of introducing coloured labour was to downgrade the job and existing staff left to go elsewhere.

He also referred to a recent investigation made by a local newspaper on this subject and the conclusion was that

> Bristol was as well, if not better off than those cities and towns employing coloured labour.

Company official and committee member T.W.H.Gailey further stated:

> there was an improved employment level in the West Indies and the better coloured labour similar to those working on the London Underground was not now available.

The minute continues:

> Views were expressed by several members of the committee and in making reference to Mr Patey's statement and appreciating the difficulties in this matter, it was not advocated that there should be any change in the existing employment policy.

In view of this situation, it is intriguing to note that the company had taken on its first black drivers in Bath during the mid-1950s!

Madge Dresser examined the background to and progress of the colour bar on Bristol's buses in her book *Black and White on the Buses*, and extracts from this book have been both summarised and used extensively in the following text. It was reported that as far back as 1955 the local passenger group of the Transport and General Workers Union passed a resolution that coloured workers should not be employed as bus crews. The maintenance section, however, voted the other way, and black people were soon taken on in the garages. Andrew Hake, then a curate attached to the Bishop of Bristol's Industrial Mission, recalled that he had confronted a member of the company management on this issue in 1956 or 1957 who had told him that they had

> no objection to employing black people ... but (that) the unions had made their position clear and the management were not prepared to face a showdown, a confrontation that would have led to strike action ... and so they were biding their time waiting for this to change.

Allegations that a colour bar existed had been made in a series of articles in the Bristol *Evening Post* in 1961 which highlighted the failure of the company to employ coloured labour and attempts by several coloured people to gain employment with the 'undermanned Bristol Omnibus Company' and the denial by the local Transport and General Workers Union officials that there was a colour bar in operation.

Some of the younger men's dissatisfaction with their treatment, especially at the hands of the bus company, resulted in the formation of a pressure group, later to be called The West Indian Development Council, and their appointed spokesman, Paul Stephenson, chose the bus colour bar as the issue to bring matters to a head. Choosing 18-year-old Guy Bailey, described as 'of impeccable character ... a Boys Brigade Officer, a cricket club member, a full time warehouseman and part time student', Stephenson arranged for him to have an interview with the bus company after establishing that there was a vacancy for someone of Bailey's qualifications: the company was then telephoned and told that he was West Indian – the interview then being promptly cancelled. Stephenson went to see Ian Patey who confirmed that the company did indeed ban the employment of 'coloured labour'. It must be remembered of course, that no race discrimination legislation was then in force and the opinions of Patey (and others) was perfectly legal at the time. Nevertheless, the matter was not going to rest as there were widely held, opposing views on the issue.

It was decided to raise the matter both nationally – with a view to getting discrimination legislation introduced – and locally with the City Council so as to get the matter raised with the company, little realising of course that as 50% shareholders in the Joint Services undertaking, the City Council were by default supporting the boycott. Raising the matter with the Council led to the exchanges at the Joint Services Committee previously referred to, and the decision that '... it was not advocated there should be any change in the existing employment policy'.

The West Indian Development Council was not to leave the matter there, however, and taking heart from actions that had taken place in the United States of America, announced a bus boycott by coloured people. In response to questioning by the Bristol *Evening Post*, Ian Patey did not change the views that he had conveyed to the Joint Services Committee, and, seemingly upset that they had not been consulted before the boycott was announced, the Transport and General Workers Union refused to meet a deputation from the West Indian Development Council, with Arthur Coxwell of the Union reportedly making it clear in a letter to Stephenson that 'the Union had no colour bar and that the decision not to employ West Indians had been made by the bus company alone ...'. He continued, 'I told him that the union had stated their view on this question so often that there was little point in stating it again'. This was the only reason why he told Mr Stephenson there was no point in an interview.

Stephenson even went as far as enlisting the help of the world famous cricketer Sir Learie Constantine, who, on the eve of the cricket match between Gloucestershire and the West Indies at Bristol's County Ground, wrote to the Bristol Omnibus Company in his capacity as High Commissioner for Trinidad and Tobago to enquire about their refusal to have black crews, even despatching an official to Bristol to 'make informal enquiries into the dispute'. Stephenson then informed the press that he might invite Sir Learie to arbitrate between the company, the West Indians and the Transport and General Workers Union. On 1st May, about 100 university students marched on both the bus station (despite this being a matter that had been raised as affecting city services, which did not use the bus station) and the TGWU headquarters at Transport House, causing Ron Nethercott, the Union's regional secretary, to tell the marchers:

> We don't want discrimination and we don't like it. There is no question of a colour bar as far as we are concerned. Without consulting the Regional Committee, I am prepared to say that if there are coloured workers on the buses, our people will accept them.

However, the headlines in the Bristol *Evening Post* of the following day, when members of the trade union met the Town Clerk and representatives of the Jamaican High Commissioner, declared that interviews with rank and file busmen had indicated that they backed the company's policies and would not work with coloured labour, regardless of what the union's policy was! This view was in fact confirmed on the following day when local television news covered the story and revealed that the busmen and women interviewed were, for the most part, unashamedly hostile to the introduction of black personnel.

Over the next few days, after recruiting a black trade union member (Bill Smith) to the South West Regional Committee, the Transport and General Workers Union issued a statement that called for 'separate and quiet negotiations on the bus issue' whilst reaffirming the union's national policy of opposing racial discrimination in any form, blaming Stephenson's campaign for 'jeopardising the welfare of the city's coloured citizens'.

The leaders of the Bristol Council of Christian Churches, the Bishop of Bristol and the President of the Free Church Federal Council appeared to blame Stephenson and the West Indian Development Council because of

> the apparent fact that social and economic fears on the part of some white people should have placed the Bristol Bus Company in a position where it is most difficult to fulfil the Christian ideal of race relations.

However, matters worsened when an article was published in *The Daily Herald* in which Nethercott 'personally impugned Stephenson's character and motives, calling him 'dishonest' and 'irresponsible' '. This resulted in Nethercott being successfully sued by Stephenson in the High Court for libel and having to both apologise and pay costs and compensation.

Towards the end of that week, at the May Day Rally held at Eastville, there was a great deal of barracking against the Transport and General Workers Union, with people calling on it to take a more energetic stand against the colour bar. Elsewhere in the city up to 200 men and women (mostly black working people) took part in what may have been the first black-led march against racial discrimination in Britain, at which the bus company colour bar was discussed.

Sir Learie Constantine remained involved in the campaign to overturn the colour bar and, after a meeting with the city's Lord Mayor did not yield 'dramatic results', snubbed Patey and went straight to the Transport Holding Company, the Bus Company's shareholder, with the result that the next day Patey denied that the company operated a colour bar and Nethercott told the *New Statesman* that

> He had reached a stage in negotiations with the main West Indian association in the city and with his own members on the buses when it would soon be possible to approach the company even though there were still white people looking for bus jobs ...

and that he

> was on the point of success at least to the extent that the ball would be played at last into the company's court ...

but that the present crisis had destroyed much of his work.

Further meetings in London between the Jamaican High Commissioner and the chairman and director of the Transport Holding Company (arranged because some un-named Jamaican residents in Bristol began to complain that their High Commissioner was not doing enough to pressurise bus officials) resulted in the two Transport Holding Company officials disavowing Bristol's colour bar policy. They also despatched a 'senior man' to Bristol to conduct 'very delicate negotiations' between Bristol Omnibus Company and the unions, which was to take many months.

Eventually, on 28th August 1963, the same day that 150,000 black and white Americans marched in protest on Washington, it was reported that the colour bar on Bristol's buses had ended. After the months of negotiations and a union meeting attended by 500 out of the city's 1,750 platform staff, agreement had been reached for the 'employment of suitable coloured workers as bus crews', with Arthur Coxwell of the union angrily denying that his members had ever passed a resolution banning black workers – he stated that the bar had been the company's policy not a union one – and with Ian Patey asserting that the public campaign of the previous May had 'delayed the opening of negotiations with the union' despite the fact that he had admitted that 'negotiations with the union had started only when a directive had been received from the London offices of the parent company'. One former branch official later recalled that the agreement had only been reached on the basis of a quota restricting coloured conductors to a maximum of 5% of the staff.

In no time at all ten coloured applicants were interviewed for the post of conductor and the first to be appointed was Raghbir Singh, a turban-wearing Sikh from the Punjab, whose appointment was even reported in an Indian newspaper as a landmark decision indeed, since the rights of Sikh busmen to wear beards and turbans had resulted in a number of racially-inspired disputes in the Midlands!

This was not the end of the matter, however, for it took some time for the platform staff to settle down to work with their new colleagues, with it being variously reported that the different races didn't sit together in the canteen, that some white women conductors were afraid to work with their coloured colleagues, and that one white driver would not communicate with his Jamaican conductor, merely staying in his cab reading the paper during layovers. It was reported, however, that as numbers increased, race relations became more difficult as 'Pakistanis' sat together in the canteen and communicated in their own language. It was also reported that one Jamaican told his Asian workmates, 'when you are around a table speak English, because I don't know if you're planning to kill me or what ...'!

Dave Bubier, who joined the Bristol Joint Services as a driver in 1967 after a period working as a student conductor in Kent, found a very different working environment to his previous experience. Staff turnover was high, the public's perception of the company low and the job was generally seen as stop-gap employment by all except the hard core of 'old hands' – generally white. He remembers that he soon found a rigid 'canteen culture' in place, and it was customary for ethnic groups to use separate tables so that you did not automatically sit with your conductor during your meal break, even though your shift married you up with that conductor for a week at a time. He recalls that:

> One flouted this at first, to some very hard looks from white colleagues. An early shock was to witness Jack Hodge, the charismatic full time union official, walk over and thump the Asian table and loudly order them to speak only English, stating that 'if the money is good enough for you, so is the language', to loud cheers.

Fortunately, he continues, he was to witness a process of integration and better acceptance develop over the ensuing years,

> but nonetheless even as late as 1975 there was a degree of management reluctance to take a chance on promoting the first, by then long well qualified, coloured Inspector.

Although the race issue largely overshadows other matters when the company's history of this period is considered, it is worth remembering how different society was then. There was no sex equality either; only men were permitted to be drivers or inspectors, but at least conductresses with the Bristol company were paid similar rates to their male colleagues. This was often not the case where men and women worked side-by-side, and during the National bus crews pay dispute of 1957, which had sought to equalise pay in companies where that situation did not already exist, the Transport & General Workers Union made a hardship payment to its members during the nine-day stoppage, which ironically amounted to £2 for men and only £1 12s 6d for women!

Only 12 miles from Bristol, Bath's first black driver (Harold Ottway) recalls that on his first day, when he was called to the canteen to meet up with his training conductor, the short walk was the longest of his life; there was not a sound from the surrounding staff and you could hear a pin drop. During his brief period as a conductor (before becoming a driver) on the Bath city services an old lady would take a stick and poke him saying 'ring the bell'. As he said:

> I'd get so mad, I grabbed the stick and broke it, saying 'where do you think you are, at the zoo or something?' Of course, the 'old man' [Traffic Superintendent Fred Dark, who gave him the job] used to pull me in and tell me off, but he was always good to me.

Whilst driving in the country from Bath to Paulton a young boy looked at his mother and said: 'That's a black man'. He'd never seen a black man before. On another occasion, having become lost near Marksbury, he got out of his cab and went round to the back of the bus where two young passengers were waiting to alight.

> They started running, and all I was going to do was ask which way the bus went! It was a boy and a girl; he [the boy] looked round, saw me coming and he took off like a scared rabbit. That made me laugh.

Harold applied for the position of Inspector at Bath four times, and although senior to other applicants and with more experience, he did not get the job.

> He [the manager] later told me that he wanted to give me the job, but that he was very reluctant to, he didn't want to be the first ...'

Although Harold experienced no problems from his Bath depot mates because of his colour, when once allocated a journey on the Bristol service during the height of the problems, he was instructed to turn short at the shopping centre and not go into the Bristol bus and coach station.

Returning briefly to more mundane operating matters the June 1962 Joint Services meeting discussed whether to convert city service 83 to operate as a circular. This service operated mainly to the east and north of the city and connected many of the Victorian suburbs with each other's local shopping centres rather than the city itself. The completed circle was to operate at 12-minute intervals in each direction at peak periods (15 minutes at off-peak times) as services 73 and 83. The new circular service (unusual in a city dominated by radial routes) was to have a timetable that allowed for no terminal layover, and so the crew duties were constructed so that in each block of work the crew only did one complete circle lasting one hour, departing from and returning to the relief point at the operating depot, Eastville, before dropping back to the following bus. This process was repeated until the end of that particular section of their shift. Geoff Gould, who as a Traffic Trainee at the time often did weekend driving to relieve the staff shortage, recalls that under these arrangements it was considered unforgivable to arrive at the relief point late since the takeover driver had no recovery time in which to return the late running bus to schedule.

1963 was a special year for the company's fleet, for apart from the regular intake of MW single-deckers and FLF double-deckers, there was a brand new coach design and four extremely interesting and unusual secondhand purchases.

No fewer than 31 standard MW5G buses were taken into stock during the year, although six of these exchanged seats with a similar number of LS dual-purpose buses before entering service and were finished with a cream roof to identify them in their new role as dual-purpose vehicles; whilst the newly bus-seated LS vehicles reverted to bus green livery. One of these new dual-purpose MWs joined the Bath Tramways Motor Company fleet, along with one of the standard MW buses, together with two (out of a total of four) further SUS4A 30-seaters.

(*right*) 1963 ECW-bodied Bristol MW 921 RAE received dual-purpose seats and a cream roof before entering service as 2019 and is seen here in Swindon. A view through the driver's windscreen seems to show that the bus is still operated with a crew of two. (*A.J. Douglas*)

(*left*) A Bath Tramways Motor Company ECW-bodied 30-seat Bristol SUS, 303 (843 THY) of 1963, is pictured leaving Bath Bus Station. Note that the destination is set for 'Service' – commonly used at Bath although not within the Bristol group generally. (*A.J. Douglas*)

The final new single-deck vehicle was the first production version of Bristol's newly developed model, the Bristol RE, with chassis number 212.001. With full chassis designation RELH6G (Rear Engined, Long-wheelbase, High chassis frame, 6-cylinder Gardner horizontal engine), this coach carried a completely new design of Eastern Coach Works luxury coach body, the first vehicle in the fleet to be built to the newly permitted 36ft length and 8ft 2½inch width. Although delivered with 47 seats, this vehicle was down-seated to 45 before entering service. It was delivered in a new Bristol Greyhound livery of cream relieved by a bright 'signal' red waistband and trim, which was soon adopted as standard for the whole Greyhound fleet.

Details of the Bristol RE chassis have been covered in other volumes, but it is sufficient to record here that the unique way in which the more powerful 6HLX engine and gearbox were mounted in the chassis, involving the use of the Lodekka-type, dropped-centre rear axle, and the higher frame of the RELH model, allowed both side lockers and a boot to be fitted, which was to be essential for its future role as an express services vehicle operating on the established Bristol to London route. This arrangement, together with its air suspension, achieved a previously unequalled stability and ride quality – which some models, even today, fail to match. Numbered 2115, this coach was to be joined by a number of similar vehicles during the following year.

It is perhaps interesting to make a small diversion here. Whilst chassis 212.001 was the first production RE to enter service, in Bristol's normal manner of developing a new chassis, trials had been undertaken with three bodied prototype vehicles. Whilst the first two, chassis REX001 (bus) and REX002 (coach), had been despatched to operating companies, the third, another coach, REX003, remained with Bristol Commercial Vehicles and was occasionally seen around the streets of Bristol whilst undergoing tests. It was unique in trialling a horizontal version of Bristol's own BVW engine; despite the future success of the RE, however, none was ever offered with this power unit.

As many as 49 of the FLF double-deckers entered service during this year, 23 of which were to join the BJS fleet, all powered by the BVW engine, whilst a further 12 with the Bristol engine went into the country services fleet along with 12 Gardner-engined examples. Three of these were for Gloucester city services whilst the Cheltenham District fleet received a further two.

The really interesting vehicles, however, were acquired half way through the year as a result of the takeover by the neighbouring, THC-controlled Wilts & Dorset Motor Services Ltd, of the long-established independent operator, Silver Star Motor Services of Porton Down, near Salisbury. Despite its small size, Silver Star had been an early operator of the rear-engined Leyland Atlantean double-decker and, by the time of the sell-out to Wilts & Dorset, there were four examples in the fleet (one of which was fitted with coach seating). Wilts & Dorset were obviously unimpressed by these buses, as, although they absorbed and operated a number of the Silver Star buses and coaches, they despatched the Atlanteans to Bristol, where Bristol's Central Repair Works set about removing the illuminated roof-mounted star on the three bus versions and repainted them into Tilling green and cream. These three were then allocated fleet numbers at the very end of the 70-seat series, 7997, 7998 and 7999, and were put to work on the busy Bristol to Weston-super-Mare service. Fred Spencer remembers them well and in particular the novelty of the semi-automatic transmission and the unusual tip-up seat on the front platform for the conductor! Even if it did ever arrive at Bristol (about which there is some doubt), the fourth, coach-seated Atlantean, was never used and was sent to an Essex dealer/operator. One can only speculate that this double-deck coach, if acquired, could have been the forerunner of such a fleet of Bristol Greyhound coaches operating on the busy Bristol to London A4 corridor, although Silver Star themselves had been unable to secure Traffic Commissioners' approval for using this coach on their own Forces Leave express services.

In their short life at Bristol (they lasted but a year) they attracted the attention of bystanders and enthusiasts alike, including both co-authors who, whilst yet to meet and then living on opposite sides of the city, were fascinated by these radically different buses, which nevertheless were running in and out of Bristol's bus station, wearing the company's green and cream colours! With their extreme front entrances, and rear engines, they were so unlike anything else operating into the area, although Ribble 'Gay Hostess' Atlantean coaches did make regular visits to the city on that company's express services.

Nos.7997, 7998 and 7999 were later removed from the Weston service and allocated to Bristol's Marlborough Street depot for use on service 85 from Bristol to Portishead, at the time of the railway branch line closure to that town, but almost as soon as they had arrived, they were gone again from the fleet!

Spotlight on the Silver Star Atlanteans

When Silver Star Motor Services Ltd of Porton Down, near Salisbury, sold out to its local BTC operator, Wilts & Dorset, in 1963, its fleet of 23 vehicles (predominantly Leylands) was distributed among four operators.

Wilts & Dorset retained the single-deckers and some coaches, with further coaches passing to Western National. Super Coaches of Upminster received three double-deckers, including an Atlantean coach. Bristol Omnibus accepted a small Trojan minibus and the three Atlantean buses.

The Leyland Atlantean represented a different approach to double-deck bus design with its engine positioned across the rear of the chassis and housed in a bustle. This allowed the entrance to be at the front, alongside the driver. The Silver Star examples were of low-height design, but unlike Bristol which had successfully developed the Lodekka with all the advantages of a dropped-centre rear axle to allow low overall height, the Leyland Atlantean still required a side gangway (on the nearside) and four abreast seating at the rear of the top deck to achieve a similar low height. They also had strip bells along the ceiling for passengers, which had yet to appear on Bristol/ECW models.

These Atlanteans were therefore unlike any other bus normally found in a Tilling fleet but looked incredibly modern alongside the FLF Lodekkas then being taken into stock. They were allocated fleet numbers as follows: 7997 (TMW 853), 7998 (VAM 944) and 7999 (1013 MW).

Re-painted in Tilling green and cream, from the summer of 1963 these buses were initially allocated to Weston-super-Mare for operation on service 24 between Weston and Bristol, and therefore were regularly seen in Bristol city centre. With 73-seat Weymann bodywork, these were the highest capacity buses in the fleet which was no doubt considered useful for carrying holiday crowds to and from the coast. They were later transferred to Marlborough Street, Bristol and appeared on route 85 to Portishead, but lasted only a year with Bristol Omnibus before being withdrawn and sold for further service during late summer 1964.

All three followed the coach version of the Atlantean, to Super Coaches of Upminster (and the associated PVS dealership) before moving on again. VAM 944 returned to the Bristol Omnibus area during the late sixties to provide staff transport for Hale-Trent Cakes of Clevedon, while TMW 853 was eventually exported to the USA. 1013 MW has been splendidly restored and is now preserved in its original Silver Star livery, and can often be seen attending rallies in the Bristol area.

It has regularly been suggested that the Atlanteans were passed to Bristol Omnibus in order for Bristol Commercial Vehicles to examine their design. There is no evidence to support this theory, however. The Atlanteans were never seen at the BCV works, which by then was planning to build a new double-decker with a side-mounted rear engine, rather than a model with transversely-positioned power unit. The latter eventually appeared from Bristol as the VRT in 1968.

The Atlanteans could easily have been allocated to a route which passed BCV's works at Brislington, such as service 33 between Bristol and Bath, but no attempt was made to do this and indeed their initial allocation to Weston-super-Mare appears to reflect little interest in these vehicles by anyone connected with Bristol bus manufacturing.

To those interested in the bus scene, the sight of Leyland Atlanteans in full Tilling green and cream was completely incongruous. 7997 (TMW 853) here races towards Weston-super-Mare along the A370. (*Bristol Vintage Bus Group*)

(*right*) VAM 944 (7998) draws into Bristol's Marlborough Street bus and coach station with the destination already prepared for its return trip. These vehicles always looked extremely modern among Bristol's front-engined double-deckers. (*Bristol Vintage Bus Group*)

(*left*) With the engine located within a bustle at the rear, in many respects Atlanteans seemed to be built back to front. 7997 is seen on its loading bay inside Bristol bus station, which was designed to be suitable for both front and rear entrance buses. (*M. Walker*)

(*right*) The Weymann bodywork incorporated shallow windows which, as in the case of the Lodekka prototype, disguised the low overall height of the design. This nearside picture of 7997 clearly shows the passenger entrance in relation to the driver. (*Bristol Vintage Bus Group*)

(*left*) The Atlanteans were always worked with a conductor, who in this case is able to converse with the driver in a manner not possible on other double-deckers of the period. 7999 (1013 MW) heads for Portishead in this central Bristol photograph. (*Bristol Vintage Bus Group*)

Geoff Lusher was the first Bristol-based driver to have one of the Atlanteans. Having driven to Weston-super-Mare on service 24 he defected his FLF at the seaside resort and, seeing an Atlantean in the back of the depot, asked to take it, convincing the depot Inspector that he had been trained to drive it. After returning to Bristol and finishing with a late journey to Nailsea and return, Geoff parked the bus up on the fuel pump, to be met with the shout from the fueler 'What the **** is this?'. The bus was parked up for the night and awaited someone from Weston depot to take it back the next day! However, when the buses arrived at Marlborough Street for the Portishead service, Geoff was called upon to do the driver training on them. He recalls:

> The Bristol Bus Station drivers didn't like them too much. They were generally very senior drivers who had become used to, and preferred the KSW. They took exception to the passengers being able to talk to them. The conductors, however, being a sociable lot, liked the fact that they could spend the trip talking to the driver!

The Atlanteans were much easier to handle than the KSWs when they were allocated to the Portishead service (although some of the SHW-registered KSWs from the 1955 batch of Gardner-engined country buses, did have a specially modified gearbox to cope with Rownham Hill). Geoff recalls driving the service with a fully-laden KSW, and being obliged to change quickly down through the gearbox as, at Bower Ashton, outbound from Bristol, you encountered first a double bend and then the ascent of Rownham Hill.

> You always took the first bend flat out and then went down through the box to first gear – people were standing looking through the window at the back of the cab at you, and you thought 'I'd better get this right'. If I'd have missed it I doubt if the bus would have re-started. There wasn't such a problem with the semi-automatic gearchange of the Atlanteans of course!

The Atlanteans were not the only acquisitions from Silver Star however, as apart from Silver Star's largest vehicles, Bristol also took their smallest! An unlikely acquisition took the form of a 13-seat Trojan mini-coach, 367 BAA, known to the Silver Star employees as 'BAA-BAA', which was numbered 2049 in the company fleet, just before the start of the number sequence for coaches, but at the end of those for dual-purpose vehicles, Wearing all-cream livery, it was sent to work on a summer service connecting two of Bath's principal tourist attractions, the Pump Room (next to the world famous Roman Baths) and the Assembly Rooms. Despite being later renumbered (to 400) and repainted (to blue) this little coach lasted until 1970.

It is interesting to note that the memory of this tentative step towards a connecting service between these important tourist attractions, which had otherwise only been served by a 'closed-door' city coach tour, formed the basis of an idea by co-author Mike Walker that resulted in Bath's first open-top, hop-on, hop-off tour in 1983. This subsequently developed over 20 years into a very highly sophisticated, high-frequency tourist facility – which was later controlled and managed by the other co-author, Martin Curtis!

With the entry into service of the three Atlanteans in 1963, another unusual vehicle left the fleet, the prototype Lodekka, LC5000, which was withdrawn from service during this year and, unforgivably, allowed to be scrapped. Considering that this vehicle was very much a prototype and included an unusual transmission arrangement that was not carried forward to either the pre-production or production models, the bus had lasted an admirable 14 years in the city of its design, development and birth. That, on withdrawal, this bus was ultimately sent to the breakers' yard, will forever be regretted by those who try to preserve examples of the major technological developments within the industry.

1963 was a significant year for Clive Norman, who had joined as a conductor in 1961, and 'passed out' that year as a driver for Gloucester city services. At the time, and for a while after successfully completing their

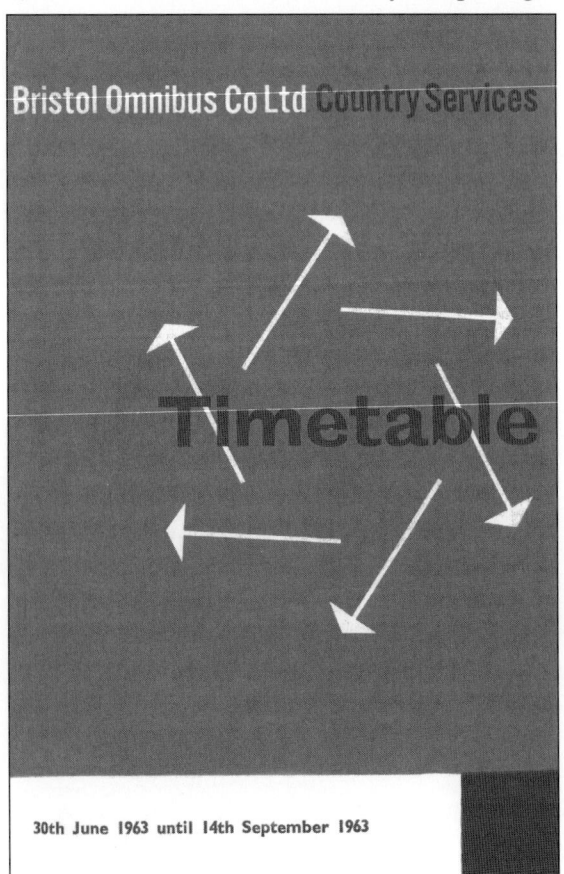

Bristol Omnibus Co Ltd Country Services

Timetable

30th June 1963 until 14th September 1963

training, drivers were still referred to as 'conductor-drivers', and could be called upon to perform either function – although by Union agreement this could only be by agreement with the individual. Depot rosters at Gloucester were divided between city and country services, with junior staff being allocated to the city roster, a system of seniority that seems to have been adopted by most of the company's depots.

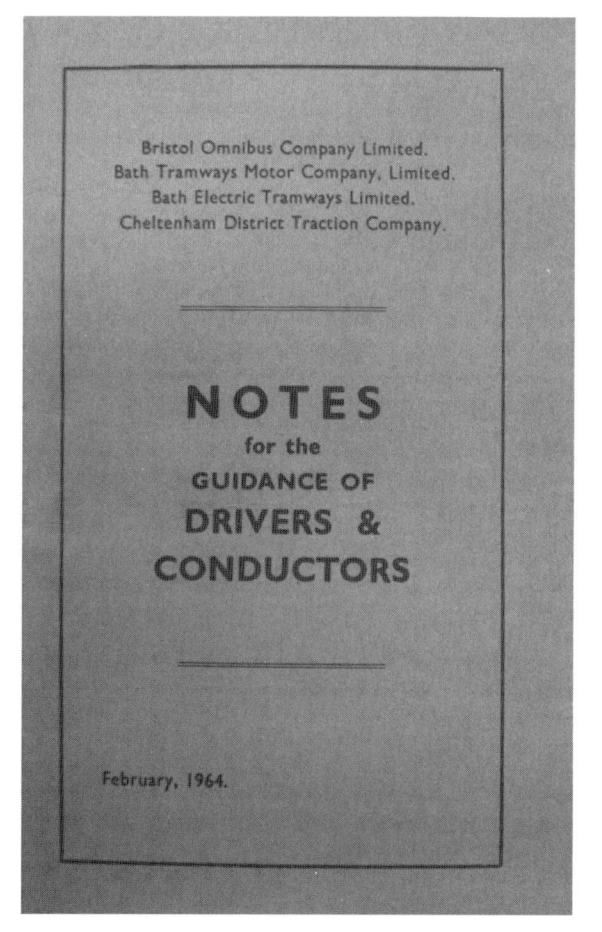

[Image: Cover of booklet titled "NOTES for the GUIDANCE OF DRIVERS & CONDUCTORS", February 1964, issued by Bristol Omnibus Company Limited, Bath Tramways Motor Company, Limited, Bath Electric Tramways Limited, Cheltenham District Traction Company.]

In the article 'Rail Replacement Around Bristol' published in *Modern Transport* for February 1965, it was reported that

> In 1963 the Bristol company carried 244 million passengers [this had fallen from the 325 million quoted to the Omnibus Society in 1952], nearly half of them on Bristol city services, over a route mileage of 5754 [the 1952 equivalent having been 3779, or 4768 if express services were included]. Despite a proportion of 70% of services which do not properly cover their costs, compared with only 50% a few years back, the company is still profitable. Over 40% of the single-deck fleet is single manned.

These figures clearly illustrate the steep fall in passenger traffic over the previous 12 years, with numbers reducing by almost 25% whilst route mileage had risen by 20% – an obvious pointer to an impending financial crisis.

1964

This year saw a programme of vehicle intakes which held few surprises, consisting of MW and SUS single-deckers, FLF double-deckers and the outstanding order for the remaining new RELH coaches.

The single-deck service bus fleet replacements comprised 14 MW5G 45-seaters, of which 2592, a Bath Tramways Motor Company bus, exchanged seats and roles with LS dual-purpose 2002 in April of that year; and two 30-seat Albion-engined SUS buses.

There were no fewer than 44 new 70-seat FLF double-deckers for that year; of those equipped with BVW engines, Joint Services took 22, whilst country services took ten and the Bath Tramways Motor Company fleet a further four. Five Gardner-engined buses joined the country services fleet. The balance of the order was somewhat of a surprise and was to remain unique in the fleet, being three with Leyland O.600 engines (an engine that also featured in the Leyland Atlanteans which were not to see out the year). Of these FLFs, 7129 was for country services and the remaining two, C7130 and C7131, joined the BJS fleet.

Along with new Bristol-built buses for operators around the country, many new Bristol Omnibus vehicles from this time featured spun aluminium wheel discs at the rear. Inevitably, such embellishments became known by staff as 'dustbin lids', though in fact they enormously enhanced the overall appearance of vehicles.

Nineteen RELH coaches were added to the one solitary example delivered in the previous year, seeing off the last of the vertical-engined L-type coaches, and settling down to become the mainstay of Greyhound routes along the A4 corridor, together with Greyhound-operated Associated Motorways express services across the Midlands and south-west.

They were joined by two further MW6G coaches from the United Welsh company at Swansea which were only a year old. These featured the new style of Eastern Coach Works body that bore a family resemblance to the new RELHs, but the pair were to remain unique in the fleet in having glazed roof quarter-lights. Although delivered as 39-seaters, one of the pair, 2136 (280 ECY), was down-seated to carry just 29 seats together with tables, and become the Swindon Town Football Team coach until mid-1966, when it regained its 39 seats.

Whilst the previous year had seen a change to vehicle registration sequences, introducing an 'A' suffix to some areas, the Bristol Licensing Authority did not start issuing new style registrations (which included the letter 'B') until 1964 when the first of the company's vehicles to enter service with a registration to include a suffix letter was C7155, registered AAE 51B.

One of Bristol Greyhound's 1964 batch of ECW-bodied, 45-seat Bristol RELH coaches, 2119 (865 UAE), at Victoria Coach Station, London. (*A.J. Douglas*)

For many years seasonal staff were employed at Weston-super-Mare. Among the seasonal conductors for 1964 were Brian Hussey and his future wife Pam. Equal pay applied for male and female personnel but this was lower for seasonal crews compared to full-time staff. Nevertheless, Brian went on to become a permanent driver, Inspector, Traffic Superintendent and Operations Manager with Bristol Omnibus and Badgerline.

The summer 1964 issue of *Omnibus* reported General Manager Ian Patey's promotion to the Tilling Group board, to be replaced by J.T.E. Robinson from the United Counties company. The next issue of the magazine, that autumn, reported that of 1,169 drivers receiving safe driving awards for the previous year, 429 were for ten years or more, and of 1,166 conductors receiving their safety awards, 462 were also for ten years or more.

Although shown here at Marlborough in 1970, this is one of the two former United Welsh 39-seat Bristol MW coaches acquired by Bristol Greyhound in 1964. 2135 and 2136 (279 ECY and 280 ECY) remained unique in the company in having roof quarter-lights built into their ECW bodies. (*M.S. Curtis*)

Dual-purpose Bristol MW 2028 (BHW 96C), along with others of the batch, was delivered in Eastern National livery, but before entering service was re-seated from 43 to 41, lasting as a dual-purpose vehicle for five years. This photograph was taken in March 1965 when 2028 was barely a month old. (*S.J. Butler collection*)

1965

New vehicle arrivals in 1965 again consisted of MW saloons and FLF double-deckers, with 44 of the former and as many as 70 of the latter!

Thirty-three of the MWs were delivered as 45-seat 5-cylinder buses, six for Joint Services and four for the Bath Tramways Motor Company (three having been diverted from a cancelled Joint Services order).

Four more MW5Gs were delivered with dual-purpose seating for 43 passengers, wearing full Eastern National livery, having been diverted from that operator. Their livery included more cream than was usual for Bristol Omnibus vehicles of this type, while in addition they sported Essex registrations and only three-track number boxes. Before being pressed into service they received Bristol registrations, fleet numbers and lettering and were re-seated to carry 41; the PSV Circle and Omnibus Society history of Bristol Omnibus Company describes these vehicles as being new from February 1965, but it was only at a meeting of the Board on 13th March that year that the transfer of these vehicles from the Eastern National's 1964 new vehicle programme was approved, at a capital cost of £22,416.

The remaining seven single-deckers to arrive from Eastern Coach Works that year were also MWs from a diverted Eastern National order, but the decision to take these vehicles had been made long before their dispatch from the chassis manufacturers since they had six-cylinder engines (Eastern National preferred the five-cylinder version of the Gardner engine) and arrived from the bodybuilders in cream and red Bristol Greyhound livery, with a red interior trim and coach seats for 39, albeit in a bus shell with folding doors and a single line destination display.

Why the company chose to take such basic vehicles for its prestigious Greyhound fleet, especially as its previous delivery of new coaches had been 20 of the new, visually stunning RELH, is unknown and, as far as we are aware, unrecorded. However, it is worth speculating that these coaches arrived at a time when the effects of Dr Beeching's railway modernisation plan were being felt and the company was involved in a series of Public Enquiries to enable them to provide rail replacement services to cover for withdrawn railway links.

One such closure at this time was the famous Somerset & Dorset Railway that meandered from Bath to Bournemouth via a number of Somerset and Dorset towns and villages, and Bristol Omnibus certainly did provide the road replacement for this over 60-mile link with a coach service that called at all of the old stations along the line of the route (some of which were still connected to the main line railway by other services).

With this background in mind, one can readily imagine why the company needed some basic coaches with power doors to provide this type of service with frequent stops and perhaps an aspiration to much intermediate traffic. At about the time of their first recertification, when seven years old, all vehicles in the batch were downgraded to green painted buses and in this form they lived out a normal life, although retaining their single line destination display and red seats and interior trim. One, BHU 92C, survived into preservation and is in the care of co-author Mike Walker as part of the Bristol Omnibus Vehicle Collection.

Bristol Greyhound's 1965 6-cylinder Bristol MW 2138, built with an ECW bus shell, 39-seat coach body, was one of seven similar vehicles diverted from an Eastern National order. These coaches never carried front wheel discs. The coach is pictured here in Bath bus station operating to Bournemouth: it survives in preservation. (*C.W. Routh*)

FLF deliveries returned to being divided between the Bristol BVW-engined variant (32) and the Gardner 6LW power unit (39). Of the FLF6B buses 18 were for BJS while three were for Bath Services (two for Bath Tramways Motor Co and one allocated to the Bath Electric Tramways), with the remainder for country services, whilst only eight of the Gardner-engined buses joined the Bristol city fleet, with six for Gloucester city, four for Cheltenham District, and the remainder going to country services.

As a direct consequence of the appointment of J.T.E. Robinson as the new General Manager, one of the Bristol Joint Services FLFs, C7186 (BHU 979C), was the first vehicle in the fleet to be delivered wearing the new Bristol scroll fleetname, matching the radiator badge, which became the new standard for the whole fleet, replacing the gold block capital design. This change had been reported to the BJS committee in March of this year, and in contrast to the apparent ill-feeling that had been created by the removal of the city coat of arms some five years earlier, this change was nodded through without comment. However, at the September 1966 Joint Services Committee meeting, the coat of arms was again discussed and it was agreed that it would be displayed in addition to the scroll fleetname on Joint Services vehicles in future! This occurred from the following year, but this time, the Corporation's official arms were used instead of the 'slightly modified' version created by the old Tramways company in earlier years.

70-seat country services Bristol FLF Lodekka 7188 was one of the last new buses delivered with the block capital gold fleetname, in 1965. Similar vehicles delivered later that year carried the new fleetname, the Bristol scroll. (*A.J. Douglas*)

Withdrawals during 1965 saw the first of the KS-types leave the operational fleet, including all of those with Joint Services, five of which went to be converted at the company's Central Repair Works into driver training buses. This involved the removal of the bulkhead behind the driver, while the control panel, normally located behind the driving seat at waist level, was turned around to face the instructor, who sat behind the trainee on a raised double seat. Unlike some companies, the Bristol concern did not employ dual controls. The fact that these five buses were only 7'6" wide made them eminently suitable as driver training vehicles as their restricted width made them far more flexible than their 8-feet wide counterparts. In livery terms, such buses had fleetnames removed; an orange band added (with 'L' plates) below the lower-deck windows; a 'No Admittance' sign fixed across the platform; and carried a new fleet number in the works 'W' series.

An interesting diversion can be made here, since about this time the company introduced a driving simulator, whose purpose was to allow novice drivers to get the 'feel' of large vehicle before they would be let loose on the city's streets, or even the depot yard. The simulator was a mock-up cab, complete with all controls, onto the 'windscreen' of which was projected the image from a small camera that, attached to an overhead gantry, was navigated through the streets of a model 'town' in accordance with the input from the controls mounted in the simulator cab. It is not known how successful this early mechanical simulator was, but Alan Peters, a driver for the company, who later became an Inspector and then Traffic Superintendent at Marlborough Street bus and coach station (before starting the successful ABus operation), recalls being told that the simulator did indeed give the feel of driving a large vehicle around the streets of the city, but the illusion was occasionally shattered on turning a corner as the camera picked up the large image of a spider walking through the street between the models of the buildings, or occasionally knocked over the model bus 'travelling' in the opposite direction! In today's world of microcomputer graphics it is difficult to visualise that such a crude system was even used in the early Concorde simulator. This was housed only a few miles from Bristol's driver training school at Lawrence Hill, on the northern side of the city at the British Aircraft Corporation works at Filton, teaching would-be pilots to land on a model airfield by means of a gantry-mounted camera that responded to control inputs made by the operator in the cockpit of the simulator machine.

Returning to the road fleet, also withdrawn from service during 1965 were the first of the 20 LS Greyhound coaches, bringing to an end the limited use of the horizontal Bristol engine in the fleet – although, of course, in its vertical form the Bristol engine still formed an essential part of vehicle deliveries.

Looking to the future, at a September 1965 Board meeting, approval was given for the building of a new Head Office on the corner of Lawrence Hill depot in Bristol, at a cost of £180,000, although it was to be another seven years before 'Berkeley House' was to replace the mock Tudor building on the Centre which had become synonymous with the 'Tramways', the 'Bristol Blues', and green Omnibuses. It would also be another four years before agreement was reached with Bristol Corporation, the 50 per cent shareholder in the Joint Services operation, that they would eventually take over the Centre offices, where, for many years the prominent clock on the outside of the building was a popular rendezvous point for Bristol couples who arranged to meet 'under the Tramway clock'! Earlier in the year, at the June meeting of the Joint Services Committee, approval had been given to move the Old Market, Bristol, canteen facilities from Careys Lane to the newly rented offices at Old Market House (which was a Bristol Division office as opposed to the company Head Office at the Centre), to allow for re-development within Old Market.

The variety of crew changeover points within a city with, in effect, two centres (the business centre and the shopping centre) of course caused problems for the company in keeping track of the punctuality of services departing from the relief points, and with a view to solving this problem the September BJS meeting considered a report which confirmed the success of a one day experiment with the patrolling Inspectors and the station (or Senior) Inspectors at the central area relief points using personal 'short-wave radio transmitters' as a means of communication. It was agreed that the sum of £720 should be spent on purchasing this equipment in an effort to improve vehicle punctuality. The following December, the position of rolling stock replacement was discussed, and it was reported that as 184 vehicles had been taken into the Joint Services fleet between 1952 and 1955, it was recommended that there should be an annual intake of 28 new vehicles each year from January 1968 in order to ensure the availability of sufficient vehicles to replace the postwar intake as their life expired. It was also reported that although there had been a major service revision within the city in November 1965, and that this had generally been a success, the services still suffered from the twin problems of staff shortages and traffic congestion – although the company had initiated a works study on the effects of the latter. An analysis of the profit and loss details for the Bristol Joint Services showed that in the 20 years since the end of the Second World War, despite the 1950s boom in bus travel, the annual profit of the undertaking before tax had barely moved, from just over £204,000 for 1945/6 to just over £210,000 for 1965, having peaked at just over £233,000 for 1963.

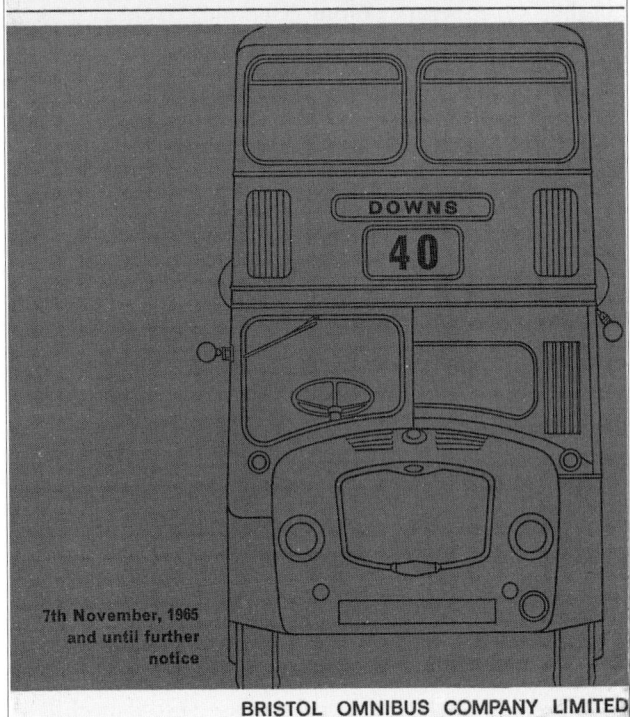

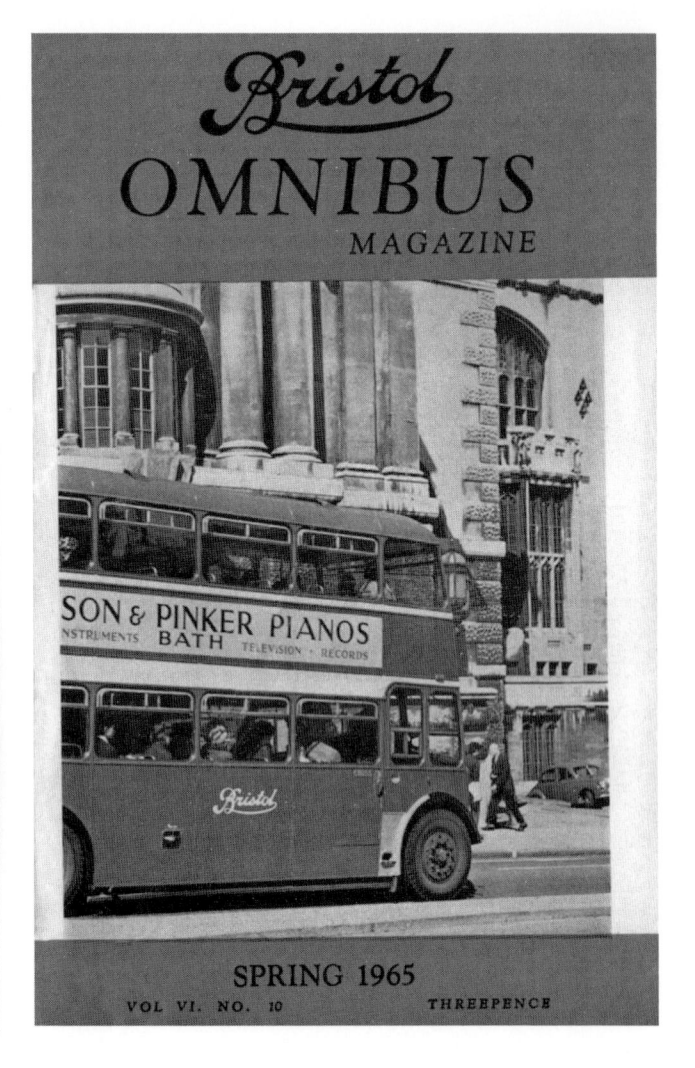

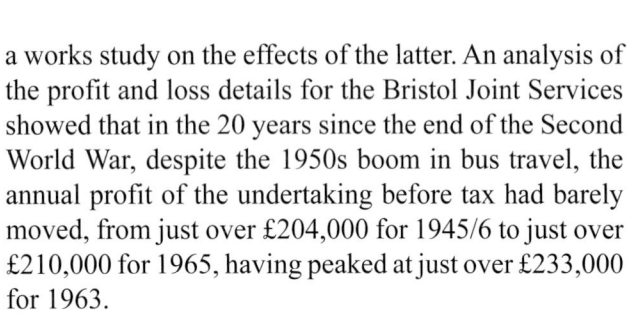

According to an interview with Traffic Manager Ken Wellman in the October 1965 *Transport Journal*, the city service revisions of the following month required 2,500 explanatory booklets, 30,000 new timetable books and 100,000 map pamphlets, with the revisions designed to provide a level of service that could be fully staffed within the available labour supply. At the time, he had stated, the failure rate on Joint Services was between 4% and 5% (due to all causes) on a total mileage in 1964 of 17,842,228. He continued:

> The current fleet consists of 1,312 vehicles, 930 of which are double-deck, 322 single-deck, 59 coaches and the Trojan used on contract to Bath Corporation for conducted tours of the city.

Compared to other sources, however, these totals look rather out-of-date, as fleet size continued to fall slowly during this period.

The February 1965 issue of *Modern Transport* reported that the Bristol company

> has scored a notable first, being appointed a full member of the Association of British Travel Agents. No other bus operating company can as yet claim this status: Bristol considers the financial gain to be relatively small but development of comprehensive travel at main offices is thought likely to encourage greater awareness of its own transport facilities.

1966
Vehicle deliveries in 1966 continued with FLF Lodekkas and MW saloons although this was to be the last year that this type of single-decker, with its engine mounted amidships, was taken into stock. This last order for the type consisted of 21 vehicles; whilst 53 of the 70-seater FLF came into service during the year.

Only two of the MWs were to the standard 45-seat bus format, whilst 12 arrived configured as 41-seat

The last batches of Bristol FLF buses for the company had only one cream band. In this view, BJS bus C7288 (JAE 628D), of 1966, with an ECW 70-seat body, is Clifton-bound from the Centre on service 18. (*A.J. Douglas*)

dual-purpose machines, although they differed from previous semi-coaches as they were powered by the 6-cylinder Gardner engines and were finished with sealed side windows and forced air ventilation, this being achieved through an air scoop either side of the destination box on the front dome that fed air to a series of small jets set into the overhead luggage racks which lined-up with each seat. A downside to this arrangement was that when these vehicles were later re-seated as 45-seat buses, the vents did not, of course, correspond with the new seat positions! Four of these 6-cylinder dual-purpose buses joined the Bath Tramways Motor Company fleet.

The remaining MWs were also fitted with the more powerful 6-cylinder Gardner engines, but were instead bodied as full coaches for the Bristol Greyhound fleet, built to the latest Eastern Coach Works design that was similar to 279 and 280 ECY – the two coaches which had arrived in 1964 from United Welsh – although they incorporated a slightly revised pattern of front end, equal depth, side windows, forced air ventilation and were built to a new length of 31 feet. A change to the Construction and Use regulations had allowed Eastern Coach Works to extend the rear overhang of the MW body, thus allowing greater comfort within the same chassis wheelbase. These coaches were to remain in

Bristol City Services FLF C7262 (GAE 883D), an ECW-bodied 70-seater of 1966, sports both front and rear wheel discs in this October 1966 view at Lawrence Weston. This bus was to be restored to Tilling green and cream livery in 1984 and used regularly in service in the city. (*M. Walker*)

After taking 20 of the longer RELH coaches, the company reverted to the Bristol MW for its 1966 Greyhound vehicles. 2144 (FHW 150D), and its six sister coaches, saw out the 1960s in the red and cream coach livery. (*A.J. Douglas*)

service for only a relatively short period, and were all withdrawn within eight years. Nevertheless, they made a particularly impressive sight soon after entering service when, on 8th September 1966, they were used alongside many of the RELH coaches (and a fleet of FLFs) to carry VIPs at the opening, by Her Majesty the Queen, of the new Severn Bridge that linked the two sides of the wide and sometimes dangerous River Severn. Together with the smaller Wye Bridge, and a new section of M4 motorway, this provided an important new connection between England and Wales. Including some vehicles hired in for the occasion, 77 vehicles were employed by the company for the opening ceremony.

Geoff Lusher was working at Marlborough Street bus and coach station at the time of the opening of the bridge and comments that 21 double-deckers (mostly FLFs) were used on a day excursion from Bristol to see the opening of the new bridge – and he was asked to drive the 22nd and last. The only spare vehicle remaining was a 1951 KS with an 8-foot wide body (nearing the end of its operational life with the company). The fully laden bus got up to quite a speed on the downhill section of the M4 – because he had knocked it out of gear! Of course, it only had a four-speed gearbox, and when (with some difficulty) he got it back in to 4th, it slowed down considerably!

Before the opening of the Severn Bridge, the only link between the two sides of the Severn as far south as Bristol was a car ferry that shuttled between Aust on the Gloucestershire side and Beachley on the Monmouthshire side. The alternative, if approaching the river from Bristol, involved a detour of over 50 miles, via Gloucester, where the river could be crossed more easily. The two small craft that formed the ferry service had to battle against both the ferocious river tide (the second highest rise and fall in the world) and the lengthy summer peak traffic queues, where a wait of many hours could often be necessary. However, on the day that the bridge opened to the public, the ferry ceased operation.

As a result of the Severn Bridge opening, and in conjunction with Red & White Services, Bristol Omnibus started running two services to connect Bristol with Cardiff, via the new bridge link. The first, service 300, operated at hourly intervals via north Bristol, the bridge, Chepstow, the A48 and Newport, with a journey time of a little under 2½ hours, whilst service 301 operated at two-hourly intervals via the Bristol suburb of Westbury, the bridge and non-stop via the A48 (or M4 when it eventually opened), and Newport, taking 90 minutes. The company presumably planned to use Bristol RE-type buses on the service but as they had yet to receive any of that type, they promptly hired some from Red & White to operate service 300, albeit manned by Bristol's Marlborough Street crews. These were manual gearbox, 54-seater Series 1 models, a type that was not to come to Bristol because by the time the company received its own RE buses the type had been redesigned; and in any case they were specified with semi-automatic transmission. Service 301 was regularly operated from the Bristol end by one of the recently delivered six-cylinder dual-purpose MWs, although the novelty of the service and the obvious attraction of the traffic objectives at each end made regular duplication necessary and extra vehicles from the Bristol end could often range from LS buses to Greyhound coaches. It

Red & White Bristol RELL bus R565 (GAX 5C) with a 54-seat ECW body, at the Marlborough Street bus and coach station in September 1966. It is operating on hire to the Bristol company and loading for service 300, the stopping service to Newport and Cardiff via Chepstow that was introduced with the opening of the Severn bridge that month. The 'on-hire' sticker is visible above the nearside sidelight. (*M. Walker*)

should also be remembered that at this time both of these routes were operated by vehicles with a crew of two.

Before the bridge opened, Geoff Lusher had been responsible for the route training of crews. A route learning party was arranged and the Bristol group left their coach at the Aust slipway, journeying to the other side of the river on the ferry. Mid-river they waved to the Red & White group on the other ferry, and on landing, each took over the other group's vehicle (both companies, of course, using Bristol MW coaches). Equilibrium was restored when both sides crossed the river again later in the day, and journeyed home.

On the first day of operation of the new services to Cardiff the 06.10 bus from Bristol reached the bridge only to find that it had not yet opened to the public! The Bristol crew (with their Red & White RE bus) were forced to wait for 30 minutes until the bridge was finally opened and they were allowed across!

The 300/301 services were not the only new company routes to cross the bridge, since the Cheltenham, Stroud, Dursley service was cut at Stroud, with the Dursley service extended by several times its previous length to operate via Berkeley, Thornbury and over the bridge to Chepstow as service 415. In retrospect, it is difficult to see the com-mercial reasons for introducing such a link – certainly there can have been little or no attraction in Chepstow to the residents of Stroud in the same way that the relative delights of Cardiff or Bristol may have attracted the residents from the other city. Nevertheless, one wonders if perhaps there was a desire to re-unite the former Red & White operations in Stroud with the head office of that company, despite this occurring some 15 years after the Stroud operations were handed over to

When new, six-cylinder dual-purpose MW 2039 (HAE 271D) was used on the Bristol to Cardiff express service 301. It is seen here entering Newport bus station, a green bus amongst red Western Welsh single-deckers, in September 1966. The air intakes either side of the destination box supply the forced jet ventilation system that takes the place of opening windows. (*M. Walker*)

Three days before the opening of the bridge, a completely unrelated new service was introduced in Bristol which became a useful addition to the Joint Services network, linking the railway station at Temple Meads, Broadmead shopping centre, the bus and coach station and the new Cannons Marsh car and coach park, situated on land previously occupied by railway sidings (on the old Bristol city docks) only a few hundred yards from the Centre. Within days of the bridge opening, and particularly on summer Saturdays and shopping days leading up to Christmas, the coach and car park became full with day trippers from Wales, many of whom availed themselves of this new service to access the shops. It was named the 'City Centre Circle' (CCC) and was launched by the city's Lord Mayor. Vehicles on the service were identified by blue coloured headboards that slotted into specially fitted brackets either side of the destination box and by the near-side headlight of the country services MW and LS types chosen to operate on the route. The service was one-man operated, and country service buses were selected because they were already modified to operate without a conductor.

Incidentally, it was reported to the June BJS committee meeting that the National Board for Prices and Incomes had submitted a report recommending that employees receive a national award of between 3% and 3½%, which could be increased if more effective use was made of manpower, making the introduction of one-person operation essential if the company was to offer greatly increased wages in order to attract more staff and reduce the ever present crew shortage. The CCC service operated at a flat fare (6d) and single value tickets were issued from specially purchased Almex single-value ticket machines (of a type that is thought to have been used in the U.K. only by the company and the Royal Parks in London) which cost £22 each.

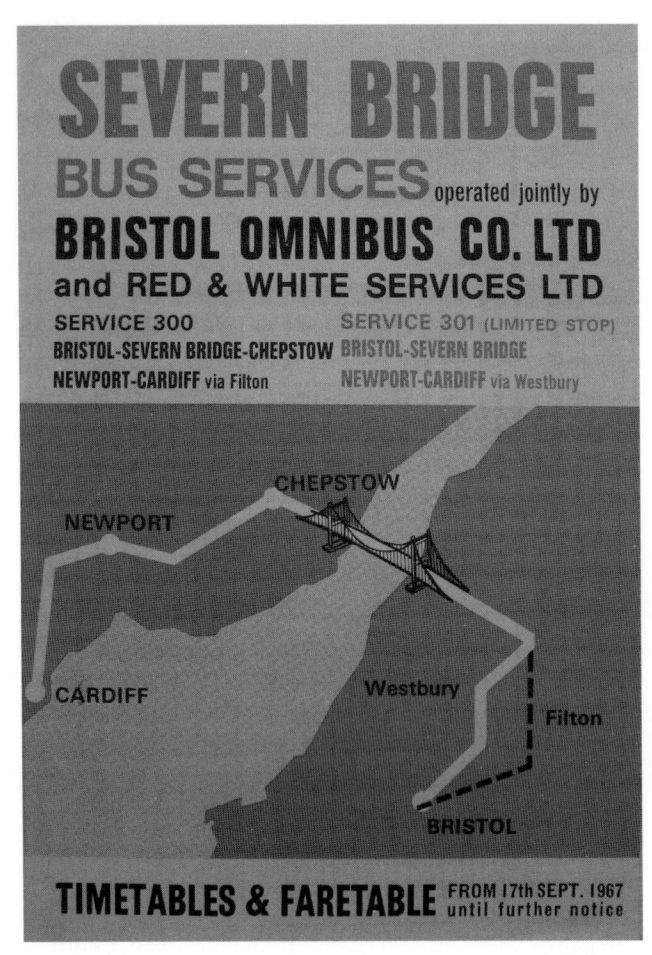

Bristol Tramways! Indeed, the Stroud to Chepstow link proved to be less than successful and in 1972 was cut back to be operated entirely on the English side, whilst the Bristol, Chepstow, Newport and Cardiff link survives today, in different forms. In fact, during the 1980s, the Bristol (Marlborough Street) operations even established an outstation at the Red & White premises at Bulwark, from which to operate two of the vehicles on its Chepstow to Bristol commuter services.

Photographed within days of the start of the new City Centre Circle service in Bristol in September 1966, is country services 2927 (YHY 85), a Bristol LS of 1958 with ECW 41-seat body. Despite being downgraded from a dual-purpose vehicle the previous month, the bus retains its high backed seats. (*M.Walker*)

Within a year or so, the regular vehicles on the service were painted into a brighter livery incorporating cream from the floorline up, with only the skirt panels and window surrounds painted green. This livery was to become the forerunner of a new, brighter 'one-man-operated' or OMO livery, gradually introduced on all of the company's single-manned vehicles thereafter. At some time during the life of the CCC service, one or two vehicles were also fitted with near-side mounted route boards but to ensure flexibility, a number of Lawrence Hill depot's 'country' MWs and LSs received the brackets for the front and rear destination boards – which were fitted when required. The CCC service became the first to be advertised on the roof of a bus, when FLF C7071 carried appropriate lettering visible to occupants of the multi-storey shops and offices in the city centre. Roof adverts also appeared for the Bristol *Evening Post*, but it is not thought that this peculiar advert position was pursued! However, earlier in the year at the March Joint Services meeting, it was recorded that city circular services 73/83 were to revert to their pre-1962 route, thus denying the city the chance to boast two separate city circle services!

Staff shortages within Bristol remained a problem, however, so when local independent operator Western Roadways decided to lodge an application with the Traffic Commissioners to operate late night routes in the city, the BJS committee decided not to object – recognising the difficulties they encountered in trying to find staff to operate this type of service.

In late 1966, Swindon's Tours and Excursions programme had been sold to Rimes coaches, a local independent operator, whilst elsewhere in the company a United Automobile Services Bristol RELL bus, CHN 336C, was received on trial during June and July, and was noted in the Weston-super-Mare area, although it is believed that it never operated in service. Brian Ede also recalls this bus operating in Stroud just before the depot received its own REs, although, again, the United bus did not run in revenue-earning service.

In Bristol, service revisions had rendered a number of Joint Services KSWs surplus to requirements and these were transferred to the Bath and country fleets (a very rare occurrence) whilst country buses 8180 and 8338 had their rear doors removed in favour of an open platform to make them more suitable for operation on Joint Services routes, whilst retaining their country ownership, presumably a means of operating BJS mileage with country vehicles in order to counterbalance the 'B' mileage operated by Joint Services buses outside of the area covered by the 1937 Bristol Transport Act.

In Cheltenham, the dark red liveried buses lost a further piece of their unique identity during May, when most of those still retaining the CDT two-digit fleet numbers were renumbered into the main company fleet system, taking numbers in the 8-foot wide series that followed on from the green Lodekkas in the main fleet. The few red buses to escape renumbering were withdrawn from service by the end of the year.

Clive Norman transferred from Gloucester to Cheltenham depot during 1966 and found that, 16 years after the Cheltenham company had been taken over, the depot was still divided into green buses and red buses, and that there was no system of transfer between the two! A new recruit might be allocated to either operation depending upon vacancies, and that was where he stayed! However, all staff could work overtime for either company and private duty changes were permitted.

Clive further commented that he found the KS and KSW type the most enjoyable to drive and the Bristol AVW engine better suited to town and city services because of its quicker acceleration and fast gearchange. 'They were consistently good performers' recalls Clive, but the Gardner engine equivalents were 'slow to accelerate with a ponderous gearchange'. On both of these observations, Geoff Lusher readily agreed.

In contrast to the KSW, Clive found the recently delivered FSF buses hard work, 'partly because of the brakes, which were difficult to control; bringing the bus smoothly to a standstill was not easy'. Geoff found them cramped compared with other types of bus.

Across the whole network there was a major renumbering of services into easily identifiable regional blocks, instead of the haphazard way in which services had been previously numbered, based principally on their time of introduction or the history of their takeover by the company. The new numbering series was:

1-99	Bristol Joint Services
100-120	Weston-super-Mare town services
121-140	Weston-super-Mare & Highbridge country services
160-199	Wells and country services south-west from Bath
200-225	Bath city services
226-299	Bath, Chippenham & Devizes country services
300-399	Bristol country services
400-499	Stroud and Swindon services
500-520	Gloucester city services
521-583	Gloucester & Cheltenham country services
585-599	Cheltenham town services (Cheltenham District Traction Company)

With some exceptions, an attempt was made to eliminate letter suffixes, so future destination equipment only needed to contain three-track number blinds instead of the four-track hitherto used, itself seen as a considerable saving in capital expenditure.

Whilst this resulted in a carefully structured geographical system, and assisted accounting, in the view of co-author Martin Curtis, it had the disadvantage of losing many long-established route numbers familiar to the public, and also meant that differing routes, operating along common roads, no longer displayed numbers which were distinctly different to waiting passengers. Geoff Lusher agrees, although when he was appointed to be the District Traffic Superintendent at Swindon, it fell to him to introduce the Swindon scheme renumbering, and where possible he kept the existing numbers with a 400 prefix. He was also able to cure the anomaly whereby the Bristol service to Oxford carried the number 74 whilst the route partner, City of Oxford Motor Services, used the number 66!

In Bristol, the elimination of route variation suffix letters was accomplished by renumbering services to carry consecutive numbers (so that, for instance, the 2 and 2A variants became 22 and 23), although a number of suffix letters were still carried and their use was explained in the timetable. Of these, 'C' indicated a journey that was going to terminate in the central area – when the majority of journeys operated through the Centre to another destination – including when staff had been advised that there was no relief crew available and they had to bring the bus in to the relief point showing 'Centre' only. The suffix letter 'L' indicated a similar journey of a 'local nature', and was sometimes used on journeys turning short at one of the depots. However, an unofficial 'D' was used by (at least) Brislington crews, for journeys terminating at that depot! More regular use was made of the letters F, J and K to indicate extensions to specific factory installations at either the Bristol aircraft complex at Filton and Patchway, or the Avonmouth or Severnside industrial estates; whilst 'H' and 'K' were frequently used for school journeys (the latter for 'kids' perhaps?).

At this juncture it is worth describing something of the nature of schools and works services. Bus services specifically for both were a reflection of the large passenger numbers that travelled to many factories and schools in the company's area. Of the works services, many dated back to the days before widespread car ownership, when most of the workforce travelled by either bus or bicycle, and there was none bigger than the huge aircraft factories at Filton and Patchway, which represented Bristol's biggest employer. It will be recalled that originally there were close connections between the Bristol Aeroplane Company and Bristol Tramways, and possibly because of this relationship, regular meetings between the bus company and aircraft works committees took place until well into the 1970s, where the needs of staff and modifications to services were discussed. Another factory with its own works services was chocolate manufacturer J.S. Fry & Sons, whose Somerdale factory in Keynsham was later absorbed by Cadburys. This was one of the more popular runs, as bus crews were permitted to make use of the factory shop to purchase extremely low priced confectionery!

School runs were often far less civilised! Co-author Martin Curtis attended Brislington School from the late

A particular problem of a large city such as Bristol, with a large number of factories and offices, was that many buses and crews only needed to work at peak times. During off-peak times many of the surplus buses and crews would be used for school games field or swimming baths contracts that may otherwise have been worked by the corporations' own fleet of coaches. Joint Services Bristol LD Lodekka LC8518 (972 EHW) of 1959, with an ECW 58-seat body, waits between contract journeys to and from Fairfield Grammar School's games field in west Bristol in February 1967. LC8518 survives today. (*M. Walker*)

104

1960s where pupil numbers peaked at about 3,000. In addition to normal services passing near by, special runs were provided to and from the school grounds, the main services being service 36K (to Stockwood) and 36H (to Brislington and St Annes). Although double-deck operated, so overcrowded were they, that the three buses scheduled for the morning 36H frequently failed to pick-up from Brislington as they were crammed full, while in the evening, pupils of all ages (and sizes) used to stampede the waiting buses for fear of being left behind if they failed to climb aboard.

Withdrawals from the fleet during 1966 were also significant, principally because of the surplus vehicles generated by the Joint Services revisions, and included the last of the K-types and the remaining L-types, resulting in the demise of the vertical Gardner 5-cylinder engine from the fleet, along with the last of the 7'6" wide KS-types. Another significant withdrawal was C8108, a 1953 KSW, which lost its roof under the St Lukes Road railway bridge at Bedminster in Bristol and was subsequently rebuilt to become the company tree-lopper, W120. The bridge, under which low-height double-deckers could safely pass, went on to claim further victims. The large number of vehicle withdrawals was also accompanied by the closure of Eastville depot with the transfer of 54 vehicles to neighbouring Lawrence Hill depot, while two decamped to Staple Hill at the eastern edge of the city.

1967

This was to be yet another landmark year for the company with the delivery of the last of over 300 new FLF double-deckers. This type would be phased out of production in the following year to be replaced by the Bristol VR, Vertical Rear-engined double-decker, albeit built to a different layout to the two prototype models that had been displayed at the Commercial Motor Show during September 1966 (Bristol and ECW by now able to sell freely on the open market once more). The VR model was, at that time, still sometimes referred to as the Bristol N-type. The two prototypes were 33 feet long with their engine placed in a novel position at the offside behind the rear wheels, longitudinally in-line with the chassis. This was coupled to semi-automatic transmission with the drive taken to the offside of a dropped-centre, Lodekka-style axle. The Eastern Coach Works single-door body seated 80 passengers, with a small shallow entrance step leading to a completely flat floor, in keeping with the layout of the F-series Lodekka. One of these two prototypes, HHW 933D, had even been displayed in Bristol Omnibus Company's livery, but it was to be a few years before the company could actually call this bus its own.

Only days after the prototypes had been unveiled, at a Board Meeting on 29th September, the capital expenditure for 28 of these new double-deckers was agreed. This was approved at the Joint Services Committee in December that year as these would be going to BJS as their 1968 order at a cost of £7,500 each. An internal memo from the Traffic Manager to the Chief Engineer stated that these N-types should be numbered into the series from C5000 until C5027, whilst the Bristol *Evening Post* revealed that the new buses would be fitted with a door across the bottom of the staircase to enable them to be used without a conductor at off-peak times. It was also reported that the city fare scale would be modified to threepenny stages to make collection by the one-man operator easier, carried under the headline 'THE THREEPENNY ONE MAN SHAKE UP'!

Strictly speaking, the use of such vehicles without a conductor at any time would have been possible, as one-man operation of double-deckers had just been legalised. However, whilst this eventually became commonplace, staff considerations might have prevented such a bold move being suggested at this early stage.

Bristol received their last Bristol FLF buses in 1967. In July 1968, BJS C7308 (KHT 956E) is seen at Bristol Haymarket bound for Filton to the north of the city. (*M.S. Curtis*)

Of 21 FLFs delivered for 1967, all were 70-seaters for Bristol Joint Services with BVW engines – a swansong for the Bristol engine, so long a favourite of the Joint Services, since neither the RE, nor the VR when it eventually reached production, were offered with this unit. Although not operated by the company, BCV had run both MW and RELH test rigs with underfloor versions of the Bristol engine, but Bristol's entire engine production was to come to an end as Leyland increased its influence over the Bristol Commercial Vehicles works.

This final delivery of FLF Lodekkas arrived without CBC heating, the lack of grilles alongside the front destination making these buses very distinctive. Their green and cream finish was also non-standard, using an attractive, slightly duller green while the waistband was pale – almost off-white. (Nevertheless, when re-painted several years later, standard Tilling shades were adopted). Other notable features of the batch were the rear wheel discs, which by this time were of a simpler glass fibre design, while wheels and wings were painted Brunswick Green which had begun to replace black the year before. This was a change that harked back to the 'Festival of Britain' livery of some 16 years earlier – and was soon to become standard, looking especially fetching when applied to the large front wings and exposed radiator stoneguard on the surviving KSW buses. The last six of these FLFs were also delivered with new, smaller, fleet number plates, and these too were soon to be retro-fitted throughout the fleet.

The remainder of the new vehicles delivered during 1967 were of the RE single-deck type, with no fewer than 60 arriving during the year. They represented a new direction for the company, and their introduction was implemented with vigour!

Seven of the batch were dual-purpose semi-coaches, fitted with a similar coach shell body to that seen on earlier RELH Greyhound coaches, adorned with much aluminium brightwork, while inside, they had green trim and seats for 47 passengers. At the front they were fitted with a high mounted dome into which was constructed a 'T' type destination box. These, together with the next batch delivered the following year, were to remain the most luxurious dual-purpose vehicles ever delivered to the company, as later dual-purpose vehicles were built within a bus (rather than coach) body shell.

The 53-seat RELL-type buses were built with the new standard, shallow flat-screen body, again with a 'T' type destination box, with wide front-entrance doors and semi-automatic gearboxes, together with what was to become the new standard engine for the company's RE single-deckers, the Leyland 0.680 of 11.1 litres. This engine and gearbox combination gave an impressive performance, leaving many a startled motorist behind as traffic lights changed to green, as they were expecting the usual pedestrian performance of an MW or even an FLF! After all, this was just a bus, wasn't it? Some near misses occurred too with other motorists pulling from side turnings in front of REs, only to be shocked at the speed of their approach!

Of the 53 buses delivered, the first four numerically – commencing a new number series from 1000 – and two later ones were for the Cheltenham District fleet, delivered in the traditional Cheltenham livery but with the cream confined to the waistband of the bus. For the small Cheltenham fleet, the intake of six buses in one year was unusual, but they were to lose their four FSF vehicles that year and this allowed a greater intake of buses suitable for one-man operation, which was the eventual intention for the REs.

1967 flat-screen Bristol RELL bus No.1006 (LAE 341E) at Bristol bus and coach station in May 1968. (*M.S. Curtis*)

Six of the others were for the Bath Tramways Motor Company fleet; while an additional three were for Gloucester city services – in which fleet buses generally were receiving a block letter 'GLOUCESTER' fleetname in addition to the established Gloucester coat of arms.

Another visiting Bristol RE during the year was LAE 770E, a Bristol Commercial Vehicles RELL dual-door demonstrator. The company was discussing the widespread use of the RE as a one-man bus with the staff representatives, and it became clear that the trade union representatives felt that for this to happen in towns and cities, buses should be equipped with a central exit in addition to the entrance at the front, and it may be that LAE 770E was borrowed to show the representatives what was available. At a Board meeting in September 1968 it was agreed that centre exits should be added to the 1969 delivery of REs and that this was to cost £300 per bus. Moreover, many REs already delivered to the Bath, Cheltenham and Gloucester fleets were retro-fitted with a centre exit so that one-man operation could be started in these conurbations with some urgency.

During the year the fleet lost its unique 1952 delivery of lowbridge KSWs (only to inherit two similar vehicles from Western National three years later!). Upon withdrawal, ex-Joint Services KSW C8071 (NHY 993) had its roof removed and was altered to have an off-side open platform by the company in conjunction with Smith's Garage (Reading) Ltd, for export to San Francisco to operate a tourist service at Fisherman's Wharf. Apparently its new owner was impressed by the open-top FS buses at Weston-super-Mare and wanted one of these, but the company was understandably unwilling to part with one! Some 35 years later this bus had moved to Tucson, Arizona, where, at the time of writing, it remains in use as a coffee bar. If you believe the information at one time given on its website it is powered by a Bristol-Gardner engine and dates from the times when the crews wore black uniforms with white stripes down the trousers and fares were 2d inside and 1d outside in the open air!

Both of the first two LS buses came to the end of their lives during 1967 and, as previously described, were kept back by the company for a possible museum, and whilst 2800 did eventually survive, 2828 sadly did not. As with the first of the LS buses, 1967 saw the withdrawal of the last of the LS coaches (of 1955) and the conversion of more country service KSWs to the open-platform layout, again presumably for mileage balancing work on Joint Services (8078, 8080 and 8179).

Although the transfer of vehicles between the Joint Services and country fleets was rare, it was quite common for vehicles to be moved between the Bath services or Gloucester city fleets and country services in order to meet changes in requirements. A bus delivered new to Bath or Gloucester might therefore end its days on country work, or vice versa.

During 1967 the company also lost its last wartime lady driver when conductress Harding retired from Staple Hill depot in Bristol after duty on 16th December. During the Second World War she had been one of a number of female bus drivers, driving Bedford buses, but reverted to conducting duties when male staff returned from the war.

In Swindon a new bus station was opened for the country services and the local offices were also moved at that time. The local municipal operator, Swindon Corporation, arranged for their central area crew reliefs

A Red & White Bristol LS, U2454 (left), has worked into Bristol's bus and coach station as a duplicate on the Cardiff service in April 1967. Alongside is Bristol's own 41-seat LS bus 2922 (YHY 80), which would later be refurbished as 3004. Coincidentally this batch of rebuilt buses received 6-cylinder Gardner engines from Red & White LS buses of the same batch as U2454! (*M.Walker*)

107

to be modified at the same time, bringing corporation crews into the new company canteen. Geoff Lusher had recently arrived in Swindon as Traffic Superintendent for the company and recalls that the new canteen was far too small for the number of crews using it, and a hasty extension had to be put in place, with the final result being a canteen almost three times the size of the one first opened! Corporation and company crews mixed quite happily in the canteen, since, after all, as Geoff recalls, a large number of the crews had worked for both operators at one time or another!

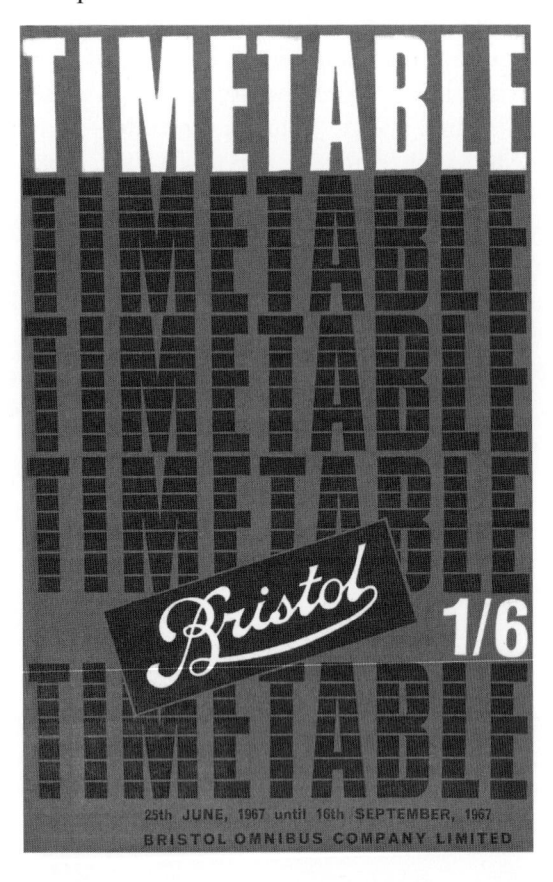

Changes were also taking place inside Bristol's Marlborough Street bus and coach station. The extra length of the Bristol REs was causing some difficulty and as more and more 36ft-long vehicles arrived, including those from Red & White, it became necessary to completely revise the internal arrangements. Gone was the second platform (rendering the passenger subway redundant) while the first platform was re-designed so that vehicles approached the platform edge head-on, instead of drawing-in lengthwise, as required by the original bay design. This allowed more vehicles to be accommodated on the first platform, when parked side-by-side, while also increasing space to reverse.

The new longer buses also required a change in driving technique since the long rear overhang of the RE was apt to swing out if turning too sharply. Geoff Lusher recalls taking a number of trade union representatives out in a new RELL bus to check its suitability for a particular route; on the return journey the party stopped for refreshments in a small market town and parked at the bus stop. When the driver pulled away from the stop after their break, he put a tight right steering lock on to rejoin the road, and the rear nearside swung in and demolished the bus shelter!

With the impending demise of the F-series Lodekka and the fact that the next new double-decker from the Bristol stable would be the VR rear-engined bus, Bristol Commercial Vehicles was unwilling to open up the production line of the shorter FSF to meet the requirements of Western and Southern National, and so Bristol, sensing an opportunity to rid themselves early of vehicles that would never be suitable to be worked without a conductor, offered to part with 20 of their FSF fleet, including the four Cheltenham examples. (No one could then foretell that only three years later, the company would receive six of them back into its fleet!)

TIMETABLE — 25th JUNE, 1967 until 16th SEPTEMBER, 1967 — BRISTOL OMNIBUS COMPANY LIMITED — Bristol — 1/6

When Bristol received its first Bristol RELL buses, those hired from Red & White and used on the Bristol to Cardiff route were returned. 1054 (MHW 858F), the last of the 1967 ECW-bodied buses, is seen at Cardiff bus station having arrived on the express 301 service. (*A.J. Douglas*)

For a number of years a 'temporary' flyover was in use to allow traffic to cross a busy junction close to Bristol's Temple Meads railway station, although it was not used by buses serving the area. In September 1967, however, the company tried a number of buses on the flyover, but in the event decided to continue to use the ground-level roads. Joint Services Bristol KSW C8163 leads an RE and FLF in this view. (*Peter Davey*)

The transfer of these 60-seaters had been discussed at Board level in May 1966 when it was agreed that a further 20 RE service buses should be added to the 1967 vehicle programme 'subject to the selling of 20 FSF buses', which brings this tale full circle and explains the rather large order for RE buses in 1967!

The Bristol Joint Services Committee discussed more vehicle orders at the May 1967 meeting, it being agreed that twelve 53-seat single-deck vehicles should be ordered for 1969 delivery 'since this type of vehicle is suitable for OMO on selected routes subject to agreement with the Trade Union'. The minute continues that

> Since there is likely to be a delay in the delivery of the 28 double-deck vehicles ordered for 1968 it was agreed that the 1968 and 1969 programme should be combined, in view of the possibility that the single-deck RE vehicles could be delivered in 1968 whereas the delivery of the double-deck vehicles could be delayed until 1969.

Operating circumstances in the city were further deteriorating, however, and it was variously reported at the Joint Services meetings that the volume of general motor traffic was increasing, causing severe disruption to the reliability of services whenever an accident occurred on a main road leading to or from the city. It was also reported that late services to the Southmead area of the city had to be withdrawn for two evenings in September due to late night rowdiness and vandalism. In respect of the former, it was later reported that traffic congestion was generally causing the loss of 900 service miles per week, whilst in January of the following year the company advised that it had made a claim against the owners of a timber lorry for losses sustained when it had overturned causing severe traffic delays (but which, in the event, was not pursued). It was also reported that two youths who had assaulted a driver and conductor had received 'sentences for periods at a detention centre and an approved school'.

1968

For the first time since 1933, the company received no new double-deckers in 1968, despite the fact that the order for 28 VR double-deckers had called for them to be delivered in that year. Due to a number of circumstances, this situation was to continue until 1972.

Service bus deliveries consisted of 51 RELL6L models with 53 seats, eight of which were for Bath (seven for Bath Electric Tramways and one for Bath Tramways Motor Co), whilst five were for Gloucester and two for Cheltenham District. The 1968 deliveries had a brighter interior than the previous year's batch, with cream Formica side panels and seat backs, and from fleet number 1061 onwards they carried their fleet number plates on the front and rear, rather than on the sides and rear. In common with all other Bristol Omnibus REs, no rear destination equipment was fitted at all. Two of the RE buses delivered in 1968 had very short lives; 1085 was gutted by a fire which started in the engine compartment when only one year old; whilst 1062 also suffered an engine fire after a rear end collision from a motor cycle and it, too, was burned out, having lasted only three years.

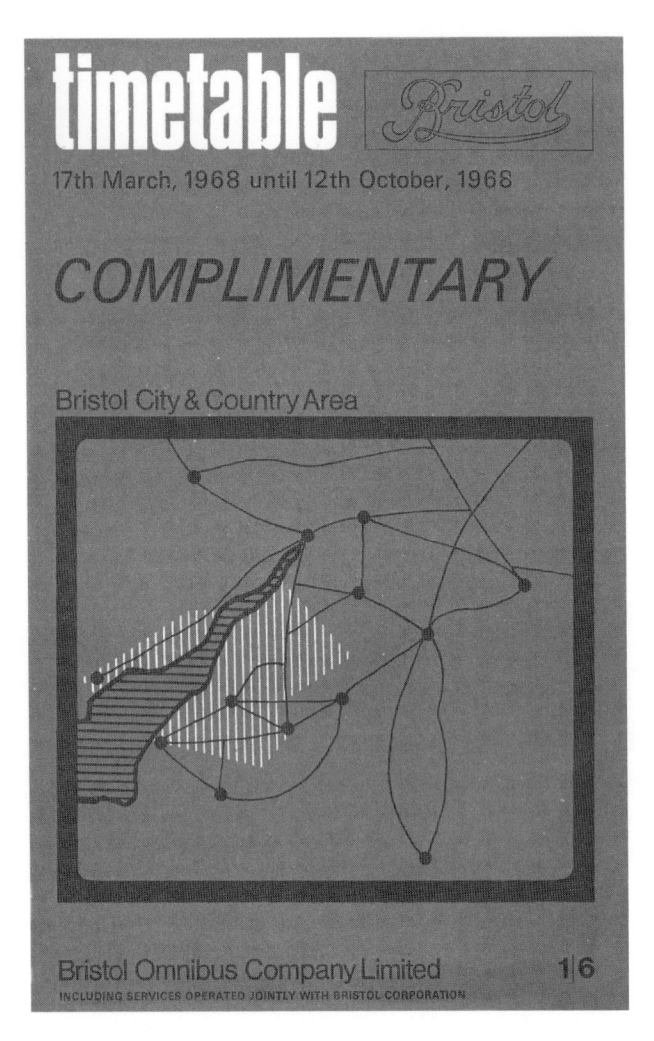

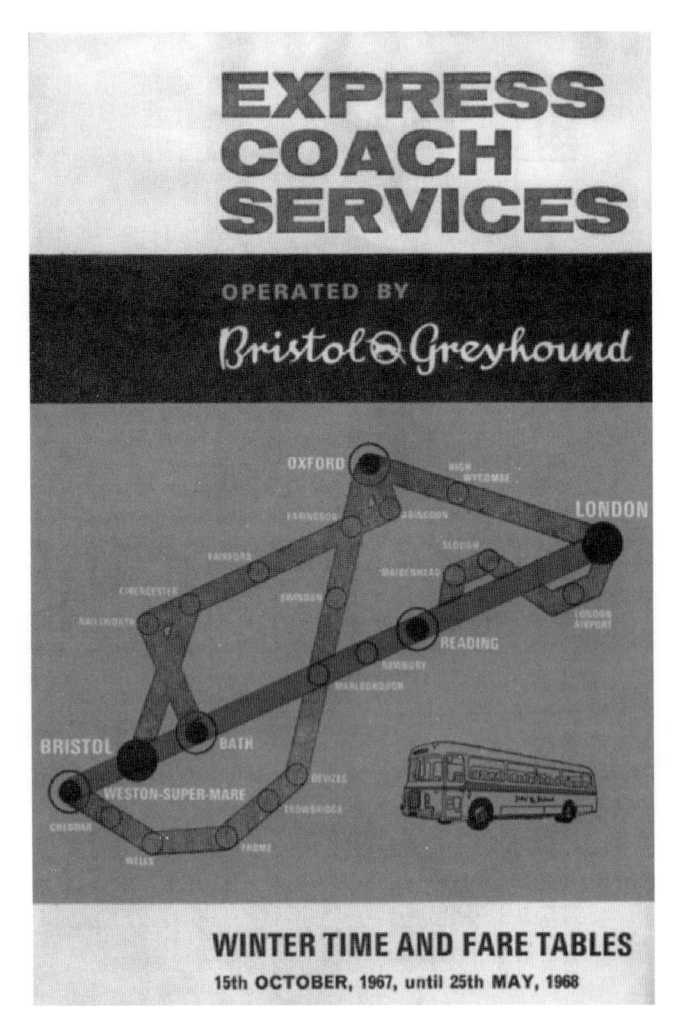

Other RE arrivals were another six handsome 47-seat, coach-shell, dual-purpose vehicles (with chassis built to RE Series 2 specification incorporating a reduced wheelbase of 18ft 6ins, rather than 19ft, although overall vehicle length remained at 36ft). Again they featured folding entrance doors which would enable them to be easily downgraded to buses if required.

These RELHs were accompanied by a further six full coach versions, with almost identical bodies, but seating 45 and painted in Bristol Greyhound's cream and red livery. These too were fitted with 'T' type destination displays and bus type doors, once again permitting a downgrade in future, but when delivered the number track box of the destination equipment displayed an illuminated Greyhound insignia beneath the standard single-line destination. With air suspension, semi-automatic gearbox and powerful Leyland 0.680 engine, to many they were the ultimate Greyhound coach, and were as at home operating the express stopping service between Bristol and London via the A4, as racing along the newly opened sections of motorway at speeds that could reach 80mph or more. Sadly, they were to be the only ones of their type. Co-author Martin Curtis recalls travelling along the A4 from Bristol to Reading in one of these coaches when it was six years old. Its performance was breathtaking, with this batch remaining unsurpassed by any later type of Greyhound coach.

Throughout the 1960s, the company proudly promoted its Greyhound operations following the introduction of the luxurious new RELHs and MWs. Unfortunately, passengers making coach bookings sometimes found that when embarking upon their journey, particularly at weekends and other busy times, inferior coaches were provided for duplication. Most common among duplicates were the lightweight Bedford/Duple coaches, in the red and grey colours of Wessex Coaches, which passengers were sometimes forced to board while a gleaming Bristol Greyhound 'service car' stood tantalizingly alongside!

Dave Clarke from Bath was by now an Inspector, and occasionally spent weekends at London Victoria coach station, supervising loading of the Bristol Greyhound services. During the rest of the week, they were cared for by the Inspectors of the Thames Valley company, who were in Victoria to supervise their own London to Reading area express buses on their services A and B.

Dave recalls an occasion when he prepared to load a Wessex coach as the duplicate for Weston-super-Mare; the driver, he recalls, was from Wessex's Chard outstation, deep in the Somerset countryside, and he had seen farmers who looked like him – a ruddy face, his shirt disorganised with straw on it, his cap perched to one side of his head – and he was told that the coach was used on school services during the week. Rather reluctantly Dave started to load up the coach, wondering what impression the Greyhound passengers would be getting of this standard of service. He despatched the Wessex coach, full, and advised him to give the passengers a break in Marlborough, but not to worry about time.

The following Tuesday he was checking a Wells to Weston-super-Mare bus when he encountered a lady he knew, because she served in the Wells canteen. 'That Wessex coach you put us on last Saturday' she said – he feared the worst – 'what a lovely kind man! We didn't go into Marlborough, but he found us a nice little café and we all bought cream teas, it was wonderful'. The next day, whilst supervising departures at Bath Bus Station, someone came up to him and said 'Have you got a twin brother working in Victoria Coach Station?'

Returning to the city of Bristol, after the successful experiment of operating one-man vehicles on the City Centre Circle, the first network route was converted to full-time one-man operation, using MW buses. During the review of the Joint Services single-deck vehicle requirements, service 19 had been formed by amalgamating two routes that were confined to single-deck operation because of low overhead bridges, and was thus an ideal candidate to convert from conductor operation to one-man as it was already using MW single-deckers; consequently, agreement was reached with the city trade union representatives and service 19 was to be converted to this type of operation on 29th September. The MWs employed were fitted with Setright ticket machines that were subsequently mated to electric operating motors. The operation was run from Muller Road depot, which was only a mile or two from the Fishponds terminus, although Winterstoke Road depot was actually closer to the Ashton terminus, and since this service had been shared between both depots whilst two-person operated, the one-man operators were drawn from both locations.

Dave Bubier, who was one of the first batch of drivers to operate the 19 single-manned, remembers that:

> Initially the MWs were equipped with standard country service manual Setright machines and minimal trays for change. I asked for, and was uniquely issued with, a leather conductor's bag and developed my own methods of operation. Eventually we got change givers and the electric Setright. However, we all suffered from aching thighs both from the heavy clutch action of the Bristol MW and having to hold the throttle down at all times to get any kind of performance out of the 5-cylinder Gardner engine. Our small fleet of city MWs included some with air suspension, which almost catapulted you from the driving seat! Another regular occurrence along Pennywell Road, which was severely pot-holed, was to break a spring and come to a crash stop as the hand brake snatched on!

Bristol City service 19 was chosen to be the first regular route in the city to be operated without a conductor, principally because it was already operated by single-deck Bristol MW buses of the Joint Services fleet. One of the reasons why single-deck buses were required on the route was the low clearance of the bridge at Ashton Vale, close to the Winterstoke Road bus depot and Bristol City football club's Ashton Gate ground. One-man operated 1961 Bristol MW C2519 is seen here negotiating the bridge. (*M. Walker*)

Problems were continuing to be experienced by city crews with vandalism and assaults, especially during the evenings, and this resulted in the acquisition of a small number of two-way radios to be fitted in the cabs of FLF buses, with these buses being allocated to work the most affected journeys. The company was already using two-way radios for communication amongst the control staff at relief points remote from the depots to ensure that the amount of delay caused by staff taking on buses late, for whatever reason, was minimised. Incidentally, it had long been practice in Bristol for some crew reliefs to take place at one of a number of points around the city centre despite the fact that staff may have started their duty at a depot on the outskirts of the city. Thus, for instance, a Muller Road crew could report to the depot for the morning peak yet be relieved for their break at the Central area, taking on there after their break and also finishing there, even though their own personal transport might be back at Muller Road, and this was an accepted format for Bristol city crew duties during the 1960s and '70s.

Some of the two-way radios really came into good use on Wednesday 10th July 1968 when an exceptional weather pattern saw torrential rain pour down on the West Country with local rivers breaking their banks and causing widespread flooding within the company's operating area. At Bath depot, according to the Traffic Manager's notes in the staff magazine *Omnibus*, the depot was flooded and evacuated of buses, except for one engineless example which was suspended between two cranes to keep it out of the water! Barbara Rex, who grew up in Bristol, and was visiting Bedminster at the time from her Hanham home, recalls that she went into a public call box to try and call home but was unable to do so because the lines were flooded, and by the time she wanted to leave the box the flood water from the nearby overflowing Malago river had reached between two and three feet deep along Bedminster Road – making it difficult to open the door! She and her companion only reached the safety of their house by walking up to their thighs in dirty water, and climbing up neighbouring gardens to vault across fences outside each house.

Those buses that could, returned to depot as there was little hope of providing a service in many parts of the city, and at nearby Winterstoke Road depot – described as like an island in the sea – even the would-be museum buses, parked as they were at the rear of the depot, were standing in two to three feet of water. Indeed, the police refused to allow the next morning run-out because they were afraid of the 'wash' that the buses would create as they used the flooded roads! Radio buses were stationed at Marlborough Street, Winterstoke Road and Brislington depots to provide communications as the telephones were cut off, whilst in the suburb of Brislington, where the A4 descends into a dip before climbing towards Keynsham, one radio-equipped FLF was overcome by water and stranded. The crew were instructed to climb on to the roof of the bus from where the driver continued to provide a running commentary on the disaster until rescue came at 1.45am! One of the company's ex-military 4x4 AEC breakdown tenders, known as 'Jumbo', was kept in constant use in the city during that day and night recovering water-logged cars and buses, and it was reported that its engine, axle and gearbox oil were changed three times during the period of the emergency!

Outside the city the River Chew became a raging torrent that swept away road bridges at Pensford, Woollard, and no fewer than four at Keynsham. In Somerset, 67 bridges were washed away, whilst almost every low-lying village or town in Somerset, Gloucestershire and parts of Wiltshire were inundated by flood water.

Jack Hodge and fellow union members organised a Bristol area fund to provide cash help to members of staff and company pensioners whose homes had been badly affected by the floods, and money was raised by means of grants from the Centre and Old Market 'machine' accounts (it was practice within the city canteens that 'fruit machines' at the depots and relief points were used for supporting the canteens and other 'welfare' benefits). In addition, there were donations from depot sports clubs and collections amongst the staff at the depots. This was perhaps one of the last times that the 'family' atmosphere of the 'Tramways' came to the fore – an atmosphere that had been synonymous with the company from the days of its formation.

During 1968 the first Lodekkas (other than the already withdrawn prototype, LC5000) left the fleet, which, significantly, was the same year that the last new Lodekkas left the factory, and was just one year after the last new examples for the company had been delivered. The first pre-production bus, L8133, joined the preservation prospects in store at the back of Winterstoke Road depot having completed a full 15 years in service, whilst L8256 was despatched to North's, the dealer, and later found a home at that renowned Bristol operator, D.R. McGregor of Sible Hedingham (trading as Hedingham and District); after 15 years, the private sector was at last able to appreciate the benefits of operating proper Lodekkas!

But what of the FLF replacement, the VR? To the great disappointment of many, it was proposed at the

December 1968 Board meeting that the order for VRs be changed for 28 dual-door REs. As a result, the 28 VRs were diverted to two other Tilling companies, Brighton Hove & District and United Automobile Services, but ironically they did appear at the Bristol Omnibus Central Repair Works (CRW) at Lawrence Hill, when brand new, wearing their new owners' colours.

Rodney Hawkins, who joined the company as Deputy Chief Engineer in 1969, having been with the BET group before the formation of the National Bus Company, when interviewed for *National Bus Company, 1968-1989* said that:

> Although the VR was advertised as being supplied with a (Leyland) 0.680 engine as an alternative to the Gardner 6LX, in fact when this was requested by B.O.C. there was concern on the part of the works as one had at that time not been fitted and there was a disinclination to do so. The close cooperation that existed between the works and the company flowed from the fact that employees' families often had members working for the works and there was therefore a direct personal relationship, which overcame many problems.

There were two reasons why these new vehicles were, nevertheless, initially delivered to Bristol. The first was that Bristol Omnibus had changed the order so late, that it was left to modify them to the new requirements of individual customers as part of the deal. This included changes to rear axle ratios. The second was that in any case, the first VRs required modification before entry into service, and in this sense, Bristol Omnibus was assisting Bristol Commercial Vehicles.

BCV had already considered an alternative engine position to that seen on the prototype VR models. However, this was accelerated when in 1968 the Government introduced its New Bus Grant scheme which initially contributed 25% (later 50%) towards the cost of new vehicles, in order to assist operators convert services to one-man operation. To qualify however, buses had to be built to certain detailed specifications relating to items such as overall length, floor height, length of front and rear overhang, entrance width, etc, which resulted in manufacturers modifying their designs in order to comply. By far the most drastic change was to Bristol's VR, as qualifying double-deck designs were required to have Transversely-positioned rear engines – rather than the Longitudinal arrangement of the first VRs. The original layout (re-designated VRL) was hurriedly modified to produce the VRT which, unlike virtually any other Bristol design, which was thoroughly tested with prototype vehicles or test rigs, went straight into production from the drawing board. Almost immediately design faults appeared and it was correcting these that caused the diverted VRs to arrive at Lawrence Hill, with the Bristol operating department and Bristol Commercial Vehicles working closely together once again. And these were not the only VRs requiring such attention. Famously, a huge batch of Scottish Bus Group VRTs for the Central and Western SMT concerns also arrived in Bristol for similar work, and were seen not only at Lawrence Hill, but other Bristol Omnibus depots which offered assistance.

Meanwhile, Bristol Omnibus persevered with its policy of introducing more RE single-deckers for one-man-operated (OMO) services. At the BJS meeting for September it was agreed that the 12 single-deck buses on order should have a central exit added, but as this was not practical at this stage of the build then the company would take the Joint Services buses when they arrived and a change would be made to the 1969 intake to provide central exit buses for BJS.

At the last meeting of the Joint Services Committee for that year, on 12th December, it was reported that the conversion of service 19 to one-man operation had been a success, with improved reliability and a resultant increase in passenger numbers leading to the consideration of alternative methods of ticket issuing for peak periods. The change-over of services to one-man operation was now getting into full swing, as there would be a further conversion of 17 vehicles on 26th January 1969, this time involving motorised ticket machines.

The prototype of a new lightweight saloon, the Bristol LH (registered NHU100F), was demonstrated to the company in March 1968 and, although tried on several routes, was not to carry fare-paying passengers. It would be four more years before the company took delivery of its first LH buses, and these would be very different from the demonstrator.

A departure from previous practice occurred when the company received its first non-Tilling General Manager on July 1st 1968, when Mr E.W.A. (Ted) Butcher joined the company from Ribble, a former British Electric Traction company, where he had been Traffic Manager. His influence was soon to pervade the company.

1969

This move preceded another change in company ownership. Only a few months later, on 1st January 1969, the Transport Holding Company was succeeded in England and Wales by the newly formed National Bus Company, which had been created to bring together

Bristol's first short Bristol RESL models with 43-seat ECW bodies were delivered in 1969; 503 (THU 349G) was one of two owned by the Bath Tramways Motor Company when new, and is seen laying over in central Bath whilst operating Bath city service 218 in November 1970. (*M.S. Curtis*)

the former Tilling group and bus companies of the rival British Electric Traction, which had recently sold out to the THC. State ownership continued therefore and once again there were, at first, few outward signs of any change – but this was a deceptive calm.

Ownership of Bristol Commercial Vehicles Ltd, and ECW at Lowestoft, also changed from this time. Leyland had already acquired a 25% share in these companies from 1965 – which allowed them to trade freely on the open market once more. From 1969 Leyland increased its stake to 50%, while NBC took over the remaining half share. Henceforth, both businesses would therefore be jointly Leyland/NBC owned, although Leyland increasingly assumed control of the firms' day-to-day affairs. This newly divided ownership was to be most significant in influencing future bus production.

There were no double-deckers again in 1969, with new vehicles consisting entirely of RE single-deckers fitted with the new standard 11.1 litre 0.680 engine, although 15 of the 59 taken into stock were of the shorter RESL type seating 43. Being both shorter and lighter than the current fleet of 53-seaters, but fitted with the same engine, the performance of these RESLs became legendary; they were numbered from 500 upwards and carried registrations in the THU-G series, which readily led them to be called 'THUGS' – and THUG number 508 survives in preservation today.

More dual-purpose vehicles were also acquired in the shape of fleet numbers 2054 to 2058, RELH chassis but this time carrying bus shell bodies with 49 seats, finished in the brighter style of livery associated with this class of vehicle, with cream roof and window surrounds.

Only five of this year's delivery were standard length, single-door buses, although the company standard was now for 50 seats with a luggage pen over the nearside wheel arch (previous deliveries had tip up seats that could be folded to make a luggage pen at this position), and they also featured the new standard ECW frontal arrangement incorporating taller, flat windscreens which necessitated side-by-side destination displays to replace the 'T' type found on previous REs. Among these, bus 1105 was used by Bristol Commercial Vehicles to experiment with a CAV474 automatic gearbox and, so fitted, the bus was used in service by the company from July 1969 until March 1970. Co-author Mike Walker recalls watching this bus drive out of Westbury-on-Trym whilst it operated the Cardiff service, with the auto box unable to decide in which gear ratio it felt most comfortable, as it constantly 'hunted' between gears while climbing Falcondale Road!

Bristol city services 15 and 83 were converted to one-man operation using country services 53-seat Bristol RELL saloons, pending the arrival of the BJS twin doorway buses. 1102 (RHT 151G) causes some congestion for following buses in this March 1969 view. (*M.S. Curtis*)

In 1969 Joint Services took delivery of a number of 44-seat, dual doorway ECW-bodied Bristol RELL buses so that one-person operation could be extended in the city. C1117 was to have been registered THW 918G, the registration number carried in this official photograph, but it became UHU 219H before entering service. This view shows the two-leaf centre doorway and the large illuminated 'pay as you enter' sign above the front nearside wheel. (*ECW*)

The remaining new buses were all to what was to become the standard for company REs, operating as OMO buses on city and town services. They were delivered in the new OMO livery of green with cream from the bottom of the windows down to the top of the aluminium rubbing strip, the required centre exit and 44 seats, with a large luggage pen replacing four seats just opposite the exit. They were also fitted with large illuminated 'pay as you enter' signs next to the entrance and a smaller one at the front, while the destination display on these buses had the number on the driver's side, unlike the 50-seaters and dual-purpose vehicles, making it much easier for the driver to change both the number and ultimate destination without leaving his seat. As with all RE deliveries, they did not carry rear route number displays, a further reduction in the quality of the information available to the travelling public, although it did become practice for a short period of time on BJS to make full use of the front destination aperture to show a series of intermediate points under the ultimate destination. Presumably the lack of rear destination display was felt necessary because during negotiations with the staff representatives it was seen as very unlikely that any agreement could be reached on them leaving their cabs to change rear number information where required, although, of course, the Conduct of Drivers, Conductors and Passengers Regulations did specify that the bus should be examined for lost property at the end of each journey, requiring the one-man operator to leave his cab anyway!

The lack of rear route information became a controversial issue. Some company managers argued that passengers didn't want to know which bus they had just missed – but as any bus user knows, this can be important in order to plan what to do next. Many passengers also approach from the rear and at a time when passenger numbers were generally declining, the failure of the company and unions to tackle this problem did nothing to reverse the loss of patronage.

Thirty-two of the dual doorway REs joined the Joint Services fleet (from C1109 onwards) and, after the success of operating service 19 without a conductor, BJS was to embark upon a rapid adoption of this type of operation, in part to ease the city of the staff shortage that had plagued reliability for many years. Significantly, this type of operation offered a higher basic rate of pay to the one-man driver which would, of course, be helpful in attracting more staff to this type of operation. Similar vehicles joined the Gloucester fleet whilst Bath Tramways Motor Company received two of the shorter RESLs, presumably deemed necessary because of the narrowness of some of Bath's more historic areas accessed by Bath City bus routes, although, of course, these only had a single door. The Bath Tramways Motor Company also received one of the dual-purpose RELHs.

The staff shortage became particularly acute during the late 1960s (and early '70s). Co-author Martin Curtis remembers a wait one summer's evening for a service 5 bus (which operated from Broomhill to Filton via

The 1969 intake of dual-purpose semi-coaches consisted of five Bristol RELH vehicles with ECW bus shell 49-seat bodies. They had flat windscreens and dual headlights: this is 2057 (TAE 418G). (*R.H.G. Simpson*)

the city centre) in the Allison Road/Sandy Park Road area of Brislington. Buses should have run every 20 mins, requiring six buses, but on that occasion the first appeared after well over an hour, with the conductor hanging from the front entrance of his FLF, announcing that theirs was the only No.5 on the road!

The extension to one-man operation of Joint Services routes had been achieved by the end of January 1969, with services 15 and 83 converted to one-person operation, although using country services 53-seat single-deckers until the arrival of the Joint Services dual-doorway buses. Service 15 ran from Shirehampton, in the west of the city, around the northwest city suburbs of Westbury-on-Trym and Henbury, through the city and on to Hotwells (near the entrance to Bristol harbour and a stone's throw from the old Clifton Rocks Railway). This service was operated by the tiny Avonmouth depot, which had a capacity of about 25 normal-sized buses, and its conversion left a small two-man roster that provided four vehicles each on services 28 and 84, the bulk of which were provided by the large Lawrence Hill depot. In fact, the very first OMO journey from Avonmouth was not on service 15 but an early Sunday morning works journey on service 27, following the same route as service 15 to Westbury-on-Trym, and returning via the depot to the factories at Avonmouth and the Severnside industrial estates as a service 27J. It then returned to Shirehampton to pick up on service 15, and co-author Mike Walker was privileged to be, he believes, the first fare-paying passenger on a one-man RE bus in the city! Service 83, operated by Muller Road depot, was what was left of the 1960s service 73/83 circular, one of the few orbital routes that principally linked neighbouring communities rather than connecting them with the city centre. (The Hanham local route network was also principally orbital, being based upon the group of Bristol suburban routes once operated by the Bence company at the time of the takeover of the bus operating business by the Bristol Tramways before the war, although these were not part of the Joint Services network.) Service 83 operated between two termini that were a mile or so apart but operating on a route that meandered around the northern suburbs of Bristol and with an end to end journey time of about an hour.

The 53-seaters continued to operate these two services for most of the first year until the dual-doorway REs were available. Initially their motorised Setright ticket machines were mounted vertically in the cab door, but this proved unsatisfactory and by the time the two-doorway buses were ready for service the company and staff representatives had agreed a new style of purpose-built ticket machine/cash tray/cash dispenser fitment that was to be manufactured and fitted at the company's own Central Repair Works, and this became the standard that was soon retro-fitted to the rest of the one-man fleet.

When service 15 was converted to single manning, Dave Bubier recalls that Avonmouth depot drivers were able to drive the MWs on Muller Road's service 19 for overtime or when spare, but the opposite was not allowed. However, the route 19 drivers were eventually given the opportunity to train to drive the REs. Dave took advantage of this, one evening finishing a piece of service 15 work at Avonmouth and, along with his service 15 takings, paid in his service 19 takings and waybill into the Avonmouth night safe. Although this was a perfectly acceptable practice (after all, both depots and services were part of the Joint Services network), it caused concern at Muller Road depot because the cash reconciliation for service 19 could not be completed until the following day when his waybill arrived from Avonmouth depot! To make a point, he went on to pay his service 19 takings at Brislington, Winterstoke Road and Hanham depots (the latter not a Joint Services operation) for the rest of the week.

As might be expected, the 36ft length of the RELL buses did cause some routeing problems (after all, they were some nine feet longer than the double-deckers they were generally replacing) and minor re-routeings did take place – including that on service 15 at the approach to Westbury-on-Trym from Henleaze to avoid a 180-degree turn! Problems were also created by the successive reduction in seating capacity from the 58 or 60 of the double-deckers, first to 53 and then to 44 when the dual-doorway buses arrived, and from co-author Mike Walker's own experiences, this did cause some overloading problems, particularly on peak-hour service 15 journeys. After all, the 44-seaters officially carried only eight standing passengers – a number that was often exceeded. It became ironic that the increased reliability of these new OMO services, largely because the increased pay rates applicable to one-man operators initially allowed these rosters to be filled, caused an increase in passenger numbers that could sometimes not be catered for because of capacity problems.

The Bristol RE entrance arrangement was low and wide, but nevertheless involved several shallow steps towards the driver and into the saloon, while the centre exits had deep steps as the floor level rose in height along the bus. This proved to be very awkward to the elderly or infirm, and was in stark contrast to the stepless floors of Lodekkas. Once again, this inevitably deterred bus travel for many potential users – despite other advantages of OMO operation.

And there was another consequence of switching from double-deckers to OMO single-deck buses. During the 1960s, a high proportion of the population (of all ages) were smokers. On double-deckers, smoking was permitted only on the top-deck so passengers selected where they travelled accordingly. With the change to single-deckers, the division disappeared – so smokers were asked to occupy the rear seats of the saloon. This meant those who disliked being in a smoke-filled environment were no longer protected to the same degree, and this eventually led to the end of smoking on public transport.

By March 1969, however, it was reported to the Joint Services Committee that the two conversions were operating satisfactory, although service 83 suffered adversely from the delays caused by traffic congestion. But BJS still needed to reduce its operating costs – before tax, the profits of Joint Services were to reduce to £120,000 for 1969, having peaked during 1966 to over £250,000, despite the introduction of one-man operation in the city with services 17 [re-numbered 41] and 40 converted at the end of November '69. It was also reported that work was in hand to reduce its commitments on evenings and Sundays. Indeed, matters were made public when it was agreed at the June meeting that a joint press release be issued stating that 'positive steps were being taken to alleviate the present difficulties facing the Joint Services.' One of these measures, agreed at the previous meeting, had been the setting up of a working party to investigate the effects of traffic congestion within the city, consisting of representatives of the company, the City Council and the Police, and another measure, agreed at the August meeting, was yet another fares increase.

Firm proposals for the reduction of BJS's evening and Sunday commitments were put to the December meeting when the company representative stated that consideration was being given to reducing the overall end to end running time during these periods. This allowed fewer vehicles and crews to provide the same frequency on a service, and to operate one-man vehicles during these times on services that would remain double-deck crew-operated during the majority of the day. At the same meeting, a demonstration was given of a new Marconi-designed bus location system, a report on which had been submitted to both the National Bus Company and Bristol Corporation. The aim was to enable a controller to identify the location along the route of each vehicle operating on a service so that gaps in the service caused by congestion or breakdown could be easily identified and remedied with the aid of a pool of spare vehicles and crews. The system worked by means of a box mounted behind the front door at the roof level of single-deck RE buses which generated a laser beam. This left the bus at right angles through a small roof-mounted window to be reflected from a plate mounted on a lamp post along the line of route, each plate being identified by a unique patterned barcode. The reflected laser beam was read by the on-bus unit and sent to the control computer over the bus two-way radio network.

It was eventually to be introduced on a number of routes in the city and the control room was initially established at the Centre offices. As a result of a competition held amongst the staff, the system was eventually launched as 'B-Line' and was to operate for a number of years, but the true benefits never materialised since the company never had sufficient spare buses or crews to fill gaps in services (especially if those gaps were caused by staff shortages anyway) and if traffic congestion was the problem, then any replacement vehicles would encounter the same congestion, negating any improvement in service. The equipment itself was also found to be unreliable, and when fitted on board vehicles, suffered from rattles and vibration that normally occur during service running.

For some weeks after delivery in August 1969 RELL C1118 was converted to a mobile staff recruiting exhibition with a reduced capacity of 18 seats, and in this form it was displayed around the city to advertise both the new type of bus entering service, and the availability of one-man operator jobs at a good rate of pay. In fact the one-man operation acceptance bonus that had been paid to staff in advance of the conclusion of the negotiations on further one-man conversions, had only recently been consolidated into the basic pay rates, meaning that it was now also able to enhance overtime pay rates.

As these examples of dual-doorway REs were being prepared for service towards the end of 1969, the Joint Services was to answer a call for help from fellow National Bus Company subsidiary the West Riding Automobile Company at Wakefield, who, together with Guy Motors of Wolverhampton, had pioneered the development of a new type of double-deck bus, the Wulfrunian. The futuristic braking and independent suspension systems of this bus were causing so many problems that it was felt necessary to replace them prematurely. Joint Services seized the opportunity to despatch 27 of its Gardner-engined, 70-seat Bristol FLF Lodekkas northwards so that it could order early replacements for them in the shape of REs suitable for more one-man conversions. However, there was an undercurrent amongst the BJS staff that they were losing some of their newer buses (the oldest of these FLFs were eight years old while the newest, only three years old) and were being expected to soldier on with older vehicles when these should have been withdrawn. Matters reached the point where the general manager was forced to issue an Official Notice to staff, extolling the long-term benefits of this move, since the Joint Services would see additional replacement REs delivered the following year, as a result of releasing these FLFs.

The company was still able to 'pull out all the stops' to cover important events, however, as Geoff Lusher recalls. During the year Swindon Town Football Club made it through to the League Cup Final at Wembley, and not only did much of the population of Swindon want to attend, many of his staff did as well! Indeed, a number of the staff were lucky enough to secure tickets, and it was decided that these would all be released from their regular duties to drive a coach to London for the day. Local operator Rimes was the holder of the Excursion and Tours licence for Swindon, and in the event Bristol Omnibus was able to supply 17

Joint Services Bristol RELL C1118 of 1969 was used by the company as a mobile recruitment office before entering service, and is shown here parked on Bristol's bus and coach station forecourt in September 1969. (*M. Walker*)

coaches and dual-purpose vehicles for hiring to Rimes for the day; the vehicles were drawn from all over the company's operating area, and lacking space in the depot, they were parked overnight at the bus station – with the depot trade union official volunteering to be the overnight security guard and sleep with them! The 18th coach was used by the Sports and Social Club and driven by Geoff. For the day, all scheduled bus duties were suspended and the entire timetabled bus operation was covered on an *ad hoc* basis with those staff who did not want to go to London, the only lost mileage for the day being untimetabled duplication on some of the busier local services. Swindon beat Arsenal 3-1!

Towards the end of the year a vehicle exchange took place with South Wales Transport which involved one of their AEC Reliances coming to Bristol, where it was used on the Bristol to Cardiff service, whilst an RELH dual-purpose vehicle went to South Wales; the exchange was in connection with saloon heating trials.

South Wales Transport was among the former BET companies which now formed part of the new National Bus Company, and the exchange of ideas, together with a gradual integration of the former Tilling and BET groups' policies was to become increasingly apparent during the next decade. The Bristol group of companies initially formed part of NBC's South Western Region.

Within the Bristol group itself, Bath Electric Tramways Ltd, and Bath Tramways Motor Company Ltd ceased to be operational companies from 1st December 1969, with vehicles and services transferred directly to Bristol Omnibus Company, rather than maintaining them under the subsidiaries. The 'Bath Services' fleetname nevertheless remained in use on a substantial number of vehicles, often appearing on single-deckers in a revised, smaller style with slanting characters, which had first appeared the previous year (in some cases surmounted by a Bath shield). The established, larger 'Bath Services' fleetname design remained for double-deckers, however. This left Cheltenham District Traction Company as the only remaining operational subsidiary company.

By the end of 1969 the fleet total had reduced slightly to 1,213 vehicles. The pattern for future deliveries into the 1970s was largely set at the September 1969 Board Meeting. The continued expansion of one-man operation was assured as the capital expenditure for 1972 deliveries was agreed. In addition to more REs, this called for the first lightweight Bristol LH buses at £5,865 each (a full 20% cheaper than the RESL buses of a similar seating capacity!), and eight VRTs for Joint Services at a cost of £8,640 each. A return to double-deckers, at least in a small way, would at last see the Bristol VR enter the fleet.

The end of the sixties had thus seen the formation of a new parent company, the disappearance of two long-lived subsidiary companies and a temporary hiatus in the purchase of new double-deck buses, with the prospect that most double-deckers could be replaced by single-deck vehicles which were deemed more suitable for the task, as more widespread one-man operation was envisaged for the coming years. The Bristol Omnibus Company Limited entered the seventies as it had other decades, changing to meet new challenges of operating public transport, but this time against a backdrop of rising car ownership, heavy traffic congestion and a labour market reluctant to take on the responsibilities of driving buses in that congested environment.

***

Many of Bristol's city depot's miscellaneous (peak hour) vehicle workings operated country services using BJS buses, adding to some of the mileage imbalance referred to in the text. 1953 ECW-bodied Bristol KSW C8136 (PHW 961) waits at Winterbourne, in the country services operating area, in late 1969, before returning to Bristol bus and coach station as country service 326. It would have reached Winterbourne by operating a school service to the nearby secondary school. (*M. Walker*)

119

(*left*) Joint Services Leyland Titan PD1 C4036, with an ECW Tilling standard 56-seat body, dates from 1948 and was withdrawn in 1961, the year following this photograph. The original 18-inch deep destination display has been panelled over to the 12-inch standard; many of Bristol's Titans ran with black radiators. (*S.J. Butler collection*)

(*below*) Bath Tramways Motor Company 8172, a 60-seat closed-platform Bristol KSW of 1954, had received a 'T-type' destination box by the time this photograph was taken in Bath. (*A.J. Douglas*)

(*right*) Bristol's last new LD Lodekka, L8546 of 1959, operating on the Cheltenham to Gloucester service. Note that most ventilators are of the hopper type, and that there are very few on the upper deck.
(*S.J. Butler collection*)

(*below*) Originally a 1946 lowbridge bus, LC3376 became C3480 in 1955 when it was fitted with a new lower radiator and bonnet line and a 1949 Tilling-style, ECW, 59-seat highbridge body that had previously been on Bristol G-type C3024. The centrally mounted gearbox of the G-type meant that the body was slightly higher than K-types, which had their gearboxes at the front, just behind the engine, and so the windscreen was of a squarer appearance than the standard K-type body, as seen on C3444 which is in pursuit in this 1960 view. C3480 lasted another three years on city services. (*S.J. Butler collection*)

(*left*) After barely a month as BJS C3449, 1950 Bristol K-type LHY 938 became country bus 3775, and then, in 1954, was transferred to the Gloucester City fleet as 1542! This 59-seat, ECW-bodied bus lasted until 1966, long enough to be fitted with a 'T' type destination display.
(*S.J. Butler collection*)

(*below*) Bristol only had four standard ECW-bodied, 60-seat, rear-entrance Bristol FS Lodekka buses. L8548 (438 FHW) of 1960 is seen here before its 1967 transfer to Gloucester City services. (*R.H.G. Simpson*)

(*above*) 'Flatback' 45-seat Bristol MW bus 2942 (932 AHY) and Bristol LD L8482 (838 CHU), both built in 1958 with ECW bodywork, pictured in the early 1960s when the block capital gold fleetname had replaced the Bristol coat of arms. (*S.J. Butler collection*)

(*right*) The driver of this BJS Bristol FLF adds water to his bus after it had boiled over at Westbury-on-Trym in Bristol in September 1967, a not uncommon sight with Bristol BVW-engined buses operating in the city. (*M. Walker*)

(*left*) Bristol received its first production Bristol LD Lodekkas in 1955, and L8279 (UHY 408) was one of the last of these to be fitted with the long radiator grille. Note the brackets holding the route number information on the stop pole, typical of the period, and what is believed to be a Swindon Corporation Leyland PD2 to the left of the photograph. (*S.J. Butler collection*)

(*left*) Bristol L-type saloon 2481 was new in late 1949 as BJS bus C2743 with an ECW 33-seat dual-door body, but was converted to a 35-seat one-man bus and renumbered as country services 2481 in 1959. It is seen here leaving Bristol's Marlborough Street bus and coach station in 1963, the year it was withdrawn from service. Note the slanting cab-side window, so arranged to allow the driver to speak to boarding passengers and work the manually operated ticket machine. (*S.J. Butler collection*)

(*below*) Many of the company's depots were built to a similar design, that of the Tilling group architects. The small Highbridge depot, in Somerset, the company's southernmost premises, was a sub-depot of Weston-super-Mare, and it was that depot which determined the vehicle allocation. In this view, one of those buses provided by the main depot for the Burnham-on-Sea to Bridgwater route was one of the four convertible open-top ECW-bodied Bristol FS double-deckers, complete in its seaside cream! (*Peter Davey*)

(*right*) The company's one-off Bristol LDL, L8450, moved to Bath Tramways Motor Company in 1963, where its additional capacity was useful on the service to the military camps at Colerne. This view shows the rear loading in use at Bath's bus station until the advent of forward-entrance buses, and more particularly one-man operation, made it necessary to load head-on. (*Bristol Vintage Bus Group*)

(*below*) Country services ECW-bodied, 70-seat Bristol FLF Lodekka 7125 of 1964, operating on the Gloucester to Hereford route. (*S.J. Butler collection*)

(*left*) 1957 Joint Services Bristol KSW C8415 (YHT 911), with a standard 60-seat, open platform body, still retains its 12-inch deep destination display and block capital fleetname in this November 1965 view at the Redland terminus of service 20. (*M. Walker*)

(*above*) For a brief while the ECW-bodied, 58-seat open platform Bristol LD Lodekka was the BJS standard bus. LC8475 (815 CHU) of 1958, is seen here at the Avonmouth bus terminal, close to Avonmouth bus depot, in November 1965. (*M. Walker*)

(*right*) This 1948 ECW-bodied, 55-seat lowbridge Bristol K-type, L4120 (LHU 516) lasted in service until 1966, and received the latest style of destination display. (*A.J. Douglas*)

(*right*) Titan PD1 C4041 had a company-built body and saw service until 1961. The destination screen on this bus has been masked rather than rebuilt. C4041 stands at Bristol's Tramways Centre. (*A.J. Douglas*)

(*above*) A closed-platform country services Bristol KSW, 8345 of 1956, at Bridgwater bus station, operating a short working on the hourly service to Burnham-on-Sea.
(*R.H.G. Simpson*)

(*left*) Leyland-engined, ECW-bodied Bristol FLF C7130 (823 SHW) of 1964 waits time at the centre in September 1969.
(*M.S. Curtis*)

(*right*) This small 30-seat Bristol SUS, 306 (846 THY) of 1963, is seen operating the former Dundry Pioneer service 80 between Bristol and Dundry with Lewis's department store in the background in November 1965. Note the lazy blind in what was, to the company, a non-standard destination display. (*M. Walker*)

(*left*) Bristol MW bus 2960 (980 DAE) of 1959, and Bristol LS bus 2911 of 1957 (XHW 427), illustrate what would have been a very common scene in the rural towns around the company's operating area in the early 1960s. This is believed to be Frampton-on-Severn. The rear destination display of the MW bus is still in use, whilst the one-man operated LS bus has a much simpler single-line destination arrangement. 2911 would go on to be refurbished and modernised in 1972 and emerge as 3005. (*S.J. Butler collection*)

(*right*) Former BJS bus C2738 (LHY 978), of 1949, became Gloucester G2496 in 1960 and then country services 2496 in October 1965, despite keeping twin doors in its ECW body throughout. It is seen here at Bristol's Lawrence Hill depot in November 1965; the destination display has been reduced to one single line. (*M. Walker*)

(*above*) 2884 (UHT 494), the A.E.C.-engined Bristol LS with a 45-seat ECW body that was used in connection with the development of the lightweight Bristol SC model. It was fitted with a Bristol MW-type grille two months before this September 1967 view, and lasted in this form for another year. (*Peter Davey*)

(*below*) The Bristol Commercial Vehicles demonstrators, LH registered NHU 100F and RELL registered LAE 770E, both with ECW bodies, were together at the manufacturers' Brislington premises in March 1969. The LH was in green and cream livery whilst the RELL was finished in caramel and cream. Both of these vehicles paid a brief visit to the company. (*M. Walker*)

(*above*) 2291 (LHY 965), a 35-seat Bristol L-type, at Bristol's Centre in May 1966. This bus was new to the Bath Tramways Motor Company, only becoming a country bus the previous year. 1966 was the final year for this type of bus. (*Peter Davey*)

(*left*) Country services bus 2636 (HHW 452D), the company's last 45-seat Bristol MW, seen here passing through Bristol's shopping centre at speed in November 1967 in the brighter livery introduced for the City Centre Circle service that year, together with a side route board. (*Peter Davey*)

(*above*) 45-seat Bristol MW bus 2514 (536 JHU) of 1961, viewed in June of 1965. The rural nature of this section of the route to Malmesbury was typical of many of the services using one-man operated single-deckers at the time. (*S.J. Butler collection*)

Part of the behind the scenes operation of any bus company is keeping the buses and coaches clean. At a large depot such as Lawrence Hill at Bristol as many as 175 buses would have to be washed and swept out at the end of the working day. Here the cleaning crew tackle the dirt on the inside of a Bristol KSW. (*Bristol Omnibus*)

Accidents

Fortunately accidents were few and far between, and fatalities very rare. Here we show a selection of those reported in local newspapers.

(*right*) One man died and 15 people were injured when Lodekka L8497 on service 339 from Bristol to Bath crashed at Durley Hill, Keynsham on 1st September 1970. Shortly before the accident the bus had been involved in a minor collision with a police car which was attempting to stop the bus in order to question one of the passengers. The bus mounted the pavement and demolished a lamp post before plunging 25 feet down an embankment and ending on its side. (*Keynsham Weekly Chronicle*)

(*left*) The remains of Bristol RELL 1062 (NHU 196F) whch caught fire at Wells Road, Pensford on 9th September 1971 following an accident. Luckily none of the passengers was injured. (*Bristol Evening Post*)

(*left*) On 19th December 1971, a large pine tree was blown by storm-force winds onto a bus travelling from Bristol to Gloucester outside Berkeley Castle. The tree sliced the bus in half, landing on the seat behind 60-year-old Hilda Coulson.
(*Bristol Evening Post*)

(*right*) Twelve people were hurt when this FLF on service 352 from Bristol to Weston-super-Mare fell into a ditch near the Woolpack Inn at Worle on 28th January 1969. (*Bristol Evening Post*)

4. The Early Seventies: Going Places With The NBC

The 1970s was a time of significant change for the bus industry generally, which was trying to counter the effects of fewer passengers and growing private car ownership, whilst also dealing with ongoing staff shortages. Bristol Omnibus was very much part of this, but was also unusual in remaining structured as a regional company operator. Most other large towns and cities in Britain were either served by municipally owned buses, or increasingly, by one of the newly formed Passenger Transport Executives, which were taking over transport in the huge conurbations outside London. The Bristol Joint Services arrangement did provide for some local authority control – although increasingly, one questioned how much real influence Bristol councillors actually had.

1970

For Bristol Omnibus, the decade started with a big freeze; an expansion of the company's operating territory; and women taking to the wheel!

The first week of January saw Bristol bus crews having to deal with extremely cold temperatures, with snow and icy conditions. This of course, was a time when many open-platform buses still had no internal heating, and staff relied on their clothing, including long winter uniform overcoats, to keep warm.

On the morning of Tuesday 6th January buses set out before daybreak as usual, to commence Service 5 from Broomhill, which involved a climb from Brislington depot up over Sandy Park Road, then upon reaching Allison Road, a descent followed by another steep climb towards Broomhill, some of the most severe gradients on any bus route in the city. Sheet ice had covered the roads and pavements overnight and the first driver descended into the valley of Allison Road only to find he was unable to complete the climb on the other side, as his bus started to slide – and then began rolling backwards. He successfully turned it at 45° to bring the rear wheels against the kerb, which avoided sliding back any further.

In the freezing mist and darkness, the following driver was unable to see what had happened until he too was placed in the same situation and had to wedge his bus on the Broomhill side of the hill, managing to avoid the first bus!

No one was able to warn other crews, and two more buses followed, each trying to pass those already stranded, only to find that they were also sliding backwards. This resulted in four double-deckers, two on either side of the road, stranded half way up the hill. There they stayed until grit and salt could be applied to the road surface which quickly enabled them to gain a grip once more, and the service resumed.

Company expansion occurred, together with the acquisition of 24 secondhand Bristol/ECW vehicles, when Bristol took over the Trowbridge depot (and Chippenham outstation) operations of Western National from 1st January 1970. In many ways this move was long overdue, as these services had remained isolated from the rest of Western National, following the Stroud area transfers to Bristol in 1950. In the February 1970 edition of *Omnibus* the Trowbridge depot correspondent said that the depot had now fallen to 'Bristolisation'!

A small complication of the takeover was that the staff belonged to a separate trade union, as Western National employees had traditionally been represented by the road transport sector of the National Union of Railwaymen, who henceforth were to be included around the negotiating table. Most of the company's other platform staff were represented by the Transport & General Workers' Union.

Amongst the vehicles acquired with the takeover were two elderly lowbridge KSWs, to which reference has already been made. These were renumbered into the series previously associated with 7'6" wide vehicles as L4155 and L4156, although they were withdrawn for

Western National Bristol KSW LTA 844 of 1952, with a 55-seat lowbridge body, became Bristol L4156 with the takeover of Trowbridge depot. Within a year the bus was transferred to the driver training fleet. (*R.H.G. Simpson*)

Eight ECW-bodied Bristol FLF double-deckers came to the company with the takeover of the Western National operation at Trowbridge. 818 KDV of 1963 became Bristol 7315. (*S.J. Butler collection*)

conversion to driver training buses within their first six months with the company. Returning to the fold were six of the FSF double-deckers that had previously been sold to Western National, and which reverted to their previous fleet numbers. These were joined by eight FLF6B buses dating from 1963 to 1966, which were numbered 7314 to 7321 at the end of the Company's own FLFs: many of these were 68-seaters with luggage racks. In time, inter-fleet movements saw these 'slightly non-standard' FLFs work in nearby Bath, and even Bristol.

The remaining buses to come from Trowbridge were eight 5-cylinder LS buses, the newest of which was almost 16 years old. One can't help wondering whether Western National used the transfer of Trowbridge as a means of ridding itself of some time-expired vehicles. The LS buses took the fleet numbers 2409 to 2416.

Nevertheless, Bristol rapidly added new fleet number plates, legal lettering and Bristol scrolls to the acquired vehicles, but because the fleetname transfers were not applied properly, the yellow area of the scroll flaked off very quickly, leaving some buses with just the black outline of the company name!

In due course the Trowbridge operation was operationally integrated into the Bath district: the depot itself, however, was to be a casualty of the cost-cutting measures of the early 1980s when it was finally closed.

Bristol Omnibus continued to strive to improve the service it offered, particularly in Bristol itself where it was often publicly criticised.

In another practical move, the company felt that its Inspectors should exhibit a higher profile within the city as a means of showing to the travelling public that they were on the move and able to respond to changing traffic situations. Shortly before, police forces generally had started to use highly visible 'panda' cars, which in the case of Bristol police resulted in the introduction of pale blue and white Morris Minors from 1967. In possibly a unique situation among bus companies, Bristol Omnibus exploited this idea by introducing four, cleverly named, green and cream Morris Minor 'Bruin' cars into the city from March 1970. Each of these 'BRistol Urban INspection' cars carried a large police-style, roof-mounted, illuminated sign displaying the Bristol scroll. They were manned by two uniformed Inspectors, fitted with two-way radio control and were launched in a blaze of publicity. They were certainly highly visible, but so like the police pandas were these cars that they were often confused by the public! For bus crews, the sight of one of these bright green and cream Morris Minors looming up behind the platform of a city KSW or Lodekka made many a conductor mentally examine his ticket-issuing procedure lest he had an 'uncollected', as co-author Mike Walker remembers only too well. Practically, apart from mobile ticket checking, use of the cars enabled Inspectors to achieve a high public profile, reach incidents quickly and move staff around the network so as to reduce lost mileage. Unfortunately, however, the travelling public

The Bristol Urban Inspection (or 'BRUIN') cars were launched to the press in a blaze of publicity. From left to right are Ken Forrister (Bristol Divisional Traffic Superintendent), Bob Pinder (Assistant Traffic Manager), Fred Dark (Traffic Manager), Bill Fenn (Chief Inspector), and mobile inspectors Roy Spencer, George Sevier, Keith Maloney, Tony Bullen, Alf Dean, Bill Underhill, Dennis Newberry and Fred Jarrett, together with their Tilling green and cream Morris Minor saloons. (*Bristol Omnibus*)

never got out of the habit of suggesting that rather than appearing at a series of stops to advise them that their bus would be missing because of staff shortages and the arrival time of the next one, the Inspectors would be better employed actually driving buses themselves. These bright Inspectors' cars lasted for only four years until they were replaced with more practical Morris Marina 'Bruin' vans in light green but retaining similar roof-mounted signs. However, despite continuing the 'Bruin' name, somehow these replacement vans did not have the same cachet. And the local police, by this time, had moved on to Ford Escorts for panda car patrol work in Bristol.

From 1970, a radical change which attracted a great deal of publicity, was the introduction of the first women bus drivers since the war. Previously, female platform staff had been confined to the role of conductress, although a small number of women had been employed driving lightweight Bedford saloons during the war years. Equal opportunities for women was entering every facet of British life, and for bus drivers, the physical effort involved in steering and braking had become far easier on the company's modern vehicles than was the case generally during the forties and fifties, when the role of bus driver was indeed considered 'a man's job'.

Bristol's first woman bus driver was Mrs Freda Somers who passed her driving test during October and was soon followed by four more women drivers in Bristol, one in Weston-super-Mare, another in Cheltenham, and yet another at the former Western National depot at Trowbridge. All of these pioneering ladies had previously been conductresses, but as their numbers increased, some women were recruited directly into the driving school.

The same equality did not yet exist in the company's offices, however, and less than two years earlier, Clive Norman applied for, and was offered, the position of wages clerk at Cheltenham depot. Having previously been a driver, this change of role meant more regular hours but provided less opportunity to enhance take-home pay with overtime. Clive recalls that there was still sex discrimination, as there was a perfectly competent and very experienced female wages assistant, yet Clive was taken on as her superior with no previous experience in that type of work. The company felt the wages clerk should be male, despite the fact that the female assistant was far more capable of doing the work. In today's age of powerful computers and the transfer of wages directly into a bank account, one must remember that calculating and paying wages both before and during the Green Years was a very labour intensive task.

Although crews worked a pre-determined roster, allowing a normal week's wages to be calculated in advance, staff shortages, holidays, sickness, unexpected absence, overtime and rest day working, breakdowns, delays through traffic and all other exceptions to the normal schedule had to be recorded on a daily basis. Expected changes to the roster, to cover for problems such as staff shortages, holidays and long term sickness, would be undertaken by the depot Duty Clerk, but covering for changes on the day was usually the responsibility of the Senior Inspector on duty at each depot or relief point, whose job it was to ensure that the timetable was adhered to as fully as possible despite problems resulting from the above. It was then the wages clerk's responsibility to work out each individual's weekly wage based upon the schedule together with recorded changes.

Even calculating the pay for scheduled duties could be time-consuming and difficult, and was often undertaken by the schedules office as part of the process of changing or re-writing duty rosters. In the period before the consolidation of all separate paid allowances into 'basic' rates of pay at the end of the 1960s, pay could consist of the standard hourly rate (different for drivers and conductors), a bonus for operating a bus without a conductor, early and late cash allowances (for a duty that started before or finished after specified times), an enhanced rate for work over the agreed weekly maximum hours or for weekend or holiday working, an additional payment for working split duties (where the two halves of a duty encompassed both peak periods, separated by a break of several hours in between the two parts) and an allowance for working shift patterns.

Once the gross pay for each individual had been calculated, the required deductions for items such as income tax and national insurance had to be made, together with deductions for membership of the trade union, sports and social club subscriptions, savings etc., although the difficulties didn't stop once the wages to be paid to each employee had been determined.

Geoff Lusher had earlier spent some time in the Bristol Division wages office in Host Street. He recalls that there was an agreement between the company and the trade union that determined how a pay packet would be made up so as to minimise the number of coins to be included. For instance, a weekly net wage of £8-18-11d would, by agreement, have to be made up as follows:

> One five-pound note
> Three one-pound notes
> One ten-shilling note
> 3 half-crowns (total 7/6)
> One shilling piece
> One threepenny piece
> Two pennies

On the day that wage packets were made up the chief wages clerk would have to calculate exactly how many of each of the notes and coins were needed to fill the packets and collect this amount from the bank: the packets would then be filled one by one until, with some amount of trepidation, the last coins were put into the last packet in just the right combinations leaving no coins over or no coins wanting! No packets were sealed however until the last packet had been filled just in case each had to be checked if there was a discrepancy in the 'coinage'. The sealed packet had a series of small round holes in it so that the employee could check that the right amount of cash was inside before the packet was opened.

Geoff also recalls that he was once asked to help take trays of wage packets out from the wages office into a parked company car and then asked to accompany the driver on his rounds of the depots. When he enquired why the driver wanted Geoff to come with him, the reply was 'security'. On this particular day the rounds of the city depots was a little later than usual and, on arriving at the first depot, Geoff recalls that the depot clerk ran to the car and snatched his depot's wages tray, beginning paying out wages to the assembled staff (many with their wives) straight away.

Such a lack of basic security in the process of moving a large amount of cash (with platform, maintenance and depot staff there would probably have been up to 2,000 wage packets in the back of the car) and the seeming disregard for employees' safety in carrying such large amounts of cash unguarded seems strange when measured by today's standards, but was common practice in the country at the time.

The company also took in vast amounts of cash, of course, much of it tendered on the bus in very small value coins for individual fares, and after counting and reconciliation (ensuring that each conductor or one-man operator had paid in the exact amount recorded on his waybill) this would need to be bagged and taken to the bank. In practically all depots at this time the cash would have been taken to the bank in a bus; spare staff would have been summoned from the canteen by the call 'bank bus', and they would have helped load the cash into the bus, accompanied it on its journey and unloaded it into the bank on arrival. Often the banks welcomed the bus's arrival since they then had sufficient small change for their day's business. Incidentally, there were spare staff available at most times of the day, albeit sometimes only for short periods, since most rosters had 'early', 'middle' and 'late' spares to be available to cover for staff who failed to turn up or who were running late for whatever reason, and a number of duties were made up with spare hours so as to meet the minimum daily hours of work agreed with the trade unions.

Collecting cash for wages from the bank and delivering takings in the bank bus were still very much part of the depot scene when co-author Mike Walker took over as Traffic Superintendent at Weston-super-Mare in 1974, but within a few years the company had employed a security company to undertake both cash movements.

This had come to an abrupt end as a result of an incident in Bristol, which co-author Martin Curtis recalls. Although perhaps inevitable as society and attitudes gradually changed, this was also partly the result of city bus crews regularly appearing on duty wearing only part of their uniform. A call one day for 'spare' crews at the Centre to carry money bags onto the bus to the bank, saw two additional individuals (wearing uniform jackets) join the line of staff; each was handed two full cash bags and then walked into the street never to be seen again. The two 'imposters' had disappeared as the real staff members boarded the bank bus as usual, resulting in some very red faces among company officials.

New vehicles for 1970, were, with one exception, of the RE-type single-decker. By far the most numerous variant was the two-doorway, 44-seater, of which 58 entered service during the year: 42 were for Joint Services, four for Cheltenham, two for Gloucester, eight for Bath services and two for Weston-super-Mare town services. Midway through the year, as these REs were being delivered, a revised front end design was introduced incorporating a BET-style curved windscreen intended to reduce internal reflections. This change added five inches to the length of the front overhang and clearly illustrated how the new National Bus Company was drawing on BET Group ideas for its Tilling-inspired vehicles. In the case of Bristol Omnibus REs, this new design also included twin headlamps. With the arrival of the RE buses, the conversion of services to one-man operation was accelerated with another seven or so Bristol City routes being so converted during the year, together with services within the rest of the company's operating area.

A further ten of the longer variant, but this time with the higher RELH frame, were finished as 49-seat, dual-purpose semi-coaches (again within bus shell bodywork), whilst the remaining six RE-types were of the shorter RESL model. The latter variant had been redesigned, not only with revised curved front, but also with re-spaced pillars, which resulted in the RESL now measuring almost 34 feet long, although the seating capacity remained at 43 with a nearside luggage pen.

The remaining new vehicle was very much a 'one-off', being a 16-seat Ford Transit, which replaced the little ex-Silver Star Trojan on the Special Service in Bath. It originally wore cream livery, but was later repainted white, and later still, pale green.

Finally, in June of 1970, and with no advance warning or ceremony, the first Bristol VRs surprisingly appeared in the fleet, and their arrival was reported to

For a short while, BJS Bristol RE buses had a full destination display, including via points. C1158 (WAE 791H), a 44-seat, ECW twin-door bus of 1970, displays this feature, along with a four-leaf centre door and twin headlights. (*M.S. Curtis*)

the Bristol Joint Services Committee meeting of that month. The minutes record the purchase of '2 VRL buses for experimental one-man operation at a total cost of £7,000'.

These of course were the two prototype VRLs that had remained in the ownership of Bristol Commercial Vehicles since they entered service after the 1966 Commercial Motor Show. GGM 431D, VRX 001, wearing Central SMT livery, had been sent on loan to that company where it worked the busy suburban services around Glasgow, whilst the Bristol Omnibus Company liveried bus, HHW 933D, VRX 002, was dispatched to Mansfield District where there was the prospect that its 80-seat capacity would be very useful on local colliery services. Neither had proved to be very reliable in use, with comments being made that HHW spent more time on the pits than actually in service! It had occasionally returned to Bristol, however, since apart from visits to the factory as part of the type's development, it came to Bristol's Lawrence Hill depot in March 1967 – and from there departed to Metz, Gloucester's twin city in France. It retained its Tilling green and cream livery but carried the GLOUCESTER fleetname in addition to the coat of arms on its side panels (believed to be the first vehicle to do so). On that occasion however, it continued to display Mansfield's fleet number 555 at the foot of the stairs, and on the exterior. Co-author Mike Walker was at Lawrence Hill depot on the morning of the bus's departure for France: a conductor, waiting to start duty, looked at the inside of the lower deck and asked 'What is that big box behind the wheels on the other side? [It was of course to house the engine.] The Bristol public will not like that!' In 1970, the Bristol public were about to find out if they did indeed 'like that'!

On acquisition from Bristol Commercial Vehicles the company painted these buses into a double-deck version of the recently introduced OMO livery of more cream than green, although somewhat surprisingly, considering the experience that the company's Central Repair Works had in all sorts of body repairs, GGM retained its Scottish Bus Group-style 'triangular' destination display. Numbered C5000 and C5001 respectively – and affectionately called Daisy-Belle and Lulu by several of the traffic trainees at head office – after some debate the two buses were initially allocated to Joint Services crew routes from Lawrence Hill depot. They operated principally on a variety of services at peak times and very occasionally remained in service all day long. Regrettably, their unreliability travelled with them, and it was rare indeed to see both of them in service at any one time together. Nevertheless, this was known to have happened at least twice (to be photographed by the co-authors), once while operating football specials and parked outside the Bristol Rovers football ground, next to the old Eastville bus depot, and on another occasion when used to bring home day-trippers from Weston-super-Mare on a Bank Holiday – duties for which their very high seating capacities were well suited.

As detailed in the report to the Joint Services Committee, the principal purpose for the acquisition of these two buses was to trial the one-man operation of double-deckers on Joint Services routes, and schedules were drawn up for each of them to operate one duty as OMO buses on either services 15, 40/41 or 83, but in the event agreement could not be reached with the trade union representatives – believed to be because the buses were of a single-door configuration – and the two of them were withdrawn in 1973, even though only seven years old at the time. In any case, by this time the first of a large number of two-doorway VRs had entered service which were being worked without a conductor. Very sadly, and as with the Lodekka prototype which also carried fleet number 5000, neither of these two revolutionary prototypes was saved for posterity.

Although measures such as more one-man operation (still widely abbreviated to 'OMO'), the introduction of women drivers and radio control were gradually making services more reliable, staff problems continued, although possibly because drivers were in closer contact with their passengers on OMO buses (rather than being isolated in their cab) it was noticeable that staff/passenger relations generally improved with one-man buses.

On crew buses, bell signals involved one ring to stop, but conductors gave two rings to start, allowing the driver to pull away safely. Unfortunately by the early seventies, standards on BJS buses had fallen to such a degree that conductors rarely gave the driver more than one ring to start, and sometimes on forward entrance buses, no signal at all. Clearly, this could compromise passenger safety.

In another situation, where services such as Nos. 1 and 5 at Brislington remained crew-operated, a top deck full of passengers could be heard to groan in unison if, on arrival outside the depot, the engine stopped and the cab door was heard to slam shut. This meant a crew change was taking place and the driver and conductor would then be seen sauntering away through the archway which formed the depot entrance. It could be some considerable time before a replacement crew appeared; meanwhile a following bus on the same route would often have overtaken the stationary one.

Spotlight on the VRX Prototypes

Two examples of a brand new Bristol model were displayed at the 1966 Commercial Motor Show, held at Earl's Court in September of that year.

These were the first bodied examples of Bristol's new double-decker, the VR (for Vertical Rear engine) although the model had earlier been referred to as the Bristol N-type. Although with engine located at the rear, unlike the Leyland Atlantean, the Bristol VR featured a Longitudinally-mounted power unit in the rear offside corner of the chassis. As prototypes, the show models were designated VRX types but by the time production of the design commenced two years later, Bristol was also building a Transversely-engined VR called the VRT. The original, side-engined layout therefore became known as the VRL.

One of the 1966 show exhibits with chassis no VRX.001 appeared on ECW's stand registered GGM 431D, wearing full Central SMT red livery. On the Bristol stand however, VRX.002 (HHW 933D) was painted in Tilling green and cream colours and displayed a Bristol scroll fleetname. When built, this bus was finished in full Bristol Omnibus livery with black wheels and carried BOC legal lettering, including the company's address. However, whilst it was usual for one of the first of each new Bristol model to join the local fleet, BOC management in this case appeared reluctant to accept this particular model and the bus very rapidly received most un-Bristol Omnibus like cream wheels, while its legal address was changed to that of BCV.

After the show, while VRX.001 went to Scotland, the green prototype did not, as earlier expected, join the Bristol Omnibus fleet; instead it was allocated to Mansfield District. Both vehicles remained the property of BCV, however.

HHW 933D, nevertheless, did visit Bristol Omnibus in March 1967 where it received a Gloucester fleetname and coat of arms (believed to be the first bus to carry this fleetname) and BOC legal address, which it then proudly carried on a trip to Metz in France. Metz had been twinned with Gloucester, and both Bristol Omnibus and BCV personnel were on board for the trip.

HHW made several other return visits to BCV but after further periods away, both prototypes came home to BCV in 1970, and were then unexpectedly sold to Bristol Omnibus to become C5000 and C5001 respectively.

They were immediately repainted into a double-deck version of the company's OMO livery but saw little service over the following three years, even though they received a further repaint during 1972.

Largely because of their livery, and their size (they were 33ft-long 80-seaters – the largest buses ever operated by the company) the VRXs were striking in appearance when newly acquired.

Unfortunately, as a result of ongoing reliability and other issues, the company decided to dispose of these prototypes during 1973, and they passed to the independent Essex operator G.W. Osborne & Sons of Tollesbury, who at first retained their livery style but repainted the green areas red. Both were eventually scrapped, however, HHW reaching the end of its life in 1981, while GGM followed ten years later.

HHW 933D in the condition in which it was displayed at the 1966 Commercial Motor Show. Whilst it wears a Bristol Omnibus scroll fleetname, when built this vehicle had standard black-painted wheels but cream was substituted for the Show. (*BCV*)

(*left*) Driving out of the gates of BCV's Chatsworth Road works on trade plates in November 1966, VRX.002 would soon join the main A4 Bath Road, where it would look very much at home in Tilling green and cream livery. (*M. Walker*)

(*right*) A view inside the lower deck of VRX.002 showing the engine postion in the rear offside corner. With the top of the cover removed, access to the engine was easy; but when replaced it formed a luggage rack. (*ECW*)

(*left*) A rear view of HHW 933D taken at BCV's Bath Road works, in April 1967. It displays the Gloucester fleetname and arms together with a GB plate, which it carried in connection with its trip to France. (*Peter Davey*)

141

(*left*) After joining the Bristol fleet, relatively little use was made of the VRXs, and it was very rare indeed to see them working together. Nevertheless, on 28th August 1972 – a Bank Holiday Monday – both were pressed into service on the Bristol to Weston route (by this time numbered 352). C5000 (GGM 431D) emerges from Weston-super-Mare bus station packed with returning day-trippers from Bristol. (*M.S. Curtis*)

(*left*) On the same day, 28th August 1972, C5001 arrives at the Bristol end of route 352 just as a newly introduced Bristol VRT C5007, on city service 23, passes by. The resulting photograph of VRT and VRL type buses working side-by-side is therefore believed to be unique. Of the two, the wrong bus has the 'pay on entry' sign illuminated. (*M.S. Curtis*)

(*right*) The VRXs were sometimes used on peak-hour journeys and would occasionally spend a whole day on a city service. Here C5001 heads along the Portway towards Avonmouth on service 99. (*Peter Davey*)

(*right*) It happened very occasionally! The two VRX prototypes are seen working together while operating football specials. Among a number of buses used to carry supporters to a Bristol Rovers match at Eastville is C5000 (nearest camera) with C5001 at the rear. Coincidentally, the advertising on the side of GGM is similar to that carried by the original C5000, the Lodekka prototype built in 1949. (*M. Walker*)

The examples given above of casual crew behaviour are a reflection of poor supervision and a general lack of regard for passengers which would never have occurred in earlier years, yet sadly was epitomised by the attitude of far too many employees of the period. In hindsight, however, it also illustrates why the company was so desperate to recruit more staff, and to make various attempts to raise standards once more. Eventually, they began to succeed, to the benefit of all concerned. It is also interesting to note that in the company's area outside Bristol itself, in Gloucestershire, Swindon, Bath and Weston-super-Mare for example, the situation was entirely different, with higher standards maintained throughout this period.

An item from the February 1970 edition of *Omnibus* adequately illustrates this point, and the still high standards expected by passengers outside Bristol:

> Overheard on a Weston country bus –
> Small boy to mother: We haven't got a real conductor on the bus today.
> Mother: Why do you say that?
> Boy: Because he's not wearing a tie.

As if commenting on the decline in standards on the Joint Services operation in Bristol, in 1971 local singer and performer Fred Wedlock released a recording entitled 'Bristol's Buses', the contents of which must have indeed reflected the view of many a city bus passenger. The words (to be sung in a Bristol accent!) are reproduced here by kind permission of the writer, Keith Christmas:

> Bristol buses, how I love you,
> In your British Racing Green,
> Thundering through our glorious city,
> Seldom heard and never seen.
>
> And your conductors, they're all so helpful,
> They sling yer change all over the floor;
> While the driver roars with laughter
> As he traps you in the folding door.
>
> 'This bus is full' said the conductor;
> I said 'how long will the next one be?';
> He said 'just the same as this one,
> 26 foot bloody three'.
>
> And if you want the bus to Southmead
> And you wonder why it's late,
> It's 'cus the crew of the 7.20
> Are riding shotgun on the 10 past 8.
>
> Now your crews are gettin' stroppy,
> Revolution's in their eyes,
> Because their mates in Wolverhampton
> Have had a 50 Rupees rise!
>
> And as the winter wind howls up the Blackboy,
> For hours I face the notice on the wall;
> It says they're running every 20 minutes
> And that's the biggest bloody joke of all!

In May 1970 the head office of the company finally relocated from the mock Tudor offices at the Centre to the newly built Berkeley House at Lawrence Hill which had been officially opened by Mr T.W.H. Gailey, National Bus Company's Chief Executive, accompanied by Mr J.T.E. Robinson, Chairman of the South Western Region. This move necessitated a change of legal address carried by all vehicles and company stationery, which for so long had displayed the Centre offices address at 1-3 St Augustine's Place. With the merger of two NBC regions later in the year, Mr Robinson was to become the chairman of the newly formed South Wales and West region.

Meanwhile, the Centre offices were not abandoned as the company's prominent booking office remained there, while Bristol Division staff also transferred to the Centre and vacated Old Market House, whose lease was due to expire. A further aspect of this move was the closure of the Old Market canteen and the relocation of the Old Market crew relief points on Joint Services routes passing through the area to either the Centre, where a canteen still existed, or to one of the operating depots. The change of relief points on approximately half of the Joint Services routes required a major change in vehicle and crew schedules, and the opportunity was taken to combine this schedule change with that required to implement the evening and Sunday reduction in running times that had been discussed at Joint Services Committee meetings in the late 1960s, and which in the meanwhile had been agreed with the trade union representatives. By lunchtime of the Sunday when the new schedules had been introduced, crews had downed tools in protest at the new running times (which had seen average speeds on Joint Services routes increase from around 12mph to 16mph during evenings and Sundays), citing them as impossible to maintain, and all buses ran into their respective depots. Despite their previous acceptance of the new running times, over the course of the next few days the trade union officials supported unofficial strike action. On Monday 3rd August, the day after the strike had started, the Bath *Evening Chronicle* reported that the schedules had already been accepted by the Transport and General Workers Union representatives, that the men were now willing to resume working the old schedules, but that the Bristol Omnibus Company would not agree. The paper also reported Jack Hodge as saying:

> The strike is unofficial, yes, but it gets my support. [He had been involved in the negotiations over and the acceptance of the revised schedules.] The strike may be against the advice of the Union at national level, but it is certainly official as far as the branch is concerned.

By the middle of the week, a new agreement had been reached with the management to reinstate the old schedules until such times as a new set of timetables could be negotiated, allowing the required savings to be made by a reduction of evening and Sunday frequencies instead. The Bristol Division schedules office (which by this time included co-author Mike Walker), having worked overtime to introduce the original changes, now had to work overtime on another set of new timetables, crew duties and bus running cards, since computer scheduling had yet to make a substantive appearance and everything had to be worked out by the human brain. However, during the ensuing few months during which the new timetables and schedules were compiled, arrangements had to be made to provide meal break facilities at the Old Market relief point where the offices and canteen had been abandoned. This was achieved by the judicious placement of an FLF vehicle in a blocked-off side street, which served as a control office and crew rest room. It was connected to the rest of the operation by a radio link and a hastily arranged telephone line, and with no canteen facilities now in existence the crews were paid through their meal break. In due course the revised service revisions were introduced, with 30-minute evening and Sunday frequencies generally being reduced to 40-minute headways to make the desired savings. The strike itself had a further detrimental effect on the profitability of the Joint Services network, and at the October Joint Services Committee meeting the parties agreed a corporate plan that recognised an urgent need to protect falling stage carriage revenue, to improve the first line management structure, the provision of better management control information, improved reliability and the introduction of a marketing function.

Generally speaking, industrial relations within the company were good, and the Bristol strike can be seen in this context as an exception. In fact, it had been reported to the September Joint Services Committee meeting that although nationally the Transport and General Workers Union had asked busmen to implement a ban on standing passengers and the working of overtime in protest at the failure of the National Council for Omnibus Industries to reach agreement on a further wage award, the Bristol City branch had refused to accept this advice and had wanted to work normally. By way of explanation, as part of the National Bus Company, wage negotiations for Bristol were carried out at national level, as opposed to working practice agreements which were handled locally.

Two further secondhand purchases arrived this year at Lawrence Hill in the shape of ex-Red & White Bristol LS6G saloons, which were acquired with the intention of rebuilding them for continued service – they were even allocated fleet numbers 3000 and 3001 – but were eventually stripped for spares and the remains scrapped.

Joint Services 1965 ECW-bodied Bristol FLF C7219 (EHT 108C), was used as a control room at Old Market, central Bristol, following the resolution of the 1970 strike, and before the introduction of revised schedules. Note the two Inspectors' 'Bruin' cars parked alongside. (*M. Walker*)

A new colour scheme for driver training buses of cream with orange trim appeared during 1970, while during the same year, National Bus Company influence on livery was also felt for the first time with the introduction of a new style for all NBC coaches in the south-west. This involved repainting coaches white, with a different colour waistband for each operator on which was carried a bold, block-letter fleetname. This allowed each company to retain its own identity while emphasising the connection between the associated fleets. For Bristol Greyhound, this meant the stylish cream and red coaching livery began to be phased out in favour of a new style of white with magenta band, involving the loss of the familiar 'greyhound in wheel' emblem which was replaced by a simple white greyhound silhouette next to the fleetname. The first coaches to receive this new livery were two-year-old, ECW-bodied RELHs, and whilst one could appreciate this livery style on the newer body designs, it never looked quite right when retro-fitted to the early MW coaches.

During September 1970, another Bristol-liveried vehicle was displayed on Bristol Commercial Vehicles' stand at the Commercial Motor Show, held at Earls Court in London. Fleet number C1180 appeared to be a standard Joint Services RELL twin-doorway bus in cream and green OMO livery, but with the addition of a small window at roof level behind the front door which would allow the laser beam from the shortly to be introduced B-Line location system, to pass to and from the roadside plates. Under the rear floor, however, this bus was a foretaste of things to come, for instead of the now standard Leyland 0.680 engine, this bus was powered by the new Leyland 0.500 fixed-head engine, which had been developed for the new Leyland National bus which made its debut at the same show. C1180 entered service the following year, while the eventual production of Leyland Nationals would impact heavily on BCV. Fitting this engine to this particular RE obviously served to forewarn the Joint Services Committee of the type of single-deck vehicle they would be expected to operate on the introduction of the Leyland National, since minutes of the September 1970 meeting reported that the next purchase of 34 single-deckers should be 'either REs or Leyland Nationals', whichever was available, and a later minute indicated that the choice of the proportion of Bristol REs and Leyland Nationals for the 1972 vehicle programme should be decided by the company's officers. This was a far cry from the postwar committee meetings at which every justification had to be presented to the councillors for the purchase of Leyland vehicles (the PD1s) whilst stressing the continuing excellence of the Bristol-built vehicles which would be the preferred choice. Whether the RE would have been the preferred choice of the councillors on the 1970 committee is not recorded, but it would have made no difference to the final outcome, as is recorded later in the chapter. The final knife was twisted into the prospects of future Bristol built deliveries when it was agreed that

> the Chairman of Bristol Commercial Vehicles should be invited to a lunch with the committee to answer any questions, technical or otherwise, about the Leyland National.

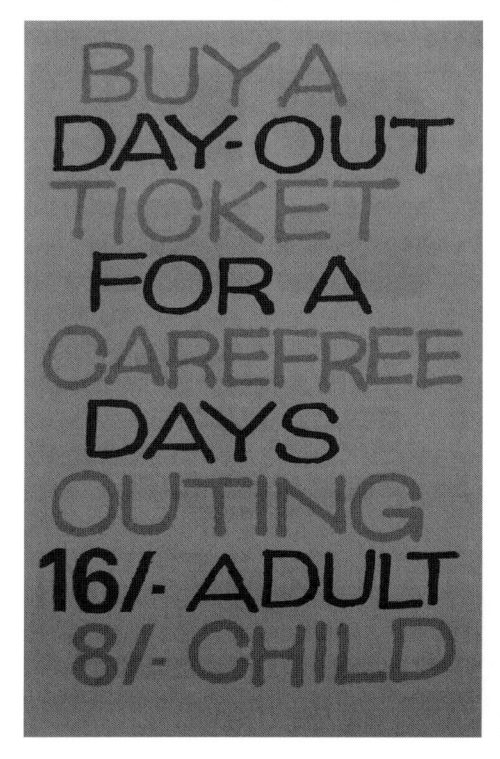

One of the Company's marketing exercises from 1970.

One suspects councillors had little appreciation of how the Leyland National project was being driven from within the highest levels of NBC and Leyland, which neither BCV nor Bristol Omnibus management could possibly influence.

Turning to a different subject, the councillors remained concerned about growing the Joint Services operation, since the March meeting records that they wanted the company to consider incorporating service 373, from Bristol to Dundry, into the BJS network. Service 373 was the latest incarnation of the route taken over with the operation of Dundry Pioneer in 1950, and whilst still wholly company operated, it spent much of its journey to and from Dundry, a village at the top of the hills surrounding the south Bristol housing estates, operating through those estates, carrying what could be considered BJS passengers. The company, however, declined this request – for the time being at least.

1971

Once again, in 1971 new vehicles were largely of the RE type, this having become the standard bus for city and country services alike. Two-doorway 44-seaters accounted for 42 of the deliveries, 38 of which were for Joint Services and four for the Gloucester city fleet. Of the Joint Services buses, C1232-36 were also fitted with Leyland 0.500 series engines and, coupled to fully automatic transmission, became additional in-service test-beds for the Leyland National. C1237 was used by Bristol Commercial Vehicles as a demonstrator for Colchester Corporation, which was obviously successful as Colchester followed its visit with orders for similar (though single-door) RE buses.

For country services, ten of the delivery were standard single-door 50-seaters and the remaining six were 43-seat RESLs.

In addition to C1180, a second company vehicle had also been exhibited at the 1970 Commercial Motor Show on the Plaxton stand, in the form of a Leyland Leopard coach (2157) wearing the new white and magenta Greyhound livery. Entering service in 1971, this coach, and its sister 2158, were the first painted in this livery from new, although by the time the next two Plaxton-bodied Leopards arrived later in the year, a detail of the livery had changed in that the Greyhound dog symbol now appeared in full colour (as it had in pre-war days) replacing the white silhouette. These new style coaches, the first full-sized, non-Bristol coaches to enter service for many years, reflected the choice available to NBC companies, and were ordered for sustained non-stop operation along the newly opened sections of the M4 motorway to London, their Plaxton bodies featuring large gently curved glass and a driver-controlled 'Webasto' oil-fired heater for the passenger saloon. Indeed, the introduction of these coaches was but one facet of proposed improvements to the old established Greyhound service (although ironically, the Leopards failed to match the performance of the later

Bristol's ECW-bodied Bristol RE buses had a window in the rear emergency door to aid the driver when he needed to reverse, as illustrated by this view of 1971 bus C1240 (AHU 734J), seen at Lawrence Weston when just three months old. (*M. Walker*)

Bristol Greyhound's ECW-bodied Bristol MW coach 2107 (formerly 2986) was painted in the final coach livery of white and magenta in 1971 but was withdrawn in 1973. (*Roy Marshall*)

RELH coaches). When operating along the A4 before the opening of the motorway west of Reading, the Bristol to London service could still take up to five hours in each direction, resulting in a coach driver receiving perhaps 12 hours pay for a return journey to London. The new motorway schedules provided for an end to end journey time of only two and a half hours, which meant that the likely day's pay for an express driver working one return journey from Bristol to London would be halved. The trade unions were not happy with this situation and before the motorway service was introduced a new pay structure was agreed, resulting in motorway journeys being paid at the rate of two minutes paid time per mile rather than actual driving time; this rate of pay, together with paid reporting, loading and layover time at each end, resulted in a daily pay allowance more akin to the previous day's work than strict duty time. Of benefit to the company, however, was the new intensity with which their motorway coaches could be worked, with it now being possible for one coach to complete two return journeys from Bristol to London in a day rather than one. The new non-stop motorway service started on 9th January 1972, and was launched by the singer Peter Noone and actor Mervyn Webb who at the time were performing in the pantomime *Dick Whittington* at the Bristol Hippodrome. What better story could be behind the launch of a new service to London? The two members of the cast were supported by three Lawrence Hill depot-based conductresses, Irene Barry, Janet Pitt and Linda Sheppard, who were dressed in the Greyhound colours of magenta and white and who, for a long time afterwards, were referred to as the 'Greyhound Girls'.

After six years of frontline service, and in accordance with previous practice for coaches, the Leopards were downgraded to semi-coaches and painted into dual-purpose livery, as well as being converted to one-man operation. They were never popular in this form, however, due principally to the lack of perceived security normally offered by the driver's cab door, which these coaches did not possess.

As happened in the previous year, a number of secondhand LS buses were acquired with a view to rebuilding them for continued use, but, again, they were eventually only stripped for spares and their remains scrapped. Despite these various false starts, however, the company did successfully rebuild LS bus 2844 which, although 17 years old at the time, re-entered service with a brighter RE-style interior, including light formica seat backs and fluorescent lights, fitted with a Gardner six-cylinder engine and renumbered 3000, the conversion taking between eight and nine weeks. It was intended to be the start of a programme of refurbishing withdrawn underfloor-engined buses, but only eight were actually completed before the process was halted.

A refurbishment programme was also taking place on FLF double-deck Lodekkas. As these became seven years old they were taken into Lawrence Hill's Central Repair Works where the interiors were re-trimmed, the chassis, engine and running units overhauled, and any remaining air suspension buses were converted to coil springs. In addition, and in a similar manner to those of LDs 15 years earlier, the front wings were shortened, which rather detracted from their appearance, but improved air flow to the front brakes, and reduced the potential for accident damage.

1957 ECW-bodied Bristol LS-type 2912 was fitted with a six cylinder engine, modernised and re-seated to 43 in 1971. It re-entered service as 3003.
(*Roy Marshall*)

In May 1971, following the appearance of C5000 and C5001 in one-man livery, this predominantly cream colour scheme was experimentally applied to Joint Services FLF C7133, although, of course, there was no attempt to convert the bus to be operated without a conductor. At the time, Lawrence Hill's paint shop was repainting a batch of AEC Swift single-deckers from South Wales Transport, into dark green and yellow on behalf of London Country Bus Services. Only weeks after receiving its new livery, it was decided that C7133 should have all its green areas repainted again in the dark London Country shade, and so it emerged with a very distinctive, non-standard paint application.

In December, an even more interestingly painted Joint Services FLF (C7109) emerged from Lawrence Hill in the form of the company's first all-over advertisement bus, finished in bright red with slogans for the local 'steak house' Berni Inns, and providing the company with £3,000 in additional revenue for the duration of the contract. C7109 thereafter became known as 'the Berni bus'. A further Berni bus (7033) was to follow, painted white and red for the Northern Division at Gloucester, and this was the start of the regular use of all-over advertising buses, earning the company valuable extra revenue.

By March 1971 it was reported to the Joint Services Committee meeting that 23% of Joint Services vehicles were one-man operated, representing 89 vehicles. This had, of course, resulted in considerable savings in crew costs, but further reductions in the cost base were required, and to this end, starting on 1st April, a survey was undertaken on the Gloucester Road group of routes, services 3 and 6 (terminating at Filton), and 36 and 98 (terminating at Patchway Estate). Under the banner headlines 'Help Yourself to a Better Bus Service', the intention was to be able to match demand with supply more easily and, probably, make savings as a result. In June 1971 the general manager also reported in *Omnibus* that lost mileage in the city had fallen from 8% to between 1 and 2% during the first part of the year.

On 3rd October 1971 many years of history came to an end when Brislington depot was closed, the proposed closure having been reported to the Joint Services Committee five months earlier. Opened in 1899, as Bristol Tramways' main works and depot – and for many years the home of Brislington's body works, where the company constructed its own bus bodies – it not only became an operational bus depot for the city, but before the opening of Bristol bus station, was also used to maintain many country services. Latterly with 54 buses, it was the operational base for 230 staff and city services 1, 5, 36, 40, 41 and 95; the crew routes (1, 5 & 36) were the first to leave when transferred to Lawrence Hill depot on 5th September, whilst the remainder were one-man operated and moved to Winterstoke Road depot four weeks later.

Just before the closure many office staff and maintenance workers became drivers and conductors for the evening to allow as many regular staff as possible to attend the depot's closure party, and co-author Mike Walker was privileged to be able to spend the evening conducting an FLF on services 1 and 5.

(*above*) In 1971, BJS Bristol FLF C7133 of 1964 had its ECW body painted into the brighter version of the livery more usually associated with one-man operated saloons. This was the only Bristol FLF ever painted in this style. The authors believe that this is the only photograph of the bus wearing its brighter livery of cream and *Tilling* green. (*M.S. Curtis*)

Following its very brief appearance wearing Tilling green with extensive cream areas, C7133 returned to the works to emerge with its green areas repainted into a much darker shade as used by London Country Bus Services. It had also undergone refurbishment and now displayed shorter front wings. It became very familiar in Bristol wearing this unique livery, and is seen here crossing the Downs during July 1971. (*M.S. Curtis*)

During the previous May, British Rail had opened a new station on the northern outskirts of Bristol close to the villages of Stoke Gifford and Harry Stoke, and the huge Filton and Patchway complexes of the British Aircraft Corporation and Rolls Royce, the former served by infrequent country services, the latter by very frequent Joint Services buses. The new 'Parkway' station, built on the London to South Wales railway line close to the point where it joined the Bristol to Cardiff line, was intended to become principally a park and ride site, although at the outset one of the Hanham local services – a pure country service operation that had seen its origins in the services of the Bence company before the war – was extended to provide a link between some East Bristol estates, the new Bristol Parkway railway station and Filton. However, by far the most interesting service to be introduced to serve the station was the first dial-a-ride operation in the country that was to link the station with the prosperous housing developments of Westbury-on-Trym and Henleaze to the north-west of the city. To operate the service the company hired three red Morris Marina cars from the rental firm Godfrey Davies and had them tested as public service vehicles – which of course required that they displayed standard gold legal lettering on their nearside front doors indicating the company's address, the unladen weight and the seating capacity of three! Suitable volunteer drivers were chosen, including at least one conductress who was obliged to take her PSV test in a similar car – the company

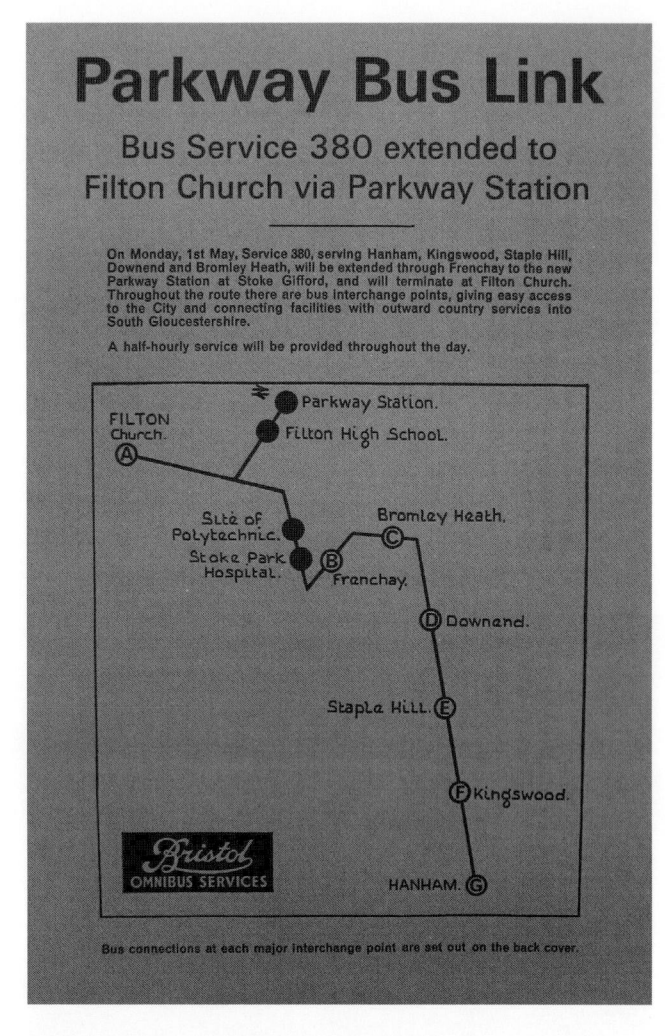

Parkway Bus Link
Bus Service 380 extended to Filton Church via Parkway Station

On Monday, 1st May, Service 380, serving Hanham, Kingswood, Staple Hill, Downend and Bromley Heath, will be extended through Frenchay to the new Parkway Station at Stoke Gifford, and will terminate at Filton Church. Throughout the route there are bus interchange points, giving easy access to the City and connecting facilities with outward country services into South Gloucestershire.

A half-hourly service will be provided throughout the day.

Bus connections at each major interchange point are set out on the back cover.

BJS C1262 (DAE 516K), an ECW-bodied, twin-doorway Bristol RELL of 1972, was used for the press launch of the extension of Hanham local service 380 to the new Bristol Parkway railway station and Filton in April 1972. Note the projection at roof level above the nearside mirror that houses the small window associated with the Marconi B-Line bus location system. (*M. Walker*)

having its own examiners to conduct the test – and the service was introduced to operate on a pre-booked basis for journeys to the station and as required within strictly controlled boundaries of operation. Naturally, objections to the service were received from the local taxi owners' association, but the Traffic Commissioners held a public hearing which resulted in a limited road service licence being granted. The service was a joint venture between the company and British Rail but, in the end, became simply an interesting experiment that soon ended. Bristol Parkway station, however, went on to be one of the success stories of the rail network: since its opening the original customers waiting 'hut' has been replaced by a first-rate booking and waiting facility and the car park has been increased many fold, whilst the bus service to the station has increased to a number of high-frequency routes that link the station to the massive newly built housing estates of Bradley Stoke, the city centre, nearby population centres and as far as Bath to the east.

During 1971 the company installed a new automatic chassis washing facility at Lawrence Hill, believed to have been the first in the south-west, and this used high-pressure water jets to clean the underside of each bus within the Bristol Division before they were presented for their annual inspection by the Department for the Environment (better known as the Ministry of Transport MOT test). Before the installation of the machine, this particularly unpleasant task was performed manually taking almost five hours, the machine cutting the time taken to under half an hour.

Decimal currency was introduced during 1971 and, as with every business, the company found it necessary to embark upon a major training programme for its staff, together with the need to alter the workings of all of the company's ticket machines; it was reported that two-thirds of the machines, some 1,500 units, had been re-engineered midway through the previous year, although it was necessary for 40 specially trained mechanics to make the final adjustments to the machines during the night before D-day. The company also found it necessary to re-design and reprint a great deal of stationery, including fare tables and waybills, and to this end the company's printing shop came into its own.

By the summer of 1971 it was reported to the staff that local authorities within the company's operating area were now paying £100,000 towards keeping un-remunerative services in operation, a source of revenue that was to become very important to the company in the following years, whilst towards the end of 1971 it was also stated that the underlying passenger loss had been halved, from 10% in 1970 to only 5% in 1971.

1972

New vehicle deliveries for this year offered more variety than in recent years, and whilst the majority continued to be Bristol REs, the first new double-deckers since 1967 also arrived. These of course were the long-awaited Bristol VRTs which arrived at Bristol Commercial Vehicles works (having returned after receiving ECW bodywork in Lowestoft) in early February. They were then quickly dispatched to Lawrence Hill in anticipation of their entry into service within a month. The Bristol *Evening Post* ran a story under the headline 'Up Periscope on the Double-deckers', as it was through such a device

The company's first ECW-bodied Bristol VRT was C5002 (EHU 361K) which was used in the conversion of BJS services 22/23 to part double-deck, one-man operation in the summer of 1972. This offside view shows the limited space of one window bay that was used for the tightly ascending staircase. (*M. Walker*)

151

that drivers could view the interior of the top deck, although there were already doubts contained in the report about whether the buses would be crew or one-man operated, even though OMO double-deckers were already common in other British cities. The press item revealed that what would happen in Bristol depended on the outcome of union negotiations. However, by the time another press report about the buses appeared five months later (in the *Leyland Truck & Bus Times* – a staff paper seen by BCV employees) they had still not entered service.

Numbered C5002-9, the VRTs were powered by Transversely-positioned Gardner 6LXB engines, with dual-door, 70-seat Eastern Coach Works bodywork painted into a similar green and cream OMO livery to that applied on the two prototypes.

Several hundred Bristol VRTs had been built by this time – largely, but not exclusively for NBC operators – but the Bristol Omnibus examples (together with a batch built simultaneously for the Southdown company) were the first ECW-bodied examples incorporating two doors and a centre staircase. In contrast to the usual high standards of ECW, these characteristics resulted in an extremely cluttered and untidy interior layout with only 10 of the 27 lower deck seats mounted at floor level. The remainder were perched above footstools and 12 of these faced sideways; while the stairs were awkward, turning through 180° within one standard ECW bay measuring just 4ft 3ins long. Upstairs, 43 passenger seats were accommodated, but again there was conflict between the position of the door gear housings and passenger legroom. Traditionally, Bristol and ECW had established an enviable reputation for working closely with operators, but this seemed to be going wrong under NBC; and for Bristol Omnibus, this was probably not the best design with which to launch OMO double-deck operation, as other manufacturers and operators had achieved far more satisfactory layouts. Significantly however, it was a lack of staff cooperation rather than passenger concerns that delayed these buses from entering service.

One plan was to allocate one each of these buses to different routes as OMO buses, but this came to nothing; however, when, on a couple of occasions, some ventured out on crew workings, they were quickly called back into the depot. One was used on 13th May, however, in connection with a visit to Bristol by members of the Omnibus Society, who were again visiting Bristol for their Presidential Weekend; this time their President was J.T.E. Robinson.

Eventually, success was achieved when the eight VRTs were allocated to Muller Road depot to launch the company's first one-man operated double-deck bus route, on Sunday 23rd July 1972. This was a complex arrangement involving the conversion of cross city service 22/23 which operated from Lockleaze in the east through Easton (passing the former Eastville depot – which once operated the service using the Leyland PD1s) through Old Market, past the bus station and Bristol Royal Infirmary, along Whiteladies Road. From there it crossed the Downs (a vast area of green open space donated to the city by the Merchant Venturers) and through Sea Mills after which the route divided to either Lawrence Weston (22) or Shirehampton (23).

The route required 12 or 13 buses – but of course there were only eight VRTs so the balance was made

This bodybuilders' photograph of the interior of the lower deck of one of the 1972 batch of twin-doorway Bristol VRTs for Joint Services shows the unsatisfactory arrangement of the 27 seats, with only 10 of them facing forward at floor level. The rest were on pedestals, 12 of those facing sideways – not a seat you wanted to sit on when the driver was making up time, particularly on some of Bristol's tight turns! The central staircase and door bulkheads add to the claustrophobic feel, made worse when the bus was carrying standing passengers. However, this arrangement was the standard for two-doorway double-deckers until the arrival of the single-door Olympians over 10 years later. (*ECW*)

up by RELLs. A further complication was that the local trade union insisted that as double-deckers attracted a higher rate of pay than single-deckers (in urban areas, a 25% enhancement on the basic rate against 20% for the single-deckers) they must be worked by a separate roster of drivers who would always receive that rate of pay regardless of the vehicle driven. The result was that services 22/23 were operated by two separate rosters, one of which could only drive single-deckers (because of the lower pay rate) while the other could drive all types, although if they were allocated a single-decker they would still be paid as if it were a double-decker! At some other depots, when double-deckers were introduced later as one-man vehicles, the enhanced pay followed the vehicle, allowing staff to be paid for whichever vehicle was allocated to their duty. The company decided that in order to ensure sufficient spare VRs for unknown eventualities – after all, these were the first of this type that the company had operated – only six of the eight new buses should be allocated for service (a 33% spares ratio) and the schedules department ensured where possible that these were allocated to the busiest journeys. It wasn't that simple, however, since when the frequency was reduced during evenings and Sundays, the Shirehampton route variant (23) needed to be allocated VRs as the end-to-end journey time was 55 minutes, resulting in a terminal layover of 5 minutes. This was the minimum necessary under the applicable agreements, and, because of the road layout at the terminus, an RE required an extra minute as it was unable to turn around in the same way as the shorter VRs. The result was that, whilst every effort was made to allocate VRs to the busiest daytime journeys, some exceptions had to be made to ensure that they ended up operating to Shirehampton during the evenings!

This particular route conversion was preceded by one of the buses and drivers making a publicity tour, and the appearance of a revised timetable booklet that gave a great deal of information about the new double-deck buses to be seen on the route. In operation, it took both the staff and passengers some time to get used to paying the driver on the double-deckers, often resulting in the bunching of vehicles on the service. The internal layout already mentioned was also unpopular, especially with elderly passengers, but this did not prevent this type of bus becoming the company's standard double-decker for operating one-man services in towns and cities. Meanwhile, in an effort to make the drivers' job easier as busier routes were progressively converted to OMO, the Joint Services Committee agreed to the purchase of control sets to convert many existing semi-automatic buses to fully automatic transmission.

This was followed by a report on the operation of one of Muller Road depot's VRs fitted with an experimental electronic ticket machine, the Setright Keyspeed, which looked rather like an old-fashioned cash register affixed to the driver's cab door. However, no orders for this new generation of electronic ticket machine ever followed.

Passenger loss remained a serious issue, however, and co-author Martin Curtis watched passenger numbers reduce as route 36 was converted from double-deckers to RELLs – with far fewer seats. Each individual RELL driver had their own policy on standing passengers, which frequently was more relaxed than the official rules, but of course affected how many passengers were carried on each particular journey. As a consequence, at bus stops along the route many regular morning peak passengers found that depending on the driver, one of three things would occur: they could board and might find a vacant seat; they could board but were required to stand, or thirdly, they were left behind completely. After a fairly short period of time, many of these passengers were gone for good – having found other ways to travel. The company seemed to have learned nothing from the service 15 conversion of three years earlier.

Amendment No. 4

NEW BUSES ON YOUR SERVICE

On Sunday, July 23rd, 1972, your bus services 22 (Lockleaze to Lawrence Weston) and 23 (Lockleaze to Shirehampton) will be changed to one-man operation. This means that the buses will not have conductors and that your fares will be taken by the driver. Can you please help us by following the passenger code:—
* Please have your correct fare ready for the driver and state your destination.
* Please *enter* the bus by the *forward* door.
* Please *leave* the bus by the *centre* door.
* On single deck buses smokers please sit at the rear half.
* On double deck buses smokers please sit upstairs.

You will have brand new buses on your service. At certain times you will have the latest two-door double decks, and at others the new two-door single deck saloons — both types in the smart cream and green livery and offering a much higher degree of comfort.

THE TIMETABLE
There are slight changes to the timetable, and for your guidance we have printed the timetables in full in this free leaflet.

TECHNICAL NOTES
The new two-door double deck buses have a seating capacity of 70 (43 upper deck, 27 lower).
Fleet Numbers C.5002 to C.5009 inclusive.
(Registrations EHU 361K to 368K inclusive).
Engine 6LXB Gardner, vertical rear transverse, developing 180 B.H.P.; 4-speed semi-automatic gearbox.
Bodywork Eastern Coachworks.
Cost £11,000 (subject to 50 per cent Government grant).

BRISTOL JOINT SERVICES.

mb d7435 6/72

The number of buses 'off' (off-the-road) during this period also continued to present difficulties, especially in Bristol itself. At the city depots, dozens of buses would be 'off' each morning owing to 'No Driver' or 'No Conductor' and if their shift pattern didn't match it wasn't always a straightforward matter for the remaining staff to be paired together by supervisors. The phenomenon of 'No Bus' would additionally occur, which was partly caused by a chronic spare parts shortage that developed during the seventies throughout the industry, and became worse with the introduction of rear-engined, automatic vehicles which required more attention than their simpler predecessors.

It was unfortunate, too, that at this time, most of the company's management were allocated company cars – the General Manager even had a chauffeur! Whilst some managers nevertheless made a point of using the services, those who did not were perhaps becoming remote from the frustrations of users.

(*left*) Both city and country services in Bristol suffered from staff shortages during the early 1970s. In this view of the inside of Bristol's bus and coach station, the blackboards mounted on the queue barriers show the considerable number of 'buses off'...
(*Bristol Evening Post*)

... whilst outside the bus station (*below*), probably a quarter of the vehicle allocation of city services 22/23 are 'off', with further buses also awaiting drivers.
(*M.S. Curtis*)

154

At the beginning of the 1970s Dave Bubier had been appointed to the position of Inspector for the Joint Services. One of his main functions, he recalls, was to 'warn' the crews of buses on their outward journeys to return showing 'Centre' only, because of the known lack of any staff to take on that journey.

> This was of course detrimental to passengers making cross-city journeys, but I do not recall any serious complaints about that aspect. We then had the problem of numerous parked up buses, shunting them down to [nearby] Cannons Marsh and later in the evenings back to the depots. Impatient passengers would sometimes want to take the law into their own hands and threaten to steal a bus to drive home.

Despite the staffing problems, the 1972 NBC Annual Report stated that 'there was a continuing improvement in [the staff situation] in 1972, except notably in respect of maintenance staff shortages, particularly in Bristol.'

As previously mentioned, the RE represented the lion's share of 1972's new bus intake but these were accompanied by the first of two very different new designs of single-deck buses; one of which, the Leyland National, was to replace the RE, not only in Bristol, but throughout the country.

The RE did not go quietly, however, with many operators preferring it to the replacement, and no fewer than 71 Bristol REs entered the Bristol fleet during this year. The largest batch of body type was once again the 44-seat dual-doorway version, with 42 entering the fleet, 26 of which were for Joint Services, five for Gloucester City services and two for Cheltenham. Fourteen of this batch were different from the normal specification in being delivered with Gardner 6HLX engines instead of the Leyland 0.680 variant, the Gardner-engined buses having been diverted from Western National. Two RE buses were fitted with 0.510 power units, another variant of the 0.500 series. Twelve of the remaining longer REs came with 50-seat bus bodies, whilst of 13 of the higher frame RELH model, 10 had Leyland 0.680 engines and 49-seat dual-purpose bodies, while three (again diverted from Western National) were Gardner 6HLX powered with 47-seat Plaxton coach bodies for the Greyhound fleet. The Bristol RE had returned to the Greyhound fleet but with coachwork similar to that of the Leyland Leopards, and failed to match the performance of the 1968

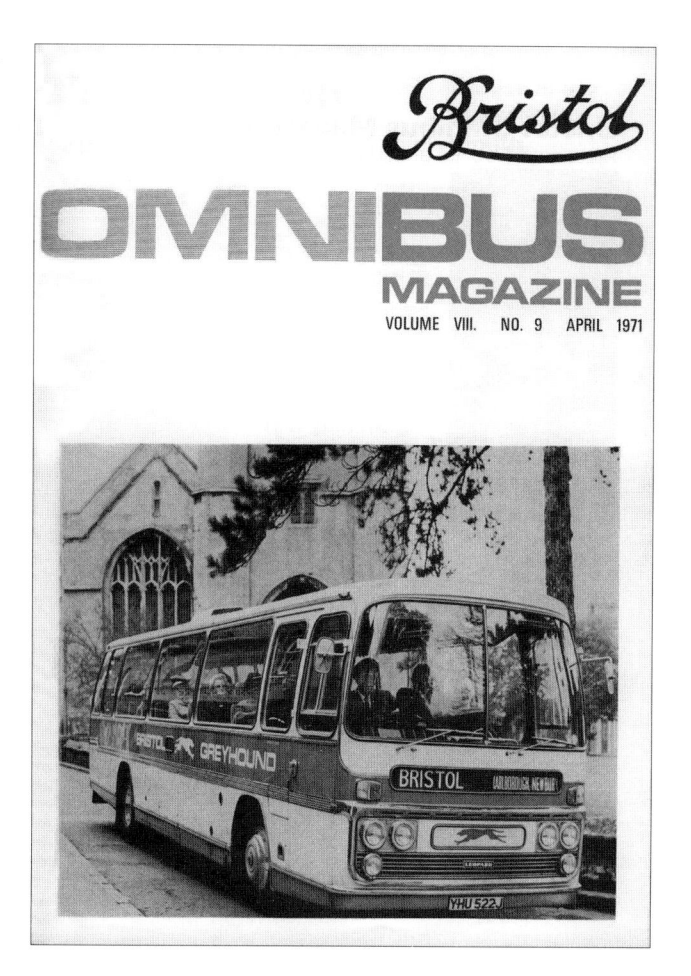

1279 (EHU 380K) was a 1972 country services 50-seat Bristol RELL, shown in the company of red Wilts & Dorset buses at Salisbury bus station having worked from Trowbridge on former Western National service 241. (*M. Walker*)

All new buses and coaches were delivered to the Central Repair Works at Lawrence Hill in Bristol to be made ready for service. ECW-bodied Bristol LH, 351 (DHW 291K), was the first of the six with semi-automatic gearboxes delivered in 1972. These buses were unique in having no green skirt panels. (*M. Walker*)

RELHs. Eventually, two of these three were converted to dual-purpose status vehicles after seven years or so but, as with the previous Plaxton coach deliveries, were seen to be unsuitable for general one-man operation, not only because of their cab arrangement but also because of the lack of performance from their Gardner engines in comparison to the more usual Leyland units. One of them was to find a home on the re-launched Bristol to Cardiff service, known as the X10, carrying route-specific branding, and when that service was extended beyond Cardiff to Swansea and West Wales, and re-named 'Expresswest' the coach was again re-liveried. Its performance remained disappointing, however, so it was soon replaced.

The Plaxton-bodied RELHs were to be the last new Greyhound coaches of any type however, as the National Bus Company had decided to introduce an all-over white livery with 'NATIONAL' branding for all its subsidiaries' coaches – countrywide. A small local fleetname was retained over the front wheels, but this read simply 'BRISTOL' in a new NBC standard block typeface, and, without the 'Greyhound', was thought by many to be a destination!

The remaining 1972 RE types were four of the shorter Leyland-engined RESL variant with the company's standard 43-seat body, and these were joined by the company's first Bristol LH buses, powered by Leyland 0.401 engines and featuring unusual semi-automatic gearboxes. The LHs spent almost their entire short working lives at Weston-super-Mare and Wells depots (they were all withdrawn within 8 years, the company intending that the service life of lightweight single-deckers should generally be up to the first Certificate of Fitness renewal at seven years), and whilst delivered in a version of the OMO livery, they differed from the rest of the fleet in having no green skirt. Although they entered service as 43-seaters, they soon had the rear centre seat removed to allow a reversing window to be fitted. Despite their semi-automatic gearboxes they were not popular, and were referred to by the crews as 'Jumping Jacks', as selection of first gear at rest caused the bus to lurch forwards as if the body was about to separate from the chassis; in due course this was cured by the fitting of 'de-bumping' equipment, which momentarily selected reverse before first, thus negating the effects of the violent movement forward! This wasn't the only problem, however, for they were blessed with very heavy steering, resulting in the trade union officials at Weston-super-Mare asking the company Chief Engineer to complete part of a shift on one of them on town services, so that he could experience the problem first-hand. Although he acceded to this request, the problem was never satisfactorily resolved.

Following the introduction of the white-painted coaches, more livery changes under NBC were about to alter the appearance of state-owned buses not only in Bristol, but throughout England and Wales.

At first, the full impact of NBC's proposals were not entirely obvious as the plans were announced during July in *Bus*, a new NBC staff newspaper. This described how throughout the group, new block letter fleetnames and a 'double N' symbol (already seen on the white coaches) would replace traditional fleetname styles, in 'cream on red or green as appropriate to existing liveries'. It went on to explain that this would be followed by all 20,000 NBC buses gradually losing their 'traditional cream' relief on repaint, to be replaced by white so that vehicles would be finished in either green, red or blue with white relief and fleetnames, a process that was expected to take up to two years.

In order to promote its new corporate image, NBC took the unusual step of commissioning a TV advertising campaign which was broadcast in the Bristol area by HTV 18 times during October and November. Buses from around the country were featured driving in formation and Bristol supplied FLF C7211 to take part in the filming, freshly repainted in Tilling green, but with white waistband and new style fleetnames. The wheels were also painted light grey, possibly the most impractical colour imaginable for bus wheels.

From a Bristol perspective, little more happened concerning liveries until September 1972, when the biennial Commercial Motor Show was again held at Earls Court. One of the exhibits on the BCV stand was a VRT chassis which was destined to become Bristol Omnibus C5010 the following year.

Among the bodied exhibits were a VR and LH on ECW's stand (for Southern Vectis and Eastern Counties respectively) whilst elsewhere at the show was a Park Royal-bodied Leyland Atlantean for London Country. For the first time, they revealed new standard hues of poppy red or leaf green, to be applied to almost all NBC fleets. It was suddenly realised that the plan to maintain a selection of individual company colours had been dispensed with – and here were the new standards!

Over two months passed and there was no sign of the new shades in Bristol, which must have been deliberate for during this period the company repainted its last MW bus into Tilling green and cream OMO livery, thereby completing the entire one-man fleet.

A visit to Lawrence Hill paint shops at the beginning of December revealed a different story, however. Alongside buses in Tilling green livery were three double-deckers being repainted National green and white; an early RELH, the first to receive NBC's dual-purpose (or as NBC called it 'local coach') livery of half green/half white; and a Cheltenham RELL, the first to receive National red. Gone was the Bristol scroll – at least on country buses – and simplified fleetnames were used for Bath and Cheltenham, although Cheltenham and Gloucester buses retained their coat of arms.

The new lighter colours appeared to be inferior to the previous rich shades, and when weathered, sometimes looked appalling. And since repainting of the entire fleet would take several years, the fleet took on a particularly shabby appearance over the next year or so, not only because of the mix of green shades but because an attempt was then made to accelerate the change by adding white bands and new fleetnames (often in cream lettering to use up stocks) to Tilling green vehicles not due for early repainting.

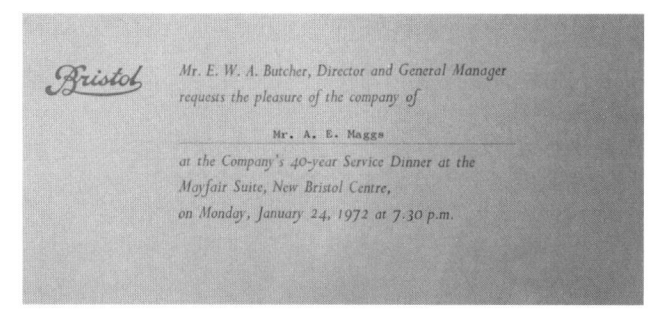

Bristol Mr. E. W. A. Butcher, Director and General Manager requests the pleasure of the company of
Mr. A. E. Maggs
at the Company's 40-year Service Dinner at the Mayfair Suite, New Bristol Centre, on Monday, January 24, 1972 at 7.30 p.m.

The new corporate colours were widely unpopular as so many delightful and historic bus liveries were lost, which in many cases represented the locality. Senior NBC management claimed the new image would soon be as popular as the old styles. They were wrong, and all over the country any excuse was seized to revive an old colour scheme. Not all was lost in Bristol, however, for although unclear whether driven by Company or Corporation, the Joint Services were not going to conform without a little resistance, of which more later.

The first of the new Leyland National single-deck buses were 44-seat dual-doorway versions for Joint Services and started a new 14xx series of fleet numbers. The co-authors, by now work colleagues, together inspected the first two to arrive at Lawrence Hill early on the morning of 1st December 1972. The Leyland National was a new design of single-deck bus that came out of a joint venture between British Leyland and the National Bus Company and was intended to replace all other heavy-duty, single-deck buses being offered by Leyland associated companies, including the Bristol RE. It was built at a newly constructed factory in the Cumberland town of Workington, an area of deprivation and unemployment that meant that the project attracted a good deal of financial support from central government. The bus itself, which, unlike any other British bus design was of integral construction and built on a production line in the same way that cars were manufactured, was to be offered in very limited forms and in even more limited colours, with only one engine choice. As a partner in its development and production, the National Bus Company insisted that its subsidiary companies received only this type of bus for its heavy-duty requirements.

The National Bus Company Divisions were re-organised from 1st April and the company's General Manager, Ted Butcher, was appointed as one of three Chief General Managers of the new Southern Region. Meanwhile, within the company a new Marketing and Public Relations Unit was formed, under the control of Brian Cooper, a public relations professional who had joined the company as the personal assistant to the General Manager, the intention being to explore new opportunities of marketing the company's services and to rejuvenate the relationship between the company and the media.

In Stroud a new bus station and shopping centre complex was completed in July 1972, described as being one of the most up-to-date in the country, but services had been forced to use temporary departure platforms for the preceding 15 months.

Returning to vehicle matters, agreement was reached at the September 1972 Joint Services Committee to make the entire 1974 single-deck order for Leyland Nationals. At the December meeting it was reported that it was the intention to negotiate with the trade union for this order to be fitted with rear route number indicators, it being admitted that agreements for one-man operation had resulted in the dropping of these number displays so far. There was also a suggestion that BJS should purchase their own coach for a city tour; however, this was not followed through.

At various times during the year, the company borrowed four Plaxton-bodied Bristol RELH6L coaches (some of which were repainted into the white and magenta Greyhound livery), together with a Plaxton-bodied Leyland Leopard and a Harrington-bodied AEC Reliance: they all came from Greenslades Tours of Exeter, a fellow West Country coach operator within the National Bus Company. Coincidentally, the Chairman of the Region, J.T.E. Robinson, retired at the end of March having spent a lifetime in the transport industry, and having been with the Bristol company since being appointed General Manager in June 1967.

Meanwhile, NBC's corporate identity was extended to include a new blue/grey uniform for drivers and conductors, complete with an American style 'blouson' in addition to the conventional jacket, a clip-on tie and, for men, an American police-style cap! Furthermore, the group promoted a new slogan which it posted on vehicles and elsewhere, proclaiming: 'We're proud to be part of the National Bus Company. Together we can really go places'. The group's marketing and promotional teams were having a field day.

NBC's new livery posed a problem for BJS however, since having achieved the return of Bristol's coat of arms to bus sides, it was felt, for the sake of civic pride, that it should stay there; while there was also a widely held desire to retain the Bristol scroll.

After the company's painters dipped their brushes into the first tins of pale 'leaf' green, BJS FLFs appeared in this shade with white waistband, but retaining dark green wings, gold scroll and arms. The first RELLs went even further: NBC green replaced Tilling green, but the deep cream in OMO style and scroll and arms all remained. Unfortunately, the dark green mudguards of double-deckers were rapidly dispensed with, but the RE layout remained for some time, although every repainted vehicle received grey wheels. The first Leyland Nationals arrived in unrelieved NBC green however, and uncertainty then followed.

The Bristol Joint Services vehicles had always closely followed the livery of the main fleet, and attractive though the idea may have been, to have a separate livery for BJS was uneconomic and after all, the main objective was to provide a bus service for Bristolians. The rigidly inflexible livery policy for Leyland Nationals resulted not only in their arrival in green but with no relief at all. Many NBC operators ran them in this form which was little better than the appearance of wartime buses, but Bristol was among those to add its own white relief. The first entered service on BJS services with no fleet markings, however, and repainted BJS double-deckers were out-shopped from March to June 1973 similarly devoid of fleetnames or other insignia, for although standard NBC green and white was extended to BJS vehicles, a debate continued about fleet markings. A series of mock-up designs had been applied to Leyland Nationals for inspection and consideration. A double N symbol was included, as was a coat of arms, and a new white version of the scroll which was slightly reduced in size compared to the gold version. At least one layout even resurrected the old design of arms last seen in the early sixties, placed in a row behind the N and scroll. Finally, it was agreed the N would be placed above driver's cabs and front entrances, with the scroll surmounted by the smaller arms in the usual way although often further forward on vehicles than before; the flowing lines of the 'Bristol' name often conflicting with angular bodywork when applied thus. Once established however, city buses became readily distinguishable from country buses in Bristol.

1973

This was to be the last year that the company took new Bristol REs, a type that Bristol Commercial Vehicles was forced to phase out in favour of the Leyland National (although BCV was permitted to continue limited production for customers in Northern Ireland, and New Zealand). For a short period therefore, RE and Leyland National deliveries overlapped for Bristol.

Thirty-four REs came into the fleet, 14 of which were Joint Services, 44-seat, centre-exit buses, and four of these were a diverted order placed by the Western Welsh Omnibus Company of Cardiff. All of the centre-exit buses were powered by the familiar 0.680 Leyland

11.1 litre engine, whilst the buses ordered by Western Welsh were the only 1973 vehicles to be delivered in the cream and green OMO livery, with the rest received in the new National green. The remaining 20 were similarly engined 50-seat, single-doorway buses, one of which, 1338, OAE 960M, remained unique as it was held back for development work on engine soundproofing and entered service in Stroud in April 1974 with a large baffle plate under the engine. More importantly, this bus was also fitted with a spring parking brake instead of the normal ratchet handbrake; this latter feature was to be incorporated into the later RE buses sold to the Christchurch Transport Board in New Zealand, but no other RE operated with this feature in Great Britain.

No fewer than 32 Leyland Nationals entered service in 1973, all of which were 44-seat, centre-exit buses, 14 for BJS, eight for Gloucester, four for Cheltenham and the remainder for Bath and country services. These buses arrived at Lawrence Hill Central Repair Works in all over green and received a slim white line painted below the windows (there was no moulding there in the fashion of previous ECW bodies) before entering service, and some of them were delivered from Workington on the back of articulated flatbed lorries. This caused some consternation as new Bristol-built vehicles were always driven to operators and Bristol Omnibus staff were also very familiar with the sight of newly completed Bristol chassis being driven on test runs or to the coachworks. The Cheltenham buses continued the red livery of the subsidiary fleet, albeit now National poppy red, whilst Bath bus 1416 caught fire before the end of the year and was stripped for spares by the company before being scrapped.

The remaining full-sized, single-deck deliveries consisted of four further Plaxton-bodied Leyland Leopard coaches, two of which were disposed of to neighbouring National Travel within the year, whilst a smaller bus arrived in the shape of a 17-seat, Ascough Clubman-bodied Leyland EA which was required for a new Gloucester City shoppers service. This little bus later pioneered the Grove Park Mini demand-responsive service in Weston-super-Mare and a community route in Windmill Hill, Bristol, lasting nine years before withdrawal.

The year also saw the delivery of a further 20 Bristol VRT double-deckers for Joint Services, all to the new dual-doorway layout and all arriving in the National green livery. They featured the re-appearance of rear route number displays but these saw little use and were soon either painted or panelled over. The chassis of the first of these VRs, C5010, was that exhibited at the previous year's Commercial Motor Show, and was delivered with a blue and chrome engine and blue trimmed seats bearing red and white National Bus Company double N symbols – a design also fitted to RE bus 1311 along with individual vehicles

BJS Leyland Nationals entered service in National green relieved by a thin white band, at the same time as some of the last Bristol RELLs were put into service in the Tilling green and cream colour scheme. Leyland National C1404, a 44-seat twin door bus, is seen on its first day of service at the Cheltenham Road terminus of service 83 in February 1973. (*M.S. Curtis*)

throughout National Bus Company. This moquette was not generally adopted however.

Once again, there were a number of secondhand vehicle acquisitions during the year, both double- and single-deck. During a year when Bristol Lodekkas were being withdrawn in numbers, it was perhaps a surprise that three second-hand examples joined the fleet: TUO 486, a Bristol-engined, 60-seater came from Western National but was only to be stripped for mechanical spares before being acquired by a local contractor for use as a staff hut. 626 HFM and 627 HFM came from Crosville Motor Services and were 1959 Bristol-engined 60-seaters with platform doors – and removable roofs! Taking fleet numbers L8580 and L8581, the two joined the convertible FS buses at Weston-super-Mare. Following a change of local management, the open-top requirement was increased by the introduction of two new town tours. They lasted between six and seven years at Weston, before succumbing to the ever-present spread of one-man operation.

The single-deck acquisitions were five Plaxton-bodied Leyland Leopard coaches from the Southdown company dating from 1966, and these initially entered service in Southdown livery before being repainted into National white, and were to last five years. Whilst still in Southdown colours they were often seen operating Joint Services routes at peak hours, with, of course, a crew of two.

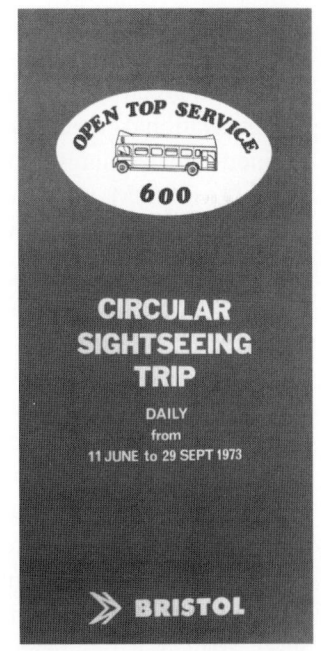

1973 saw the eventual introduction of the much publicised Marconi B-line bus location system – rather later than intended. Up to 600 staff had attended a special training course in connection with the system, and 40 of the BJS RE buses operating on three routes were equipped with the laser-generating and transmission equipment and its associated additional roof-mounted window, at a projected cost in 1970 of an additional £650 to £1,000 per vehicle – a not inconsiderable sum added to a vehicle already costing around £8,000. The ground-floor front of the mock Tudor, Centre offices were modified to take the controller's office and his staff, together with all of their equipment and the supporting computer system. Being the early days of such technology, this computer occupied a large room of its own, and required constant water for cooling. The amount required occasionally caused a problem for the Bristol Division office staff as it affected the supply to their cloakrooms.

Former Southdown Plaxton-bodied Leyland Leopard coach EUF 201D of 1966 became Bristol's 2171 in 1973; it was repainted into National white one month after entering service in Southdown's green livery. (*Bristol Vintage Bus Group*)

Another momentous event took place during the year, with the mounting of the 'Bristol 600' exhibition on Durdham Down, to celebrate 600 years since the granting of the city's Royal Charter which gave Bristol its City and County status. Lasting for much of the summer, the exhibition brought together many of the organisations and companies that had made Bristol their home, as well as hosting a number of arena displays and events. Naturally, Bristol Omnibus took an active part in the celebrations.

Firstly, the company took a stand at the exhibition to display the details of the services they offered, and exhibited a motorised large-scale model of a Bristol tram which ran along a length of track, the stand being manned by volunteers from Bristol-based staff, including the authors and the company 'Greyhound Girls'. Secondly, the company converted life-expired country services Lodekka L8394 to open-top and painted it in light blue and white with an all-over design featuring aspects of the city, for use on an hourly service connecting the central area with the exhibition. The bus was renumbered into the open-top series as L8582, and the service, appropriately, was numbered 600. In following years the same vehicle was used to provide a city tour on a hop-on, hop-off basis, taking the year as its route number. After withdrawal it spent many years at the premises of North's, the Leeds area dealer, before being exported to Holland – where in 2002, it was viewed by co-author Mike Walker, still in its withdrawn condition with sign-written views of Bristol on its sides.

Following the success of the first 'Berni' bus, no fewer than six over-all advert FLFs entered service during the year, and there were to be many more over-all advert buses in the years to follow.

Still anxious to improve passenger comfort, a new Cirencester bus station was opened during the year. However, the Company was already examining the use made of rural services by asking the one-man operators to complete a census form (looking not unlike a rather large fare table) so that details could be obtained on the passenger carryings of every journey on every rural route. The 1968 Transport Act had already given local and central government the powers to support bus services financially in rural areas that were considered by the company to be uneconomic to operate but considered by the authority to be socially necessary, and the 1972 Local Government Act had extended those powers to encompass the provision of service networks. National Bus Company had a duty to 'break even taking one

The City and County of Bristol organised a large exhibition on the Downs in 1973 to celebrate the 600th anniversary of their founding Royal Charter. The company linked the site to the central area of the city with service 600, operated by a specially converted and painted 1956 Bristol LD Lodekka, formerly L8394 (WHY 947), which became L8582. Although not a BJS bus, L8582 carried the earlier style of Bristol crest on its rear panels. (*M.S. Curtis*)

year with another' and so the company were continuing negotiations with the authorities to get any financial support for which they felt they were entitled.

The 1972 Local Government Act was also to introduce a new local authority, Avon County Council, formed in 1974 from Bristol, together with sections of Somerset and Gloucestershire; ironically removing Bristol's County status celebrated only the year before. Avon was to play a very large part in the development of the company's services in future, but the wrangling between this authority and Bristol City Council would be the downfall of Bristol Joint Services.

Meanwhile, the use of one-man buses continued to increase, and an interesting statistic occurred on 1st October 1973 when Bristol city depots (including Hanham) had exactly the same number of crew as OMO buses: 215 of each.

As a result of tensions over oil supplies in the Middle East, involving Arab states belonging to OPEC, lower speed limits were introduced temporarily at the end of 1973 and fuel rationing was proposed. The company was directed to prepare contingency plans to retain buses beyond their normal life, to employ staff beyond retirement age, to reduce service levels and to contract out maintenance so as to switch labour to other duties. In the event, the emergency was fairly short-lived and none of the contingencies was put into operation. However, despite the possibility of the emergency causing car drivers to switch to public transport, and the continued savings made by service reductions and one-man conversions, the company reported to the Joint Services Committee at the end of 1973 that the 1974 full year forecast showed a loss of £63,350; an early fares increase was now a necessity. Even so, in July 1974 it was reported that the financial position had worsened, due in no small part to recent threshold increases in staff rates of pay brought about by an increase in the Retail Price Index, Government diktat controlling the changes to wage conditions associated with changes to this index. At the July meeting the 1974 deficit for Joint Services was to have been reported as over £600,000 and a further fares increase proposed, this time a blanket rise of 1p per fare, but a subsequent further increase in the Retail Price Index had triggered another wage rise and now a 2p rise on fares over 10p was essential to eliminate the deficit. Bristol Joint Services were heading towards deep financial problems.

Throughout the whole of its operating area, the company sought to promote itself and become involved in local events of all kinds, doing its best to maintain staff numbers while attempting to retain and even expand its customer base, which nevertheless seemed to be reducing further. The number of licensed motor vehicles in the UK had by then reached 15 million, having tripled in 20 years. This would have been a difficult situation for any business, but with greater local government involvement generally, Bristol Omnibus was trying on the one hand to continue providing important public services while increasingly having to deal with falling passenger numbers and associated economic difficulties.

***

1964 Bristol RELH coach 2126 (972 WAE) received local coach livery of National green and white in 1973 but continued to run into London's Victoria Coach Station; the following year it was painted into National white. (*A.J. Douglas*)

(*above*) 1967 53-seat ECW-bodied Bristol RELL 1030 (MAE 33F) leaves Wells bus depot dressed for Bristol on the 376 service. Delivered in Tilling green with a cream band, this batch of buses received the brighter 'one-man' livery in 1970 and National green in 1973. The forward position of the fleetname allowed for placing an advertisement. (*R.H.G. Simpson*)

(*below*) ECW-bodied, 30-seat Bristol SUS 307 (AHW 226B) of 1964 had received the brighter 'one-man' bus livery by the time that this 1970 photograph was taken in Swindon. (*R.H.G. Simpson*)

(*right*) It was unusual to see a Bristol MW running on BJS one-man operated routes other than service 19. 1961 43-seat C2520 (355 MHU), is seen on service 17/18, normally an RE route, in Clifton in October 1970. (*M. Walker*)

(*left*) 1963 one-man operated ECW-bodied, Bristol MW saloon 2573 (932 RAE), photographed in March 1971. The manually operated Setright ticket machine can be seen through the driver's windscreen, by his left arm. (*S.J. Butler collection*)

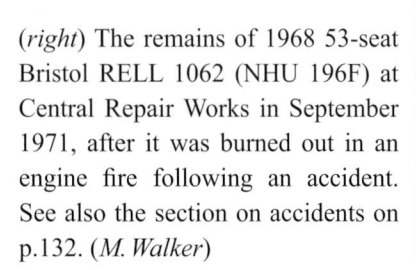

(*right*) The remains of 1968 53-seat Bristol RELL 1062 (NHU 196F) at Central Repair Works in September 1971, after it was burned out in an engine fire following an accident. See also the section on accidents on p.132. (*M. Walker*)

(*left*) Greyhound coach 2138 became bus 2428 on recertification in 1971, although this entire batch of 1965 ECW-bodied, 39-seat Bristol MWs retained their red interior and trim. The bus is seen in May 1972 working the Portishead local one-man service, to the south of the city and in Somerset. (*M. Walker*)

(*right*) ECW-bodied, 49-seat, dual-purpose saloon 2068 (WHW 380H), a 1970 Bristol RELH, pauses at Westbury-on-Trym, outbound to Cardiff in August 1972. (*M. Walker*)

(*left*) For many years the crews of the Bristol to Gloucester and Cheltenham service swapped buses at Berkeley, although the bus and passengers travelled through. The crews then returned to the depot from which they had come on each journey. In this August 1973 view, RELL 53-seater 1063 leads 50-seat RELL 1207 and 1965 Bristol MW 2432 (former coach 2142), all with ECW bodies. The MW is on a connecting local service. (*M. Walker*)

165

(*above*) Amongst the Joint Services depots was Staple Hill, towards the eastern edge of the city, seen in this 1971 view. Like Brislington, Staple Hill was a former tram depot. (*M. Walker*)

(*below*) Brislington depot was integral to the company's operation from its earliest days, being the body-building works, an operational tram and bus depot, and close to the Motor Constructional Works (BCV), but it closed in October 1971. (*M.S. Curtis*)

(*left*) Country services 1959 ECW-bodied Bristol LD Lodekka L8513 (967 EHW) leaves Wookey Hole for the city of Wells in November 1971. (*M. Walker*)

(*right*) The Whitchurch terminus of Bristol City route 3 was for many years on the busy Wells Road (A37) to the south of Bristol. Even as late as February 1973, this high-frequency service reversed in order to turn around. 1956 Bristol KSW C8363 (WHW 804) performs this reverse manoeuvre in February 1973, already dressed for the return journey through the Centre to Filton. (*M. Walker*)

(*left*) Cheltenham District's 1965 ECW-bodied Bristol FLF 7184 retains its traditional livery in this 1973 view, despite carrying an advertisement for the National Bus Company. (*M. Walker*)

167

When female drivers were first introduced into Joint Services in 1970 it was seen as extremely newsworthy. From left to right, front row: M. Ruddle, P. Godfrey, C. Blackford, H. Poole, P. Harris, F. Somers. Second row: D. Pickles, B. Schubert, K. Worth. Back row: I. Bush, K. Frost, V. Turner, D. Shute, L. Jones and S. Davey. (*Bristol Omnibus*)

A Bristol uniform lapel badge, and Inspector's cap and lapel badge, both worn throughout the period.

5. The Later Seventies: Into a Second Century

As already recorded in the introduction, the Bristol Tramways Company commenced operations during August 1875, and as the direct descendant of the original tramways company, Bristol Omnibus was able to celebrate its centenary 100 years later with a Centenary Luncheon attended by the Minister of Transport, Fred Mulley; Bristol's Lord Mayor, Cllr. Bert Peglar; NBC Chairman, Freddie Wood; and other senior company officials. This served to demonstrate that 'Bristol' was among the oldest road transport companies, not just in the NBC, but anywhere. However, perhaps somewhat strangely, the company decided to mark the occasion not only with the luncheon but also a bus rally, special publications and other events, after 99 years of service, in 1974, which was actually the anniversary of the company's formation, rather than the inauguration of the first service.

1974

From the beginning of 1974 a new general manager had taken over from Ted Butcher, who had returned to BET, having accepted a senior position with United Transport Overseas. His replacement was Richard (Dick) Roberts who had previously been General Manager of the Eastern National Omnibus Company. One of the first changes he made was to reintroduce blue buses, not of course for service purposes; with NBC's rigid corporate livery policy such an idea would have been unthinkable. A new blue livery was adopted, however, for the fleet of driver training buses, which was in the same style as that used by Eastern National.

Within a year, another Eastern National practice had also been adopted, involving new depot allocation plates. Following the introduction of smaller fleet number plates during the mid and late 1960s, the background colour of these plates came to distinguish to which area a particular bus was allocated, with green for Bristol Division vehicles; yellow for the Northern Division of Cheltenham, Gloucester, Stroud and Swindon; and blue for the Southern Division which included Bath, Trowbridge, Weston-super-Mare and Wells. This was later refined by adding a second colour to the plate to denote exactly where buses were based. For example, Lawrence Hill depot in Bristol displayed green with red: those of Cheltenham District and Cheltenham country buses were painted yellow and tangerine; while Wells depot carried plates with blue and black.

With the Eastern National system, all plates displayed polished numbers (and letters if applicable) on a black background with an additional two-character plate alongside with depot codes as follows:

WE   Avonmouth (as a sub-depot of Winterstoke Road)
HN   Hanham
LH   Lawrence Hill
MH   Marlborough Street (Bristol bus station)
MR   Muller Road
SH   Staple Hill
WE   Winterstoke Road
BH   Bath (including Devizes & Warminster)
CM   Cheltenham (including CDT)
GR   Gloucester
SD   Stroud
SN   Swindon
TE   Trowbridge (including Chippenham)
WS   Wells
WM   Weston-super-Mare (including Highbridge)

The fleet total in February 1974 showed a very slight, further reduction to 1,195 vehicles, which included 410 Bristol Joint Services vehicles, and 36 Cheltenham District buses.

For the first year ever, new vehicle deliveries in 1974 were all of Leyland manufacture – with no Bristols being taken into stock.

The 1974 arrivals included no fewer than 11 Leyland Leopard coaches, fitted with stylish Plaxton Panorama Elite III 47-seat coachwork, finished in National white livery. Appropriately, these coaches were fitted with a feature known as a 'Bristol' dome, with the destination equipment moved from under the windscreen to above it at roof level. This arrangement was so named as a result of the redesign work that was necessary to the earlier Plaxton Panorama body when fitted to Bristol RE or LH coach chassis, since the front-mounted radiator precluded the fitment of destination equipment beneath the windscreen.

The bus single-deckers were, of course, all Leyland Nationals with 44-seat bodies – although 10 of the 23 were of the shorter 10.3 metre-long type with only one door. Eleven of the longer, twin-door, 11.3 metre-long buses went to BJS where, by February 1974, it was reported that half of the fleet now benefited from the fitment of two-way radios, whilst the remaining two buses were for Gloucester City services.

Withdrawals during the year included the first of the MW buses, now approaching 15 years old, and the first RELH coach, being only 11 years old. The entire batch of

ECW-bodied, 50-seat Bristol RELL 1338 was the last such bus to enter service with the company in February 1974. It had an additional baffle plate mounted beneath the engine for noise reduction, and was the only Bristol RE chassis in the UK to be fitted with a spring parking brake instead of the more usual ratchet hand brake. Allocated to Stroud depot, it is seen here at Nailsworth loading for a journey through Stroud to Cheltenham. (*M. Walker*)

early RELHs was sold to neighbouring NBC subsidiary, Western National, where all except one (dismantled for spare parts) were used for further service. In July of this year, the company dropped the 'L' prefix from the fleet numbers of low-height buses, since there were very few highbridge KSWs remaining, and the survivors' days were numbered. Other 'withdrawals' were the retirement from the Bristol Joint Services Committee of the Town Clerk and the City Treasurer, both of whom had served the committee since the 1940s, having seen the entire Green Years of the company thus far!

Two vehicles came on loan to the company during the early part of the year, both of which were used at Weston-super-Mare. In January, the town was host to UOO 658L, a Ford R192, fitted with a Willowbrook 45-seat bus body and painted in a red livery, whilst in April/May the guest was a Bedford YRQ (WXE 264M) fitted with an Alexander 38-seat coach body painted in green/cream colours. Both were used in service, believed to be on the town services to Sand Bay (100) and Worlebury/Uphill/Bleadon Hill/Hutton (104/114/115), where comparisons could be made with the LS and MW saloons which regularly operated on these routes. Whilst other NBC companies did order both Ford and Bedford lightweight buses, no orders were forthcoming from Bristol.

2178 (RHY 766M), a 47-seat, Plaxton-bodied Leyland Leopard coach new in 1974, at Bedford. (*A.J. Douglas*)

(*right*) 1964 ECW 45-seat Bristol RELH coach 2132 (978 WAE) received its final livery, National white, in 1974, but was to pass to Western National later in the year. (*M.S. Curtis*)

(*left*) Very few Bristol KSWs lasted in service long enough to receive National green livery: 1957 bus C8428 was one such example, seen here operating service 74 between Patchway and the Centre, which was one of the final haunts of Joint Services KSWs. (*M.S. Curtis*)

(*right*) Vauxhall Motors Bedford YRQ demonstrator WXE 264M with an Alexander coach body spent a month or so at Weston-super-Mare in 1974 running on town services, and is seen here at the Town Hall operating from Uphill to Worlebury. (*Bristol Vintage Bus Group*)

8583 (GHT 127), the much modified 1941 tram replacement Bristol K-type, became a regular performer on the Weston-super-Mare open-top town tour at the end of the decade. Finished in traditional Tilling cream, in this 1974 view the bus also carried the town's coat of arms, and does brisk business on a hot August day. (*M.S. Curtis*)

Three AEC Reliance buses were also borrowed from Swindon Corporation (soon to be known as Thamesdown) early in the year but due to the incompatibility of ticket-issuing equipment, they were returned within days and never used.

For a fleet now composed of a high proportion of rear-engined single- and double-deckers, a very unusual vehicle entered service during 1974, although it had actually been acquired by the company as far back as 1969. GHT 127 was a 1941 Bristol K5G double-decker that had first seen service as a wartime tram replacement motor bus, passing eventually to Brighton Hove & District where, along with a number of sister vehicles, it became a much refurbished open-top bus for operation along the Brighton sea front. In 1965 it was sold to Thomas Bros. of Port Talbot, South Wales, to perform a similar role at the seaside resort of Aberavon. It was the Bristol company's Regional Chairman, J.T.E. Robinson, who brought the bus back to Bristol, where it was eventually painted cream, allocated fleet number 8583 (in the 8 foot-wide series) and sent to Weston-super-Mare, where it was used for one season before being painted Tilling green and used only for special events. It has been suggested that the intention was to use this bus on the Bristol open-top tour, although even if that had been the case, such an old vehicle probably wouldn't have been accepted by the city trade unions.

Nevertheless, in 1978 it was again painted into Tilling cream livery and sent back to Weston, where it was often used on the seafront service and the town tours, until, at the turn of the decade, and along with all other front-engined, open-top buses, it was withdrawn. After a period with the Bristol Omnibus Preservation Society, the bus re-entered service in 1990 with Badgerline for use in Bath, but is now on permanent loan to the Bristol Vintage Bus Group, where it again sports the Brighton livery. During its final two-year stay in Weston it became popular amongst certain drivers as the depot 'pet', and although no one was expected to drive it against their will, there was never a shortage of staff willing to take the bus out when it was required. A shortage of one-man buses saw it working for a period of time (with a crew of two) on the winter service 100 along the seafront to Sand Bay. The bus even took part in the BBC drama series *Shoestring*, starring Trevor Eve, and marking an early TV appearance by Toyah Willcox. It was driven for the programme by co-author Mike Walker, with the bus continuously plodding along the seafront whilst the actor Richard Griffiths discussed 'dirty deeds' with his colleague on the top deck! A media career obviously suited the bus, and it later went on to star in an episode of the drama series *Soldier, Soldier*.

On a more serious subject, the early seventies was a time when Britain experienced one of its worst periods of industrial unrest. Disputes in the coal industry had already resulted in interruptions to both domestic and industrial power supplies. By late 1973, ongoing unrest was causing coal stocks to dwindle which, coupled to the world oil supply difficulties already mentioned, culminated in the industrial three-day working week during the early months of 1974. This resulted in commercial consumption of electricity being cut to three consecutive days each week in an effort to conserve fuel supplies. Some industries, such as transport, were exempt from these measures although power supplies to the company's offices, etc were nevertheless affected.

Bristol Omnibus showed a considerable degree of ingenuity during these times and among the steps taken by the company following these problems was the purchase of secondhand fuel tankers which could not only store additional diesel fuel but could move stocks between depots if necessary. It also led later to the conversion of a Bristol MW saloon into a generator bus, which was parked behind the company head office next to the central works at Lawrence Hill, and could be used to restore electricity supplies if a power cut occurred. Not only did the bus services keep running, therefore, but so too did many essential functions behind the scenes, including maintaining the staff payroll through the wages department at head office.

At the August 1974 Joint Services meeting, the general manager indicated that there would be a delay in the completion of the 1974 vehicle delivery programme and that this delay would also spill over into 1975 deliveries, although there was a possibility of exchanging vehicles with one of the Scottish group of companies, as they were experiencing difficulties with regard to conversion to one-man operation. Tentative proposals had been put forward that some of their OMO vehicles might be exchanged for two-man vehicles from the city fleet. The intention would be to release to the Scottish company Bristol FLF double-deckers in exchange for their Daimler Fleetline double-deckers which were approximately three years old. With its transversely-positioned, Gardner rear engine and dropped-centre back axle (allowing a low overall height), the Daimler Fleetline was broadly similar in mechanical terms to the VRT double-deckers already in the Joint Services fleet. It was stated that the transaction would be carried out at book value with a corresponding cash adjustment, and it was agreed that the General Manager should investigate the position further. However, an opportunity should be made for the Council committee members to see the type of vehicle involved before making a final decision on the exchange. It was recognised that modern requirements for one-man buses necessitated that they should be driver-friendly, high-capacity vehicles such as Daimler Fleetlines, rather than the slow, ponderous, Bristol MW with its manual gearbox and heavy steering, which launched one-man operation in the city. In this regard, the meeting approved the sale of ten time-expired MWs from the city fleet, at a total price of £5,280.

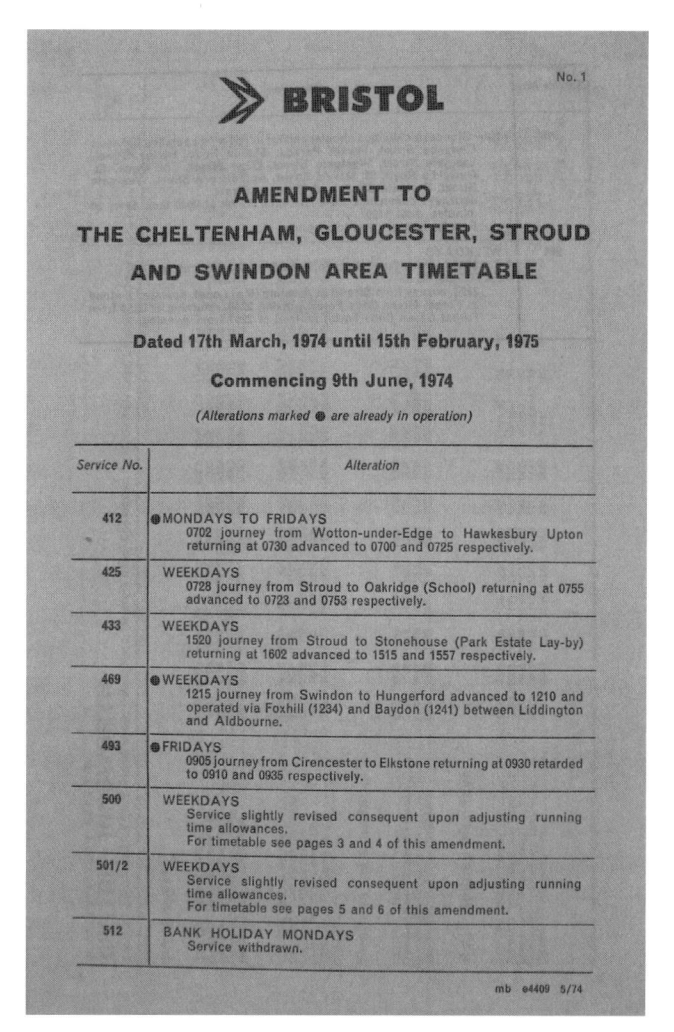

At the 15th October BJS meeting the committee agreed their 1976 vehicle requirement of 28 VRT double-deckers at a cost of £13,730 each (although, of course, the government would pay half of that amount under the Bus Grant scheme), but there was some bad news concerning the proposed exchange of buses with the Scottish group. The General Manager reported that whilst the Scottish company's initial reaction to the transfer of 35 FLF buses from Joint Services had been favourable, they had subsequently indicated that they preferred vehicles with Gardner 6LX engines, which were rather more powerful that those fitted to the Joint Services buses, and that they did not wish to continue with the transfer. Of course, the Scottish group's antipathy to the Bristol engine in both its AVW and BVW form was well known, and whilst the majority of the Joint Services FLFs were fitted with the BVW unit, it does seem likely that an internal swap could have been made within the company so that Gardner-engined vehicles were sent to Scotland. Even so, this would have resulted in FLFs being offered with the less powerful 6LW Gardner unit. With perhaps some anxiety at seeing the opportunity to make further, cost-cutting, one-man conversions slipping from his grasp, the chairman of the meeting suggested that the SMT Co Ltd (the first minute that had mentioned the name of the Scottish company involved) might be prepared to change their mind after a visit to the city of Bristol to see the type of operation on which Joint Services vehicles were engaged, and the General Manager agreed to approach the SMT Co accordingly. However, at the subsequent meeting in December it was reported that he had again been in correspondence with the SMT Co and that they had effected the exchange from within their own group.

As was much publicised at the time, elsewhere in NBC an exchange of no fewer than 106 Bristol FLFs had already been arranged for a similar number of Scottish VRTs, but this did not involve Bristol Omnibus. It is also not entirely certain which Scottish company Bristol was dealing with. References to SMT (Scottish Motor Traction) are somewhat ambiguous, since the original SMT had become better known as 'Scottish Omnibuses Ltd' during the 1960s and in any case traded under the 'Eastern Scottish' name. There were also 'Central SMT' and 'Western SMT' companies: all had been involved in the earlier Bristol FLF/VRT exchange, and all had Daimler Fleetlines at the time of the discussions, so precisely which operator was involved is not clear.

For the time being at least, the Bristol Omnibus Company was not to operate Daimler Fleetlines, and in a further blow to the Joint Services, the General Manager went on to report that the 1975 replacement programme for 30 double-deck VRTs could not be met by the manufacturer and that only seven of the BJS order would be delivered. However, an additional five double-deckers were obtained as a result of diverting an order from Maidstone & District Motor Services Ltd, which would slightly enhance the 1974 delivery programme.

The prospect of a delay in conversions to one-man operation in the city was not helped by the fact that the estimated loss on Joint Services was now more than £400,000 for 1974 and projected to be over £900,000 in 1975, principally because of the recent pay award that had again been dictated by the changes to the Retail Price Index. This meant further fare rises were inevitable. However, it was reported that at the previous fares application public hearing, the Traffic Commissioners had cited Section 203 of the 1972 Local Government Act and the need for discussion between the operator and local authorities. Unfortunately, whilst every effort had been made to interest the new Avon County Council in appointing a representative to sit on the recently constituted Traffic Operations and Fares Working Committee, to date there had been no positive response. Concern was expressed that co-operation from Avon County Council was not forthcoming.

It must have been difficult for the Bristol City councillors to have accepted the involvement of this new local authority, as previously matters were dealt with entirely within the City and County of Bristol. Nevertheless, the committee agreed to write again to the county, with a copy to the Secretary of State, since without the new authority's involvement the Traffic Commissioners might not grant the proposed fares increase, which would have devastating consequences on the financial performance of the Joint Services.

1975

The 36-vehicle Cheltenham District fleet had been rapidly repainted into poppy red within two years, resulting in the claim that it was the first NBC fleet to be completely repainted in the new corporate colours. However, in January 1975, Cheltenham District RELL 1043 was repainted again at the Lawrence Hill paint shops – this time into standard NBC green with the Cheltenham name but no longer displaying a coat of arms. The remaining Cheltenham District buses then followed at an even faster rate, transforming it into an entirely green fleet by the end of the year. Consequently, not only had Cheltenham's town buses lost their individuality, but they had also received two complete re-paints in less time than the parent Bristol fleet had received one.

Bristol-built buses once more made an appearance among the new arrivals for 1975, which comprised ten VRT double-deckers and eight LH single-deckers. The double-deckers consisted of four single-door, 70-seat versions with Gardner engines (the first single-door VRTs in the fleet) and six of the two-door variant (two for Cheltenham District, their first double-deckers for nine years and first new green buses ever; and four for Joint Services). The two-door buses were of the new VRT Series 3 design with 'quiet pack' rear end to reduce engine and transmission noise. Furthermore, they were fitted with the vertical version of Leyland's 501 engine, which resulted in a very un-VR like sound. The single-doorway versions, numbered 5500 to 5503, entered service at Weston-super-Mare depot as crew-operated buses on town services 108/109 between the town centre and the Bournville Estate where, being operated with a conductor, their rear-mounted route number blinds

Bristol's first batch of single-door, ECW-bodied, 70-seat Bristol VRT double-deckers were initially allocated to Weston-super-Mare. 1975 bus 5502 (HTC 728N) is two-man operated on town services 108/109 in this February 1976 view. (*M.S. Curtis*)

were actually used for a while before being painted or panelled over. These particular buses were intended to be used to convert the Weston-super-Mare allocation on the busy Weston to Bristol service from one-man single-deckers to double-deckers (the half-hourly basic service required four vehicles from Weston depot, with one operating from Bristol), but in the event negotiations with the trade union representatives reached a sticking point on the rate of pay to be offered. Existing national agreements called for a 15% enhancement on the basic rate of pay for the operation of single-deck buses on rural and non-urban services, 20% for single-deckers used on urban routes or double-deckers used on rural and non-urban services, and, as has previously been stated, 25% for double-deckers on urban services. Whilst the trade union had been happy to accept that the busy Bristol service from Weston was paid at the 15% enhancement whilst single-deckers were used, they argued that if the service was busy enough to need double-deckers then this inter-urban route should be re-classified as urban and paid at the 25% enhancement; the company, not wishing to create a precedent, did not agree. Consequently, it was to be another few years before one-man double-deckers were allocated to this route (after the company conceded the point on rates of pay), and the VRs soon moved away from Weston. Two of them were dispatched on loan to the Cheltenham fleet in September to inaugurate one-man, double-deck operation in that town on service 590, as delivery of their own centre-exit examples had been delayed until October. Two returned to Weston in due course to inaugurate OMO double-deck operation at the depot with a peak-hour journey on service 123, operating between Clevedon and Weston-super-Mare. This included a heavily loaded, but short-distance school movement within Weston's boundary which required duplication if it was not a double-decker. This pathfinder journey was soon followed by the conversion of a vehicle working on the Weston to Bridgwater service that carried peak loads of school children to and from the King Alfred School at Burnham-on-Sea; there was no argument from the trade union representatives on the payment of the 20% enhancement for these vehicle workings since they were conceded as being principally rural services. The Weston allocation of these early VRs went on to operate on busy Weston-super-Mare cross town service 105 where their lack of power steering soon proved to be unpopular.

The new lightweight LH buses differed from the six delivered in 1972 in having manual gearboxes and power steering, and interior trim to the latest National Bus

Company standard of brown and tan, including vinyl seat coverings – hardly the most welcoming for passengers.

Even though it had become the standard, heavyweight single-deck bus for the fleet, an eclectic mix of Leyland Nationals appeared during the year. Bristol Joint Services received nine 11.3 metre-long, dual-doorway, 44-seat buses, whilst Cheltenham District received two 44-seat, single-door, 10.3 metre ones, a seeming break from previous practice that OMO operation on urban services should use dual-doorway buses. A further sixteen 44-seat, 10.3 metre buses entered the country services fleet, while a new variant for the company was the 52-seat, 11.3 metre version, of which it received eight examples. Part way through the delivery of the single-door buses, the company changed its fleet numbering scheme. These buses had been numbered within the 14xx block, but a new series from 550 onwards was introduced for the shorter model (following on from the RESL buses) and from 3010 onwards for the 52-seater, 11.3 metre buses (following the modernised LSs), with single-door buses originally numbered in the old series, being re-numbered to conform to the new arrangements.

In June 1975 Frank Pointon, who for the past three years had been NBC's Southern Regional Director (following another change of regional boundaries), attended the Bristol Joint Services Committee and gave them further bad news. He indicated to the meeting the financial position of the National Bus Company and that no further subsidies would be available from Central Government. He explained that the only courses of action available to improve the finances of the Joint Services would be to drastically cut services, increase fares or obtain whatever grants were available from the local authority. The council members decided they should ask representatives from the Resources and Coordinating Committee to join them for a special meeting the following month, the result of which was the submission of a document to the next Joint Services Committee detailing proposals for reducing services to ensure the undertaking's financial viability. A discussion document was also tabled based on reducing off-peak fares so as actually to encourage growth in traffic, or at least to return passenger carryings to previous levels.

At the August meeting the general manager pointed out that the likely deficit would reach over £950,000 for the current year if no fares increase was forthcoming, although an increase proposed for introduction during October 1975 could yield over £1 million. This would return the Joint Services to a break-even situation.

The November BJS meeting considered proposals to cut 40 peak vehicles from the network, almost 10% of the fleet, incorporating depot staff reliefs where possible so that a further saving could be made in central area supervision and facilities. However, it was also reported that an increase in National Insurance contributions would cost the Joint Services a further £750,000, which, with a shortfall in the vehicle replacement fund, would actually yield a full year loss of over £1 million, of which the proposed vehicle reductions would only save £25,000. Subsequently, their was a wage award to the staff and so another fares increase was inevitable, proposed for February 1976, with the suggestion that children's fares should be abolished during peak periods. It was reported to the December meeting that news of this untenable situation had leaked to the press, and, as a result, the company and the City Council were getting a very rough ride indeed from the media.

On a lighter note, 1975 was a year when both a VR and an RE joined the fleet of FLFs painted into all-over advertisement colour schemes, whilst a number of the 1968 batch of RELH coaches were downgraded to dual-purpose status and repainted from National white express livery to the NBC green and white semi-coach colours, only to be repainted back into National coach livery in 1977; and revert to green and white in 1979. Over this period various directives were received from National Travel which sought to stop 'local coach' liveried vehicles entering Victoria Coach Station in London, designed to discourage the use of vehicles beyond a certain age on these services.

Sadly during May 1975, Bath driver Ray Cormack was killed and his LD bus L8516 destroyed when it was hit by a falling tree at Corsham in Wiltshire during a violent storm (*see below*). Later that year, in a moving ceremony at Bath Bus Station, Traffic Superintendent Mike Penny unveiled a plaque to commemorate the incident and drew attention to the risks taken by the platform staff every day of their working lives. At the time of writing, the plaque is in store awaiting the building of the new Bath bus station.

(*Wiltshire Fire Brigade Museum*)

1976

This was a bumper year for new vehicle deliveries, with the manufacturers catching up on delays in fulfilling previous years' orders. There was a mixture of single-deckers and double-deckers, buses and coaches, comprising 108 vehicles. The year also saw out the last of a particularly stalwart and traditional type of bus.

The largest component of the year's intake consisted of VRT double-deckers, of the now standard Series 3 design. Forty-five dual-doorway versions joined the BJS fleet (five of which were those diverted from Maidstone and District), with three each for the Cheltenham District and Gloucester city fleets. Nine of the BJS buses were fitted with the Leyland 501 power unit, the remaining two-doorway vehicles having the Gardner 6LXB. In addition, 12 were single-door 70-seat models, five of which received the 501-series engine with the remainder having the Gardner unit.

Part way through this batch, power steering was introduced to the intake of VR buses, an event which was to throw into sharp focus the fact that previous deliveries were not so fitted, with dire consequences to the operation of Bristol City services. Heavily loaded Bristol VRTs could be extremely difficult to steer if not fitted with power steering, and such 'heavy' steering was to prove a problem not just for the growing number of female drivers, but for a great many staff. The extent of this problem could vary considerably from vehicle to vehicle but became the cause of these buses being 'blacked' by staff towards the end of the decade until the matter was resolved. Until retro-fitting of earlier VRTs with power steering was put in hand, this problem caused more vehicle shortages during a period when BJS could least afford further unreliability and the resultant loss of revenue. Bristol Omnibus was not alone in suffering this problem, as other NBC operators of Bristol VRTs experienced similar difficulties.

One of the single-door buses, 5507, was also to encounter a far more serious problem, as it was destroyed by a fire on the outskirts of Bath in July 1983, the aluminium melting into the blackened tarmac road surface, marking the point of its destruction for a considerable time thereafter.

As may be expected, heavy-duty, single-deck buses were of the Leyland National type. All but one were 52-seat, single-doorway vehicles, five of which were for Gloucester city services, again breaking with the newly established tradition that urban services should receive dual-doorway OMO buses. The one exception was a 48-seat, centre-exit vehicle for Joint Services that was the prototype for the 'Phase 11' version of the Leyland National and was delivered in all-over white

Cheltenham District 5045 (LEU 270P), a 1976 ECW-bodied, twin-door Bristol VRT, operating Cheltenham town services during the following year. (*M.S. Curtis*)

177

with a rear route number box. Before entering service in the city, C1800, as it was numbered, lost four seats to allow the installation of a luggage pen, had its rear number box hurriedly painted over (it was said before Council members on BJS saw it, as they had been led to believe Leyland Nationals were not available with rear route displays), and was repainted into standard National green, making it virtually indistinguishable from the other Joint Services Leyland Nationals.

Conversion of routes from crew to one-man operation continued with these new vehicle deliveries, although as a reflection of sex equality, the term 'OMO' was gradually replaced throughout the bus industry by the term 'driver operated' or 'one-person operated' (OPO) as the decade progressed. By this time, the company had also appointed its first lady Inspector, Mrs Valerie Turner, who had earlier been a conductress before passing her PSV driving test.

Lightweight single-deckers arrived during 1976 in the shape of 25 Bristol LH buses (powered by Leyland 401 engines) with standard Eastern Coach Works 43-seat bodies, all but one of which were withdrawn after only six years service, although they were to find willing purchasers (the company in any case considered that the lightweight LH should have a maximum life of only seven years). Fleet number 373, however, was retained by the company and converted into a towing lorry, carrying the works number W108. This was a most unlikely conversion considering the lightweight nature of the chassis, and in this form it passed to the newly formed Badgerline company in 1986, notably with the addition of several very heavy weights along the top of the floor to improve adhesion.

The remaining new arrivals were three Leyland Leopard coaches with Plaxton coach bodies for National express services, this time seating 49. As usual, these were later downgraded to green and white semi-coaches (in 1981) but once again proved unpopular on bus services, particularly because of the cab arrangement. One, however, was specially lettered for the 1981 re-launch of the Bristol to Gloucester express bus service, 820, before again being repainted into a revised local coach livery, and National Express livery.

A further Ford bus came on loan during the year, appearing at Stroud for a day in July and then for a week in November. YHA 309J was a Plaxton 45-seat R192 that had been borrowed from the neighbouring Midland Red company and was used on local services in the area.

Weston-super-Mare open-top Lodekka buses lost their familiar cream during the year as they were repainted into a variety of colours each loosely recalling

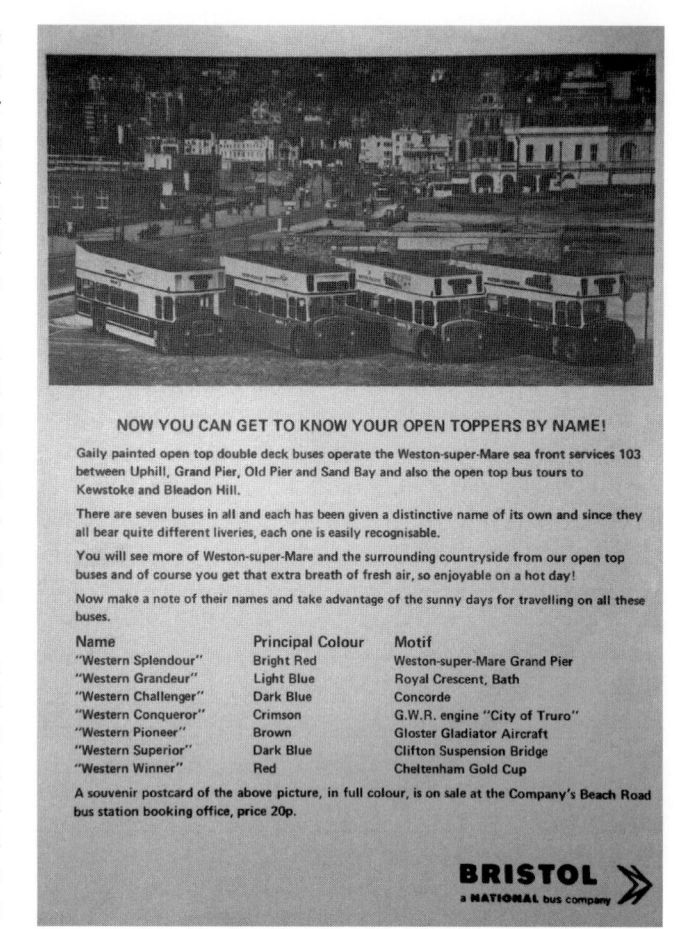

NOW YOU CAN GET TO KNOW YOUR OPEN TOPPERS BY NAME!

Gaily painted open top double deck buses operate the Weston-super-Mare sea front services 103 between Uphill, Grand Pier, Old Pier and Sand Bay and also the open top bus tours to Kewstoke and Bleadon Hill.

There are seven buses in all and each has been given a distinctive name of its own and since they all bear quite different liveries, each one is easily recognisable.

You will see more of Weston-super-Mare and the surrounding countryside from our open top buses and of course you get that extra breath of fresh air, so enjoyable on a hot day!

Now make a note of their names and take advantage of the sunny days for travelling on all these buses.

Name	Principal Colour	Motif
"Western Splendour"	Bright Red	Weston-super-Mare Grand Pier
"Western Grandeur"	Light Blue	Royal Crescent, Bath
"Western Challenger"	Dark Blue	Concorde
"Western Conqueror"	Crimson	G.W.R. engine "City of Truro"
"Western Pioneer"	Brown	Gloster Gladiator Aircraft
"Western Superior"	Dark Blue	Clifton Suspension Bridge
"Western Winner"	Red	Cheltenham Gold Cup

A souvenir postcard of the above picture, in full colour, is on sale at the Company's Beach Road bus station booking office, price 20p.

BRISTOL a NATIONAL bus company

a livery of one of the former tramway undertakings in the company's area and given a name representing the town or city associated with the livery. The new liveries and names were the result of a competition among staff designed to change the identity of the open-top fleet, but to many the loss of their distinctive and distinguished cream livery was a retrograde step, not least because it allowed them to be seen approaching from a great distance on Weston's seafront. When the K-type 8583 re-entered service in 1978 it retained Tilling cream livery, and local management ensured that the subsequent arrival of rear-engined, open-top buses reverted to the long established cream, although they wore a paler shade than applied to the Bristols. One open-top bus which was never to receive the cream livery however, arrived at Weston during that summer in the shape of former BJS Bristol-engined FLF C7148; this bus had sustained accidental roof damage when it collided with a low bridge in Bristol, so was converted for service at Weston, renumbered 7900. Local management were keen to operate 70-seat, open-top buses, particularly on the town tour, since more upper deck seats could be offered for the same crew costs, but 7900 was to remain unique, despite the fact that fleet number plates were produced for 7901 and subsequent vehicles. 7900 also became a TV star (it must be something to do with Weston-super-Mare) as it featured in an edition of the evening news and magazine programme *Nationwide* that was broadcast from the town, with comedian Richard Stilgoe dressed in a Tilling summer jacket, carrying a Setright ticket machine and cash bag and singing a song that bemoaned the lot of a bus conductor!

Withdrawals from the fleet during the year were significant, with the departure of the first FLF, C7000 – after 17 years service – and the first of the LS 're-builds', bus number 3000. The end of an era was marked when the last of the KSWs also left the fleet, a small number of which had soldiered on, particularly on busy Joint Services 73 and 74 that ploughed up and down the congested Gloucester Road (services that had been modified following surveys undertaken earlier in the decade, the result of which had been to break some of the cross-Bristol routes in the centre in an attempt to improve reliability on either side of the city). The oldest KSW withdrawn during the summer of 1976 had achieved 20 years of continuous service, eight years longer than originally intended. When the last KSWs were delivered in 1957 the type accounted for almost three-quarters of the Joint Services fleet, and became synonymous with the operation of Bristol City services during the fifties and sixties.

1976 was not to be a happy year, though, for Bristol Joint Services. Whilst the fares increase to be implemented early in the year would result in a considerable reduction in the deficit, and the proposed vehicle reduction would substantially lower costs, at the January BJS meeting further additional costs of over £650,000 were highlighted, and relationships between Bristol City Council and the new Avon County Council were getting no better. It was reported that, in relation to public transport matters within the city, and despite proposing a financial grant towards the city services as part of their responsibilities, Avon refused to accept Bristol City Council as a Joint Public Transport operator – notwithstanding the 1937 Act and the latter's role as a 50% shareholder in BJS. Until this matter could be resolved, allowing the city to be involved in public transport discussions with Avon in their capacity as operator, the city members of the committee stated that they could not support the fares increase. This was intended to yield £625,000, even accounting for a 3% loss in passengers, to reduce the current deficit. Councillors indicated that they would be prepared to take their concerns to the Traffic Commissioners if necessary. It was thus reported that the Joint Services deficit would in part be absorbed by the Avon grant, even though this appeared to be contrary to its condition of payment.

In addition to the previously reported leaks to the press, the General Manager now stated that the press were speculating whether the 1937 agreement might be terminated. Although the company had made no such suggestion, it had subsequently received a request from the city to consider such a move, and it was agreed to set up a sub-committee to look at this possibility. It seems that the city saw the termination of the agreement as their way out of the conflict of wanting to provide a cheap and reliable public transport service, whilst remaining a 50% shareholder in an operation that was suffering from declining use and rising costs, with the inevitable pressure to break even from both their fellow shareholders and Avon County Council.

At the April meeting, Avon seemed to have driven a further wedge between itself and the city, when it was reported that they intended to finance and introduce an experimental limited stop service into Bristol, but of which the City Council had no knowledge. There were now three people in this marriage! It was also reported that, in accordance with its requirements under the 1972 Act, the company had submitted its bid to all the local counties for inclusion in the newly introduced Transport Policy and Programmes. This was an arrangement by which counties were to consolidate all aspects of transport, such as traffic management, road building and public transport, into one single document which would then be submitted to central government for consideration of future spending requirements. As part of this, the company had notified the authority of a possible operating deficit within Bristol of over £1,100,000.

There was better news at the June meeting. It was reported that as a result of planned service reductions, staff problems had at last been overcome, with a shortage of only 16 drivers in the city for an establishment of 800; whilst there was a surplus of 50 conductors (as a result of the trade union being against compulsory redundancies in the pursuit by the company of further one-person operation). Dave Bubier comments that during his period as a Joint Services Inspector the continuing switch to one-person operation brought the staff position under control, and that one evening the astonishing news was broken by one of his colleagues: 'We have every journey covered.' The downside, he recalls, was that fares had risen at six-monthly intervals to the point where the passenger drain was noticeable.

> Having spent some weeks in the depot I went on my Westbury beat one morning to find half-empty buses, no queues, but delays because of car traffic jams across the Downs. I was convinced then that the bus industry was in terminal decline.

In addition to the improvement in the staff shortage, it was revealed that the further fares increase (which had presumably been introduced against the wishes of the city) would yield over £580,000 in a full year, and whilst still looking at further opportunities to save running costs, the company would consider the possibility of substituting standee vehicles for double-deckers.

However, management may not have taken into account that the trade union would seek the double-deck rate of pay for operating high capacity single-deckers (a matter that certainly came to a head at one country depot in the early eighties) as subsequently there was no let up in the delivery of new double-deckers.

When the BJS committee met in December 1976, the company reported that a further fares increase was proposed for February the following year with an anticipated yield of £283,000, but, once again, the city members of the committee stated that they would not support the increase without a meeting with Avon. They again hoped to convince the county to support the city financially and, of course, resolve their outstanding differences. This statement allowed NBC's Frank Pointon to deliver his trump card: the company would be unwilling to take over the entire operation of Bristol Joint Services if a further deficit resulted from the City Council delaying an application for this fares increase. It appeared the dissolution of the agreement was now imminent with discussions progressing on the basis that a financial settlement between company and corporation could be achieved by transferring the ownership of the buses to the company and the property to the corporation. The company could then lease back those premises they required to continue operations.

1977

The regional structure of NBC seemed to be constantly changing, with yet another review taking effect during 1977, which resulted in Bristol finding itself in the centre of the new Midlands and West Region. Four regions were created from this point, with companies arranged in quite different groups to those which had applied the year before. This represented the fourth 'regionalisation' scheme for NBC, an organisation that had only existed for eight years.

A change of General Manager also occurred during the year when Ken Wellman, who had previously held management positions at Bristol during the 1960s, returned to the company to succeed Richard Roberts.

1977 saw another large intake of vehicles, again split between heavy- and lightweight and between double- and single-deckers. Thirty-three VRs joined the fleet, 25 with 70-seat, dual-doorway bodywork, 15 of which were for Joint Services, eight for Gloucester City and two for Cheltenham District (to be their last new double-deck buses); the remaining eight were single-door 74-seaters. All were delivered with the favoured Gardner 6LXB power unit. Twenty of the single-deckers were again Leyland Nationals, six being 44-seat, two-doorway buses for Joint Services with the remainder being 52-seat, single-door examples, of which three were for Cheltenham District and two for Gloucester City – it seems that the norm for one-man urban operation outside of Bristol was for double-deckers to have two doors, whilst single-deckers could be one-person operated with only one door. One of the Joint Services buses, Leyland National C1456, was exhibited on the Leyland stand at the 1976 Commercial

Gloucester's G5090 (NWS 287R), a 1977 two-door, 70-seat Bristol VRT, seen in January 1978, displays the National logo, the Gloucester fleetname and the city crest, although they have been placed on the between decks panel because of the limited space available between the front wheel and centre doors. (*M.S. Curtis*)

BJS Leyland National C1456 (NWS903R) had been exhibited at the 1976 Commercial Motor Show, and was the second Leyland National to carry that number, the original bus being a 44-seat, 10.3-metre bus that was renumbered 556 in 1975. The bus entered service in the silver livery in which it was exhibited, and was also an advertisement for the company's Rover Cards and Fare Cards, in addition to the Silver Jubilee insignia. (*M.S. Curtis*)

Motor Show in silver livery. It entered service in 1977 in this livery, initially working in Cheltenham for two years where, being dual-door, it often ran for the Cheltenham District company. Appropriately, in view of its silver livery, this bus became the first of three company vehicles used to celebrate the Silver Jubilee of Her Majesty Queen Elizabeth II. Advertising was also carried by this vehicle promoting the company's Fare Card and Rovercard off-bus ticketing range.

Eighteen lightweight Bristol LH saloons of the now standard 43-seat layout formed the remaining single-deck bus arrivals, many of which lasted in the fleet for only four years before being rendered surplus to requirements by service reductions resulting from the Market Analysis Project (or MAP). MAP was a process by which National Bus Company subsidiaries identified their viable service network, following very detailed surveys of every journey operated.

One LH, number 404, followed 373 in being adapted as a towing vehicle, although in this case the conversion was not nearly so drastic, the bus simply being fitted with a towing hook at the rear whilst remaining in the operational bus fleet. It subsequently carried the fleet number W404.

Two more Plaxton-bodied Leyland Leopard 49-seat coaches also joined the fleet during the year: they were delivered in National white livery but received the Kingfisher blue and pale blue striped local coach livery in 1983. One of them, PWS 492S, had its body destroyed by fire during that same year and, as a result, received a new Plaxton Paramount 3200 body.

Over-all advertisement buses continued to make their debut, and while these were usually double-deckers, they included a Joint Services RE extolling the virtues of Fare Cards and Rovercards.

In addition, two very distinguished silver double-deckers joined the Leyland National in celebrating the Queen's Silver Jubilee, one being a country services VR and the other a Joint Services FLF. These double-deckers were made available to most depots during the Jubilee year, and co-author Mike Walker, by then District Traffic Superintendent at Weston-super-Mare, ensured that the silver VR was at his depot for Her Majesty's visit to Weston in July. When the Queen alighted from her official car on the sea front, the VR was parked on the depot forecourt where it was in full view of the Royal party.

A number of 'used' vehicles came into the fleet during the year, some for service and others not. The Thames Valley & Aldershot Omnibus Company (Alder Valley) supplied five 43-seat, ECW-bodied, LH buses, which, with their Leyland engines and manual transmission, were mechanically similar to the majority of those already operated by the company, but featured an earlier, slightly narrower body style incorporating a flat front. They were numbered in the series preceding the company's first new LHs (as 346 to 350) and were allocated across the company's operating area. They were all withdrawn within two years, one of them following two previous company LHs in becoming a towing vehicle – but this time for Citybus in Hong Kong.

The Daimler Fleetline finally made an entrance – of sorts – into the fleet, following the failed Scottish exchange of three years earlier. Six Daimler Fleetline double-deckers were acquired, two from City of Oxford and four from the Potteries Motor Traction Company. However, these were bought for chassis spares only, their Gardner engines and rear axles being considered of particular use in the VR fleet, as Bristol Omnibus decided to conduct trials by installing old Fleetline rear axles into

(*above*) 1969 Bristol city services ECW-bodied, 44-seat Bristol RELL C1138 received an overall advertisement for the company's Fare Card pre-purchased, multi-journey tickets in January 1976, and carried this red, white and blue livery for just over two and a half years. (*M.S. Curtis*)

(*below*) Country services single-door Bristol VRT 5512 (LHT 722P) of 1976 was painted for Her Majesty's Silver Jubilee in 1977, and spent some time at a number of the company's depots. In this January 1977 view the bus is operating on Joint Services route 88 across the Downs. (*M.S. Curtis*)

346 (VMO 227H) was already eight years old when it was acquired from the Thames Valley & Aldershot company (Alder Valley) in 1977. It was a Bristol LH with a flat windscreen, ECW 43-seat body, and is seen heading across the Centre on service to nearby Nailsea, in Bristol's commuter belt, in November 1978. Along with the other four acquired at the same time, 346 was withdrawn in 1979. (*M.S. Curtis*)

VRTs, to compare their service performance. Having removed the required parts, the remains of the Daimlers were mostly sent to a local dealer and scrapped.

During 1977 the company borrowed two separate single-door VR double-deckers from neighbouring Western National, both of which came in exchange for Bristol Omnibus VRs. This occurred in order that over-all advert buses could be seen over a much wider area, one from the Bristol fleet temporarily moving further west while those from the Western National fleet did the reverse, one of the latter returning again the following year.

Discussions towards the dissolution of Bristol Joint Services continued, but good housekeeping measures were still necessary, regardless of final ownership of the city services, and at the March BJS meeting it was agreed that unremunerative services would be examined more closely.

The City Council representatives were still against any reduction in mileage however, while a further difficulty was the city's method of dealing with depreciation, which conflicted with the county's policy and gave Avon further grounds to withhold support. The Department of the Environment became involved in this argument later in the year.

Meanwhile, the demise of Bristol Joint Services was becoming noticeable on the streets to sharp-eyed observers. During the previous year new VRTs for Bristol Joint Services had arrived with standard NBC style 'BRISTOL' fleetnames rather than BJS markings, while from the summer of 1977 repainted city vehicles were similarly turned out with standard NBC names. After all the debates in earlier years over whether or not the city arms should be carried on BJS buses, it gradually began to disappear, along with the 'Bristol' scroll.

Meanwhile, the Joint Committee was looking for further additional revenue if approved by the Traffic Commissioners while it was also reported that Avon had included £600,000 for revenue support for the whole of the county in 1977/1978 of which just £115,000 was for Bristol Joint Services.

The committee continued to look into the future, however, and at the December Joint Services meeting agreed to the 1979 rolling stock programme. A further 28 VRT double-deckers were sought, now costing almost £33,000 each, less, of course, the government grant. All sides must have known, however, that the committee probably wouldn't exist by the time these vehicles were received and indeed the City Clerk reported on this possibility, with agreement reached that independent property valuers would be engaged to assess the relevant properties. On this basis, a five-year profit and loss forecast was to be made in order to test the implications of the committee's break up. And it seemed nothing was too minor for discussion, with the point made that whatever happened to Bristol Joint Services, the clock on the Centre outside the mock Tudor offices was already safe in the city's ownership.

1978

By the time new vehicle deliveries commenced in 1978 another minor livery change had begun to occur throughout the entire fleet. This concerned the NBC double N symbol which, in line with a new directive to be followed countrywide, was now applied in red and blue within a white box, matching the version carried by the white coaches. Previously, this symbol had usually appeared in white (affixed directly to the green paintwork). Although this was a relatively minor modification, it was surprisingly effective in brightening up what were otherwise fairly dull livery styles.

Once more a mixture of Bristols and Leylands joined the fleet: double-deckers were again all of the VRT Series 3 model with the by now ubiquitous Gardner 6LXB engine, 13 being dual-doorway 70-seaters (ten of which were for Joint Services) while four were single-door versions with 74 seats. Bristol-built single-deckers comprised another 26 of the 43-seat LH type, delivered only one year before the first of the LHs were withdrawn. Indeed, 15 of this newly delivered batch were themselves to last only three years, with the majority withdrawn by 1984. Only two survived long enough to be transferred to the new Badgerline fleet where they were to act as minibus 'spares'. The arrival of the 1978 LH buses also displaced the last rebuilt LS types, ending the experiment that saw these buses refurbished and brought up to date to allow for an extended life.

Leyland provided 28 vehicles, 25 of which were more Leyland Nationals, all 52-seat, single-door versions numbered in the 3000-series, including five for Gloucester city operations (which continued to receive G-prefixes to their fleet numbers). Two of the Leyland Nationals (nos. 3061/2) were for Cheltenham: 3061 carried 'Cheltenham' fleetnames and was destined to be the last new vehicle so delivered. Sister vehicle 3062 was delivered with 'Bristol' names, signalling the end for another segment of Bristol's activities.

A number of the VRs and Leyland Nationals delivered during the year went on to receive over-all advertisements later in their lives, whilst in a strange vehicle exchange, six 1978 Leyland Nationals (3053-55 and 3064-66) were effectively swapped with sister NBC subsidiary Hants & Dorset Motor Services the following year, the latter taking over their leases while a similar number of Leyland Nationals passed to Bristol. The vehicles did not actually move between companies at all but the Bristol buses received Hants & Dorset legal lettering while the Hants & Dorset buses, conversely, received Bristol's company name and address. It is believed this was done for financial reasons, as transferring ownership responsibilities from one company to the other ensured that lease payments on the vehicles could be met more easily.

The remaining three new vehicles from Leyland were 49-seat, Plaxton-bodied Leopards with Supreme Express bodywork, featuring two-piece folding doors, whilst a number of secondhand Alexander-bodied Leopard coaches, together with a Bristol LH from Hants & Dorset, were acquired and stripped for spares parts.

Two further vehicles, both Fords, came from Hants & Dorset for short periods during the early part of the year for evaluation: one was a Plaxton 43-seat, bus-bodied R1014 and the other an Alexander 27-seat, bus-bodied A-series – the latter is recorded as spending only a day at Bristol, but the full-size bus stayed for up to a month.

A poignant event during the year was the company's departure from its offices at St Augustine's Parade, or 'on the Centre' as it was more often described. These offices were known to every Bristolian and had been occupied by the company for over 80 years. They contributed towards the area being popularly known first as the 'Tramways Centre' and then simply as 'The Centre' although no official map includes either title. First acquired in 1896, from 1935 these premises succeeded nearby Clare Street House to become the company's Head Office, as which they remained until themselves replaced in that role by Berkeley House in 1970. With their mock Tudor façade, from which was suspended the famous company clock, they remained among the most recognised buildings in Bristol.

At Bristol Joint Services, matters were reaching a conclusion. During the January committee meeting it was reported that the full year 1977 operating loss was just over £131,000 on a turnover of over £7.5 million – close to break-even but not close enough. Labour councillors continued to oppose any fare increases despite further forecast losses and a planned wage increase for staff. The councillors sought a further meeting with the Secretary of State, this time at regional level, to resolve the difference of opinion as to the use of replacement depreciation in grant calculations.

All sides clearly had difficulties in suggesting how the losses should be covered. As a way out of the impasse, John Hargreaves, the latest NBC Regional Director, proposed giving urgent consideration to making the Joint Services undertaking financially self-supporting. As is often the way with council bodies, and in the hope of finding a previously unexplored solution, it was agreed that a Transportation Steering Group should be set up to examine the whole transport scene in Bristol, comprising leading members and officers of the City Council, Avon County Council and the company.

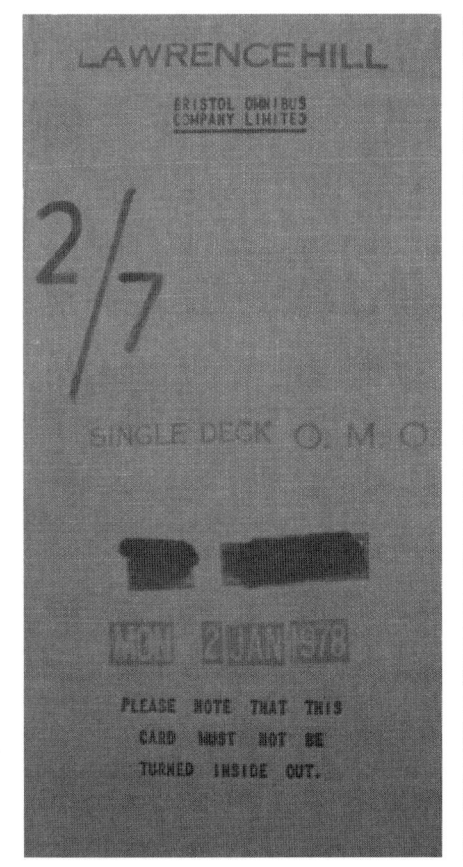

A 1978 bus duty card for bus 2 on services 7 and 8 from Lawrence Hill depot. Encircled times were added by staff to show their changeovers.

Among items considered at the April committee meeting was a grant from the Urban Aid Fund that had been approved to provide a bespoke, experimental service to the deprived and difficult to access Windmill Hill area south of the city centre; the £5,100 estimated operating loss was to be borne in three equal parts by the Urban Aid Fund, Bristol Joint Services and Avon County Council. Despite the ongoing problems of network support for Joint Services, at least these three parties demonstrated they were able to work together on implementating service improvements on the ground.

Meanwhile, when deliberating further on the future of BJS, the committee heard Avon County's latest view; that it was 'not the right time to proceed [with the Transportation Steering Group] because of the possibility of the dissolution of the Joint Services agreement'.

Plans for new vehicles continued to receive attention, nevertheless, and it was noted that the 1979 vehicle programme was to cost £943,019 and had been amended to 23 VRT double-deckers and 5 Metrobuses, rather than the 28 VRTs discussed at a previous meeting. No further mention was made of the Metrobus double-deckers, nor indeed had they been previously mentioned in Joint Services minutes, but when they did arrive they were instead allocated to Bath and not Bristol – believed to be because they were built as single-door buses and not to the twin-door specification that the city trade union expected for driver-only operation. Council representatives appeared to have no influence over the Metrobuses since their inclusion followed the placing of an experimental order by the National Bus Company. Apart from the Bristol examples, other NBC Metrobuses would go to Maidstone & District, whose batch of five cancelled VRT double-deckers had been diverted to Bristol Joint Services a few years earlier.

Whilst financial problems prevailed, the BJS committee could congratulate itself on a number of operating statistics presented at the April meeting, detailing that in recent four-weekly periods, 99.5% of mileage was operated, despite the problems of traffic congestion, and that the number of conductors employed was almost up to establishment, although there remained a requirement for over 50 drivers, representing a shortfall of over 6%. Maintenance staff employed were up to or close to establishment in almost all grades. Not such good news however was that passenger numbers had again fallen by over 2.5% from the previous year, with passengers per mile falling from 3.79 in 1977 to 3.77 in 1978.

Discussions to finalise the end of Bristol Joint Services were eventually held during June when it was agreed to dissolve the 1937 agreement: a draft legal document had been prepared on behalf of the council to be submitted to the company, who in turn would be required to submit it to both the National Bus Company and the Secretary of State for their approval.

BJS finally ceased operations on 15th July 1978 with the company already closely examining any areas of overlap between the former Joint Services and their own, in an attempt to achieve greater flexibility and inter-working between city and country services. Within two months, it was announced that Hanham depot, located just outside the city boundary to the east, would be closed and services in the area revised to take account of the new situation.

The final meeting of the Bristol Joint Services Committee was held exactly one month later, on 15th August 1978. With the dissolution of the 1937 agreement, the City Council representatives stated that they wanted to set up a consultative committee between Avon County, the company and themselves to continue the close relationship that had existed for over 40 years. (They suddenly appeared concerned that they were about to lose their influence over individual services.) Whilst agreeing that this could indeed be further discussed, the company representatives stated they should have due regard for the wishes of Avon County Council, and that they were not in favour of altering any existing agreements. However, the company stated that it would always be prepared to meet with representatives of the City Council if requested.

This meeting was held at one of Bristol's premier restaurants (The Foster Rooms in Small Street) and it is presumed that the city councillors joined the company representatives afterwards over lunch to commiserate at their loss of more than four decades of influence in the running of bus services within their city.

Life went on, however, with Bristol's city bus services now completely under Bristol Omnibus Company ownership. The 'C' prefix to fleet numbers had been removed by the end of the month but, interestingly, it took over a year for the Bristol scroll and coat of arms to be completely replaced on the sides of city buses.

Although never before considered necessary, another change in 1978, which might have been taken for granted outside the bus industry, was that ignition keys were introduced for Bristol RE, VR and LH models (Leyland Nationals having already been delivered from new with this feature). All keys were identical, to enable drivers to transfer easily between vehicles, but they improved security following instances around the country – one in London in particular – where members of the public had climbed into a cab and driven away.

1979

In the final year of the decade, once again a mixture of Bristol and Leyland vehicles were added to the fleet, although on this occasion accompanied by two Fords.

The Fords were Transits supporting 17-seat Reeve Burgess bodies with high-backed seats. They took the fleet numbers 302 and 303, following on from the Transit used for the Bath tourist link. As part of local authorities' new responsibilities towards public transport, Gloucestershire County Council actually owned these two minibuses while the company ran them on their behalf to operate a group of services in and around Nailsworth, near Stroud, in areas that had earlier seen the operation of the small SUS buses and before that, the Bedford OBs. In common with many services within the company's operating area, these routes were considered to be uneconomic, and, again as a result of the Local Government Act, received grant aid from the local authority to enable them to continue as they were considered socially necessary. Brian Ede remembers the Transits:

> They must have been heavy – they were fitted with an overdrive switch lever – if you used overdrive they slowed down. They didn't look like Transits, but under the bonnet you could see the real Ford Transit inside.

A further ten VRs joined the fleet during the year, all being to the dual-doorway layout with Gardner 6LXB engines, and, although no longer identified as such, intended for operation on Bristol City services, the company of course now having much greater flexibility in being able to transfer buses around the area of operation at will. The remaining Bristol deliveries were once more 43-seat, Leyland-engined, Bristol LH single-deckers, most of which would serve the company for under three years before the service reductions of the early 1980s would see them sold off as surplus to requirements. One of them, 434, passed to the Weston-super-Mare depot Carnival Club. The autumn carnival season is a very important two weeks for towns in the southern outposts of the company's operating area; a time in which richly decorated and illuminated floats parade through each of the participating towns on successive nights. The season starts in Bridgwater and ends in Weston-super-Mare (although for a few years during the early eighties, it also extended to Bristol), with participants collecting for charities. Stroud was another depot which participated in its area's own series of carnivals, whilst immediately prior to Christmas, Bristol, Bath,

Stroud depot was the home of the two Reeve Burgess 17-seat Ford Transit minibuses supplied to the company by Gloucestershire County Council and painted in a yellow and green livery. 303 (VFB 189T) is seen here at Nailsworth in February 1979, a month after entering service; one can understand Brian Ede's comment on these buses, that the real Ford Transit was somewhere inside! (*M. Walker*)

Stroud and Weston staff regularly manned converted open-top double-deckers, festooned in coloured lights (usually powered by an on-board generator taking the place of the lower deck seats), to sing carols and collect for children's charities. This practice started in Bristol during the 1920s when a specially illuminated tram travelled over the network collecting for the Lord Mayor's fund, and was revived from 1969 with 'carol buses'. These were just some of the many ways in which staff at the company's depots worked together outside their normal duties both aiding local voluntary groups and cementing depot camaraderie. Before, during and after the Green Years staff throughout the operating area regularly organised competitions in chess, bowls, snooker, billiards, pool, darts, football, cricket and many other sports, often with inter-depot competitions. For many employees, not only at depots but also at the head office and even at BCV, the sports and social clubs were an important part of company life which, in addition to the sporting events, organised dances, buffet evenings and outings whilst providing a welfare function that helped to support many an employee and their family during times of hardship. The 'Tramways Company' (or later the 'Bus Company') was not just an employer, to many it was also like a family. In fact, it was not uncommon at many depots for several members of one family to work for the company.

By 1979, of course, the VR double-decker and the LH single-decker were the only chassis being built by Bristol Commercial Vehicles that were available to the National Bus Company. The RE continued to be built for New Zealand and Northern Ireland but was not available to most UK customers in order to protect Leyland National sales. Ironically, the Bristol Omnibus Company therefore remained unable to buy the large single-decker model still being constructed in its own operating territory, by an associated company that had once been its chassis manufacturing department.

Two lengths of Leyland National were delivered during 1979, with ten of them being 11.3 metre, 52-seaters, two of which were destined for the Gloucester city fleet, and 15 being the short 44-seat, single-door version. These, however, were different from previous years' 10.3 metre Nationals, as they were of the newly introduced B series design. The B series was a less highly specified version of the bus intended, in due course, to replace the Bristol LH. One particular change was the replacement of the integral saloon heating and hot air circulation system with standard under-seat heaters, a change which meant that some drivers no longer felt it necessary to drive along with the doors open on hot days trying to reduce the saloon temperature, failing to appreciate that the resultant current of air reaching the saloon temperature sensors at the rear of the bus simply caused them to react by increasing the temperature! This was always a dilemma for drivers as, strictly speaking, their instructions required passenger doors to be closed while travelling, although on occasions intense saloon heat could itself result in passeners being overcome, in which case drivers attempted to increase ventilation.

The B-series Leyland Nationals and this year's delivery of LH buses were trimmed inside with the new pattern of orange patterned moquette seating, replacing the rather dour brown plastic covering that had previously been supplied as an NBC standard, and which continued to be fitted to the VR deliveries.

1975 44-seat, 10.3-metre Leyland National 568, which had been renumbered from 1468 when two months old, loading at Weston-super-Mare High Street whilst operating on town service 105 in August 1979. At the time, in common with many busy services, 105 was two-man operated during weekday daytimes and one-man operated at other less busy times. This both reduced operating costs and enabled the operating staff's take home pay to be increased by means of productivity bonuses. (*M. Walker*)

A short Bristol 35-seat LHS bus was borrowed from neighbouring Western National towards the end of the year and was tried for a week on Bristol's Windmill Hill Community Bus service, the route which accessed a very hilly inner city area towards the south of the centre that had been started using the Leyland/Ascough Clubman 17-seater. This was the little bus that had previously been transferred from Gloucester to Weston-super-Mare where it had inaugurated a demand-responsive service into another hilly suburb, that of Grove Park. However, the surprise secondhand purchases of the year were four low-height Leyland Atlantean PDR1/2 double-deckers that had been acquired from Hants & Dorset but which started life with the famous independent operator, King Alfred Motor Services. This was not the first time that the company had acquired Atlanteans from an independent company operating in the Hampshire/Wiltshire area, of course, as the Silver Star Atlanteans had preceded them by 16 years!

The Leyland National B series was initially easily recognised by the lack of a roof-mounted pod and the restyled front panel. 1979 bus 705 (VAE 504T), a 44-seat, 10.3-metre bus, was photographed whilst operating on the Bristol to Portishead service in June 1979. Despite being only four months old at the time, the bus does seem to be receiving the attention of company mechanics who have arrived in the Ford Transit van parked behind the bus. (*M.S. Curtis*)

By the end of the seventies, local management at Weston had been considering the conversion of the seafront open-top service to one-person operation, since the majority of buses operating the services were by now 18 years old, with the two former Crosville buses even older. Only the solitary FLF was newer by two years, and no more FLFs had followed. There had been talk of new convertible open-tops being acquired and, indeed, a batch of VRs so equipped had been built by ECW for NBC in 1977/1978, but the company held the view that time-expired, driver-only double-deckers would best fit the bill, since the normal seasonal increase in vehicle requirements at the seaside town could then be met quite simply by re-licencing the open-toppers during the summer months and de-licencing them for the winter. At that time, however, the Weston convertible open-toppers were released from ordinary service work during the summer months, by drafting in a selection of time-expired buses from other depots that would otherwise have been withdrawn, but which often required considerable mechanical attention to allow them to last the summer.

Attention was paid to the first generation of rear-engined, convertible open-toppers, the Devon General 'Sea Dog' Atlanteans, and although Bristol, as a fellow NBC subsidiary, might have claimed the buses at book value, none was available. There was also a suggestion by the company's engineering department that the first former Joint Services two-doorway VRs, C5002 to C5009, could be made available for conversion, but this also came to nothing.

Consequently, the former King Alfred Atlanteans joined the fleet with the intention of converting them for OPO seafront operation. In the event only three of the four were so converted, one of them by the Hants & Dorset company before the bus was despatched to Bristol. The fourth bus was never converted but instead was acquired by the Avon Fire Brigade to use for emergency practice, lasting long enough to be purchased by the Friends of King Alfred for preservation. Together with one of the open-top variants, it remains active in their historic fleet. The conversion of one bus, 8600, was completed by the end of the 1979 summer season, being painted all-over cream and sent to Weston for trials; agreement was reached with the trade union for the conversion of the seafront service to take place for the following season, even retaining a reverse terminal manoeuvre at the Uphill terminus (where the company agreed to arrange for a street light to be erected to allow the driver to see more clearly). The bus was put into service without a conductor (or a roof, of course) on the winter seafront and Sand Bay route 100, for a month or so to test out driver reaction, and was then returned to the Central Repair Works for the winter to have the first nearside window enlarged upwards (to improve the driver's view to the extreme left at a complicated junction at Kewstoke) and to be thoroughly waterproofed (operational experience had revealed that rain water on the top deck found an easy exit down the periscope hatch and into the drivers' lap when braking). The three buses, eventually converted to open-top, came back to Weston-super-Mare for the 1980 season, where driver-only, open-top operation was finally introduced, which will be dealt with in more detail in the next chapter.

Another innovation in the south of the company's area was to have a profound effect on the peak vehicle requirements of Weston depot in particular, and to some extent Marlborough Street in Bristol; the local authority covering the area of Avon south-west of Bristol, Woodspring District Council, introduced a cheap fares scheme for residents for which they budgeted £340,000 for the first year. Residents were able to purchase a photo pass which enabled them to travel after 9.00am (all day on Saturdays, Sundays and Public Holidays) from or to any point within the District Council area for a low flat fare, and on its introduction post-peak morning buses into Bristol from such places as Weston, Clevedon and Portishead became very full, often requiring many extra duplicate buses, so much so that at Weston the winter morning peak period shifted from before 9.00am to after 9.00am! *National Bus Company, 1968-1989* reports that the scheme was monitored by the NBC Research Department as well as by Avon County Council: some off-peak fares came down by as much as 75%, and 75% of residents bought the pass. Preliminary results from household travel diaries suggested that people were travelling both further and more often!

Of greater long term significance however, would be the political influence of a new Government. Although Labour had been in power since 1974 (having replaced Ted Heath's Conservative government), a General Election called during May 1979 saw Labour defeated. A new Conservative government took control, led by Britain's first woman prime minister, Margaret Thatcher. Her policies were to have a profound effect on British manufacturing industries generally, on the ownership and control of transport, and specifically on the structure of the National Bus Company and the conditions under which bus services would operate throughout the country. Although unknown at the time, these policies were to result in a total change to the composition of the Bristol Omnibus Company and, indirectly, to the end of the Green Years.

***

(*above*) 1958 ECW-bodied Bristol LD Lodekka G8459 (YHT 946), was transferred to the Gloucester fleet from Bath Electric Tramways Ltd when a year old. In this August 1975 view, the bus carries the Gloucester fleetname and coat of arms in addition to the National logo; it was withdrawn from service during the following year. (*M. Walker*)

(*below*) All of the 1960 batch of ECW-bodied Bristol FSF double-deckers were withdrawn from service in 1976; BJS C6014 (713 JHY) unloads at the Centre during its last year. (*M.S. Curtis*)

(*right*) Highbridge depot's last two-man crew, driver Jim Cottey and conductor Harold Lewis, at Bridgwater bus station ready to work a service 140 journey to Burnham-on-Sea with country services Bristol FLF 7190 of 1965. (*M. Walker*)

(*below*) 1966 ECW-bodied Bristol FLF 7275 (HHW 458D), photographed at the Whiteshill terminus of service 435 from Stroud in February 1979. The FLF driver would have experienced a continuous low-gear climb to reach Whiteshill, and then a reverse manoeuvre before descending the hill to return to Stroud, only to do the same again 30 minutes later! This tight scheduling at off-peak meant that service 435 remained two-man operated for a while even after the departure of the depot's last FLFs double-deckers the following month. (*M. Walker*)

(*above*) The outstation at Clevedon, on the Severn estuary, was for some time based in the local quarry. The operation was controlled by Bristol's Marlborough Street depot, and in January 1975 the two vehicles parked up here are refurbished Bristol LS 3006 (YHY 74) and 1963 Bristol MW 2580 (940 RAE) – both with ECW bodies. (*M. Walker*)

(*below*) 47-seat Bristol RELH dual-purpose 2044 (KHW 313E), of 1967, in Dursley, Gloucestershire, in August 1975, by which time its rich Tilling green and cream colour scheme had been replaced by the local coach livery of National green and white. (*M. Walker*)

(*right*) The little Leyland 440EA minibus with a 17-seat Ascough Clubman body, G402, later G301 (PHU 647M), was delivered in 1973 for use on a shoppers' service in Gloucester, By 1977 the bus had moved to Weston-super-Mare as 301, to operate the Grove Park Mini demand-responsive service to and from the north of the town, financially supported by Avon County Council and using specially selected drivers. The service departed from a bay at the front of the bus station, as seen here in April of 1977. (*M. Walker*)

(*left*) The Gloucestershire market town of Wotton-under-Edge boasted a small depot, serviced by the larger depot at Gloucester, and 1965 Bristol MW service bus 2615 is seen parked there in February 1979. By the early 1980s the depot had closed, a small number of the senior staff had transferred to a new outstation site in a nearby school playground, and the operation was controlled by Bristol's Marlborough Street depot – and, in fact, the outstation became the home for two double-deckers! 2615 itself had a history, as it had been a Joint Services bus until 1974. (*M. Walker*)

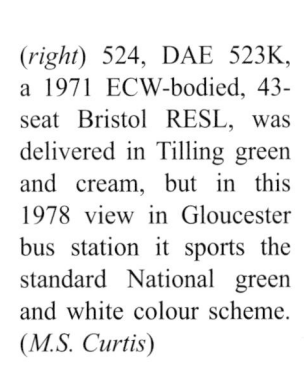

(*right*) 524, DAE 523K, a 1971 ECW-bodied, 43-seat Bristol RESL, was delivered in Tilling green and cream, but in this 1978 view in Gloucester bus station it sports the standard National green and white colour scheme. (*M.S. Curtis*)

(*above*) A standard Bristol LH bus was used to replace the Leyland 440EA minibus when the demand-responsive route at Weston-super-Mare was rerouted and rescheduled to run as a normal service. 428 (SWS 774S) was photographed at the special bus station forecourt stop in September 1978. (*M. Walker*)

(*below*) A September 1979 view of Weston's Beach Road bus station and depot. The advertising boards that can be seen between the LD open topper and the first LH show details of the tour programme operated by the local coach operator, Baker's Coaches – the company was one of their agents. When the building was pulled down in the late 1980s to make way for flats, the depot clock was saved and now stands in the seafront gardens, a few hundred yards from the depot site. (*M.S. Curtis*)

(*above*) The 1970s was the final decade of the Central Repair Works (CRW) at Lawrence Hill, a facility that handled most types of repairs and refurbishments of chassis, units and bodies in order to keep the fleet on the road. This photograph shows fuel pumps being stripped down and overhauled in the Pump Shop. (*Bristol Omnibus*)

(*below*) Most destination linens were made in the paint shop – another of the many tasks undertaken by the CRW (*Bristol Omnibus*)

... although (*below right*) mistakes were sometimes made! (*M.Walker*)

6. The Early Eighties

The Bristol Omnibus Company entered the 1980s with a total of 1,035 vehicles, the fleet having been further reduced during the preceding years. And the fleet total continued to fall, with drastic cuts in vehicle numbers occurring over the next five years.

1980

Early in the year, the Cheltenham District Traction Company was, finally, fully absorbed into the main Bristol fleet, 'Bristol' fleetnames having increasingly replaced those of 'Cheltenham' during the previous two years, although CDT legal lettering could still be seen on the town's buses. With the Cheltenham identity now completely lost, for the first time ever the entire Bristol group was Bristol Omnibus controlled. No longer were any activities conducted through subsidiaries.

Seventy-six new buses entered service in 1980, including a completely new type for the company and a revised version of the Leyland National.

Lightweight single-deckers consisted once more of Eastern Coach Works-bodied Bristol LHs. Thirteen of these arrived, including fleet number 466 (AFB 597V), which was not only the last of the batch but also the last standard-length Bristol LH ever built. Most of this batch didn't last long with Bristol however, as all but three were disposed of the following year to the Hants & Dorset company, with some then rebuilt for operation on the Sandbanks ferry, a modification that saw the front panel reduced in depth to allow for the 'dipping' effect as the bus drove down the slipway and on to the chain ferry.

Heavyweight single-deckers were also taken into stock in the shape of the latest incarnation of the Leyland National, the Leyland National 2, which (like the B series) had lost the roof pod in favour of underseat heating. Bristol's versions of this model were delivered with Leyland's TL11 engine, the replacement for the popular 0.680, instead of the fixed head unit previously employed – a change of power pack that certainly seemed to suit the bus. The Leyland National 2s started a new numbering series at 3500. Fifty of these buses had been ordered by the company, but in the event 15 were diverted elsewhere. All but the first few of the batch reverted to moquette seating, and it was intended that they should carry 22 standing passengers, although negotiations with the trade union representatives resulted in not more than eight standing being agreed, apart from in a very few exceptional circumstances. Certainly within the Southern Area of the company, agreement for 22 standing was only reached at the small depot of Wells where Leyland National 2s ousted Bristol REs on the busy Street-Glastonbury-Wells-Bristol route, although the agreement also allowed for the payment of double-deck one-man operator's rate of 20% in order that these buses could work to a higher passenger capacity. Of course, double-deckers would have been preferable, but, with the continuing drive to convert the remaining crew-operated services in the company to one-person operation, there were too many calls upon the available Bristol VRs. At Weston-super-Mare, where it was planned to use the standee National 2s to convert crew-operated local route 105

1980 saw the arrival of the very last standard-length Bristol LH to be built, which was fitted with a standard ECW 43-seat body and became 466 (AFB 597V), shown here at Central Repair Works in July 1980. (*M.S.Curtis*)

Bristol received 35 of the revised Leyland National 2 52-seaters in 1980; 3509 (AAE 653V) is seen here in Brislington in March 1981 returning from Keynsham on service 349. The destination linen is showing 'East Harptree', having slipped from 'Bristol', which is just visible underneath. (*M.S.Curtis*)

– the busiest in the town – to one-person operation, the trade union refused to accept them as being suitable. As it happened the local management agreed with them and VRTs were eventually found. In normal operation, however, in this and other cases where trade union agreements limited standing capacity, many drivers in reality simply accepted more standing passengers if they felt it to be necessary!

Twenty-eight double-deckers arrived, in line with one of the last orders placed by Bristol Joint Services, although, of course, the company was now liable to pay 100% of the cost with the withdrawal of the Government's 'new bus' grant. Twenty-three were standard dual-door, 70-seat VRTs with Gardner 6LXB engines, several of which were to go on to be painted as over-all advertisements; whilst one of them, 5146, actually went new to Weston-super-Mare where it inaugurated a one-bus working without a conductor, on town route 105. This service had a requirement for seven all-day crew operated FLFs with one or two peak extras; the extras had been converted to double-deck OPO a little while earlier, and as with many services within the company the evening and Sunday timetables were operated without a conductor. However, there was pressure upon the depot management to convert one of the all-day buses to operate without a conductor and it is interesting to further examine the reason for a 'part conversion' such as this.

During 1980 the Weston-super-Mare seafront service was scheduled to be converted to driver-only operation, and for the most part the service was operated as such, although some unreliability of the secondhand, rear-engined, open-top buses acquired for the service, did result in crew-operated FSs substituting for driver-only buses where necessary. The agreements relating to one-person operation had set thresholds at which a further OPO acceptance bonus should be paid to the staff at a depot (including the conductors whilst they remained employed) depending upon the reduction in the number of conductor's jobs. At Weston, although the seafront conversion involved four vehicles, these only operated for part of the year, and so it was deemed that the threshold in relation to the reduction of conductors had not been reached with this conversion alone. The answer was to convert one further bus working, and as service 105 remained the only two-person route at the depot, agreement was easily reached with staff representatives to convert this one bus, to enable the depot operating staff to receive the next stage in their bonus payments. The conversion was not without problems, however, and the one all-day driver-only operated double-decker on the route was occasionally seen being overtaken by the FLF timed to run 12 minutes behind it, whilst a queue conductor was often employed at the principal central area stops to ensure that fares were taken before the bus arrived. The reluctance on the part of the trade unions to accept compulsory redundancies meant that one or two spare conductors were usually available after a one-man conversion, although the surplus often vanished as a result of driver training or natural wastage. The conversion of the rest of the service was to follow at a later stage using former BJS dual-doorway VRTs that had been cascaded from Bristol depots following service revisions, many of which were later converted to single-door and either fitted with coach seats for country area trunk services, or converted to open-top for the additional open-top requirements that the company eventually faced.

(*above*) The Weston-super-Mare one-man operated open-top fleet was an eclectic mix of secondhand double-deckers. 8605 (LHA 623F) was one of two 1967 former Midland Red, Alexander-bodied Daimler Fleetlines to come to the seaside, the first arriving in late 1980, and is pictured inside Weston's combined bus station and depot. (*M.S.Curtis*)

(*below*) Three of the Weston open-top fleet were the former King Alfred Motor Services, Roe-bodied Leyland Atlanteans of 1967 that had come via Hants & Dorset. 8602 (HOR 590E) is about to pass 8603 (HOR 589E) in this July 1980 view. The seafront is to the left of the picture and Weston's bus station and depot is just behind 8603. (*M.S.Curtis*)

The five Metrobus double-deckers delivered in 1980 were initially painted into all-over advertisement liveries for the company's range of off-bus tickets. Here 6004 (DAE 514W) operates Bath cross-city service 213 in February 1981. (*M.S.Curtis*)

The balance of five double-deckers delivered were 76-seat single-doorway MCW Metrobuses with Rolls Royce engines; the previous chapter describes how these were included in the liabilities of the Bristol Joint Services, but the company was now free to do with them as it liked, and they were sent instead to Bath (despite some driver training having been conducted in Bristol). At the time of their delivery they were the first conventional 'highbridge' buses in the fleet since the final KSWs were withdrawn, as they were 14 feet 6 inches high, a full foot higher than the VRT and Lodekka models. They were delivered in a variety of colours, but with yellow fronts, and were finished as all-over advertisements for the company's range of pre-purchased multi-journey tickets.

Finally, 1980 saw a number of secondhand purchases for continued service comprising two further single-deckers and no fewer than 21 double-deckers, with four more saloons as a source of spare parts.

As stated in the previous chapter, only three of the ex-King Alfred Leyland Atlanteans were eventually converted to open-top, and although the local management had decided that the open-top Town Tours (as opposed to the seafront service) in Weston-super-Mare were no longer financially viable, there was still a requirement for additional OPO open-top buses, particularly as a new route, service 137 (later 146), had been introduced between Burnham in Somerset and the neighbouring holiday resort of Brean Down, operating at hourly intervals during the summer holidays. Initially this route had used one of the Lodekka open-toppers and was manned by Weston crews who achieved their relief changeovers by working a single-deck bus out of Weston on service 138 towards Burnham and effecting a spot changeover with the open-top bus when they met it in the narrow roads around Brean! However, on conversion of the Weston seafront service to driver-only operation, service 146 transferred to the small, six-vehicle Highbridge depot where it replaced a one-man duty that would have otherwise worked a school bus. This left the open-top bus to work a 138 journey to Weston when required, for fuelling or mechanical servicing.

Consequently, three additional vehicles were sourced and converted to open-top, one of which was a former Maidstone & District 76-seat, Weymann-bodied Leyland Atlantean (612 UKM), that was already 17 years old when acquired. Lawrence Hill's central repair works embarked upon a major conversion of the bus, and it did not finally enter service on the sea-front until the spring of 1981, painted cream with a green band, and allocated fleet number 8604. Despite

This former Maidstone & District Motor Services Weymann-bodied Leyland Atlantean, 612 UKM, was already 17 years old when acquired by the company in 1980 for open top operation at Weston-super-Mare. This view shows the amount of work undertaken in Bristol before the bus was ready to enter service from May 1981 with fleet number 8604. (*M. Walker*)

the amount of work undertaken in the conversion, it proved difficult to move the destination winding gear to a position where it would be accessible by the driver, and so the bus entered service with route number tracks only, and as a result, it usually operated the service 146 from Highbridge depot since it could then carry a 'lazy' destination board showing both ends of the route, as it was the only open-top bus in the area.

The other two open-top conversions were carried out on Daimler Fleetlines that had started the job themselves by hitting low bridges, and both came from the same source and were from the same batch. Former Midland Red vehicles LHA 615F and LHA 623F were the first Alexander-bodied buses to be taken into stock by the Bristol company, and the first Daimler Fleetlines to be used in the fleet as opposed to being acquired for spares. They took fleet numbers 8606 and 8605, and are remembered by many staff as having the heaviest steering of any vehicles in the fleet in recent times. They entered service in cream livery relieved by a thin green band but, after trials with a white livery relieved by NBC green, later adopted a revised seafront livery of blue and white. During the mid 1980s both were transferred to the Bristol city open-top tour, receiving Great Western Railway style chocolate and cream livery as part of the GWR's 150th anniversary celebrations, and were renumbered 5000/1 respectively. During their time at Weston, one featured in a local West Midlands television programme as 'the grand old lady from Birmingham who went topless at the seaside'.

Three further Daimler Fleetlines were taken into the fleet, in closed-top form. These were acquired from City of Oxford Motor Services, had Northern Counties 72-seat bodies and received fleet numbers 7000-7002, in the FLF series! They were also initially allocated to Weston-super-Mare but were not liked by the staff, principally because they also did not have power steering, and although they found use on a variety of work there, including the busy Weston to Bristol route and town service 105, they did not last long. 7000 passed to the Bristol city operation for use on a special service for university students linking halls of residence with lecture rooms, where it lasted until late 1982 until being broken up for spare parts, as was 7001. 7002 passed to a private operator; all had gone by the end of 1982.

The next source of secondhand buses was London Country Bus Services. Although part of NBC, this company had its roots in London Transport and had followed a very different vehicle purchasing policy. However, it had received one batch of Bristol/ECW VRTs just three years earlier which were non-standard among the other types operated by London Country.

The opportunity was therefore taken to transfer their entire batch of 15 to Bristol Omnibus – though they were forever referred to as the 'London Country VRs'. Coincidentally, this was the same number of vehicles as the balance of the order for Leyland National 2s sent elsewhere, presumably because of the difficulty in getting staff to accept them as standee buses that would have given them the capacity of a double-decker.

(*left*) In addition to the two open-top Daimler Fleetlines, Weston-super-Mare depot also received the three 1968 Northern Counties-bodied examples that were acquired from City of Oxford Motor Services in 1980. 7002 (KFC 374G) is shown here operating Weston-super-Mare town service 105. (*M.S.Curtis*)

(*right*) The entire 1977 batch of London Country Bristol VRTs came to the company in 1980. 6509 (PPH 470R), appears to be having a driver changeover in central Bath in this December 1980 photograph. (*M.S.Curtis*)

(*left*) 1976 Bristol VRT 5511 (LHT 721P), (with a Cheltenham allocation plate), is parked next to former London Country VRT 6511 (PPH 472R) at Bath bus station in September 1981. This rear view show the difference in design in the ECW body that was necessary to accommodate the extra height of the London Country buses. (*M.S.Curtis*)

What is certain, however, is that along with other National Bus Company subsidiaries, the Bristol company had embarked upon the viable network MAP project already mentioned, the results of which showed that the use of double-deckers on certain routes could actually make the operation of that route more economic by providing a greater capacity for more or less the same crew costs. These results changed the company senior management's views as to the necessity for double-deckers, particularly outside of Bristol. Indeed, for many years many local managers had been trying to influence a change of company policy, away from relying mostly on single-deckers for OPO conversions, but it took the Market Analysis Project finally to achieve this!

The London Country VRs were unusual in being to the highbridge specification, unlike any of the company's other Bristol VRs. This layout did not take advantage of the low build of the VR chassis, and in the higher form the Eastern Coach Works body looked somewhat odd. At Bristol, they were allocated a new fleet number series from 6500, although vehicle 6501 was later renumbered 6516 as it was allocated to Bath which was also the home of low height VR, 5601, and the similarity of the two fleet numbers could have caused a disastrous accident if the highbridge bus had been taken in error to operate a low bridge route. Although these non-standard VRs were eventually overhauled, many entered service in the condition in which they were delivered, already in National green, with many sporting Essex area advertisements. Upon arrival, all these buses remained fitted with their original Leyland 501 fixed head engines, most of which were later replaced by Gardner 6LXB units, and two of them also received experimental Maxwell gearboxes. This necessitated the repositioning of the gear change lever to the driver's right, Leyland National style. Some of these buses also went on to be painted as all over advertisements.

London Country also supplied the remaining two secondhand buses to enter service during the year. These were two short-wheelbase Bristol/ECW LHS buses seating 35. With registrations RPH 105-8L they were allocated fleet numbers 304-5 (being renumbered 1500-1 in February 1984) and set to work in Bristol on the Windmill Hill Community Bus service.

The vehicles acquired for spares were four RELH6G dual-purpose single-deckers from Crosville, dating from 1964 or 1966.

In addition, three further vehicles were borrowed from Western National. One was a VRT that was exchanged with the company for five months as part of the arrangements for increasing the coverage of overall advert buses; while two were midi-buses which were tried on the Windmill Hill Community bus service, one being a Marshall-bodied Bristol LHS and the other a Ford A-series with Alexander 27-seat body. It was these trials that led to the purchase of Bristol LHS types from London Country.

The first part of the Government's policy to change the way in which buses and coaches were operated in Great Britain also materialised during the year in the shape of the 1980 Transport Act, the principal result of which was to deregulate long-distance express services, those covering a distance of more than 30 miles. Although this produced competition for the National Express market, National's high-profile marketing and service delivery enable their passenger numbers to increase, providing the Bristol company with additional coach work. The Act also allowed for trial areas to be set up in England in which bus services would be deregulated to test a system of bus operation that the government was considering for the country as a whole. These trial areas were not to affect the company directly, but the results went on to influence every bus operator in Great Britain (outside London) in the years to follow.

In preparation for this possible deregulation of local bus services, the 1980 Act also changed the proof of need under which an operator might apply to the Traffic Commissioners to operate a local bus service; before the implementation of the Act the onus had been on an operator applying for a Road Service Licence to provide a local bus service to show that there was a public need for the service, but the Act changed that emphasis so that the incumbent operator now had to show that any new service would actually be detrimental to the overall provision of public transport within an area. In 1981 an application to the Traffic Commissioners of the Western Traffic Area for a Road Service Licence under these new conditions came from Swanbrook Transport, a Gloucester-based independent, who wanted to operate a number of Bristol city bus routes in competition with the company. Despite Swanbrook presenting a case to the Traffic Commissioners based around the poor quality of the services operating in the city, the company's solicitor was able to convince the Traffic Commissioners that if new, competing services were allowed within the city, it would be detrimental to the operation of the whole network by reducing the revenue from fares, and would result in cutbacks of city services by the company. The application by Swanbrook for the new licences was consequently refused by the Traffic Commissioners.

The company's last new ECW-bodied Bristol VRTs came in 1981, and were fitted with Leyland's 0.680 engine. 5546 (EWS 754W), numerically the last ever new VRT for the company, was also fitted with the 'Transign' electronic destination display, and is about to leave Weston-super-Mare for Bristol in this September 1981 view. (*M.S.Curtis*)

The 1980 Act also liberalised the system by which the company was able to change its fare structure, removing the necessity for fare changes to be presented before a public hearing of the Traffic Commissioners, thereby allowing the company to revise fares more easily to meet changing cost levels – and introduce commercially-based fares where it saw an opportunity to exploit a particular 'marketplace'.

1981

New vehicle deliveries during 1981 were entirely of Bristol VRT double-deckers, the last year new examples of the type arrived in the fleet. Nineteen 74-seat, single-door examples were received, unusually equipped with the upright version of Leyland's 0.680 engine, the horizontal version of which was used to power most of the company's Bristol REs.

The 0.680 engine had originally been listed as an option for early Bristol VRs, and although installed to relatively small numbers of VRL chassis, no VRTs had ever previously been fitted with this engine, although it is believed Bristol Omnibus considered this possibility when ordering its first VRTs.

The entire batch of vehicles was an order diverted from Hants & Dorset, and Bristol was one of just two companies to take VRTs with the 0.680 engine, possibly because the engineering staff were already so familiar with its design. The option of this power unit came about at such a late stage because of supply difficulties with Gardner engines.

Despite this familiarity, a start was made on replacing the engines with Gardner 6LXB units before the vehicles were two years old. The seats of these and subsequent vehicles reverted to a moquette covering, a far more passenger-friendly material than the brown vinyl of previous deliveries. The last two of the batch, 5545 and 5546, were equipped with a new style of destination equipment, manufactured under the name 'Transign', and operated electronically from the cab. These were to be the last new Bristol VRs taken into stock, and amongst the last produced by Bristol Commercial Vehicles.

It is perhaps worth taking a diversion here to examine the experimental destination equipment fitted to these last two vehicles: since before the Green Years, the destination equipment in use by the Bristol company, and indeed by most companies throughout the United Kingdom, consisted of a white linen (later paper or even plastic) roll on which the relevant destination or number information was masked and the surrounding area painted black. It was then fitted on rollers into the aperture at the front or rear (or even side) of the bus and changed by means of a geared winding mechanism that was accessible to the driver and/or the conductor. At night, the lights behind the display would light up the unpainted words or letters of the destination, but, of course, if the bus was not on service and had no interior illumination, then no destination would be easily visible. Although this arrangement had served the industry well, there was a reluctance upon the part of one-man operators to change the destination display at the rear of the bus as it meant leaving the cab, and their takings, whilst it was often the case that the driver of a late-running bus forsook the opportunity to change the display at a terminal point in an effort to get the bus back onto its scheduled time. Some companies had experimented with electrically operating this type of destination equipment to make matters easier for the driver, but the linen or paper roll was apt to stretch over time with the result that the wrong destination was often shown.

The Transign equipment was an attempt to overcome all of these problems and consisted of a single-line destination display, together with a separate number display, which was made up of a row of single character apertures employing a number of separate vertical display segments, each of which carried small white on black characters which, when read together in various combinations, would represent the letters of the alphabet, each segment being brought into position by a small electric motor activated in a pre-programmed sequence by the driver dialling a code into the activation unit in the cab. The beauty of the system was that as every letter of the alphabet could be represented in each of the character displays then a new or changed destination display could be accommodated simply by means of changing or replacing a code, thus making the equipment not only universal but likely to be able to last for the life of the bus. The latter was not to be the case however, as the system was unreliable in operation and proved difficult to illuminate clearly during the hours of darkness. Ultimately, it was replaced by standard roller blinds on these and subsequent buses delivered with this system.

Two of the final VRTs were later fitted with experimental Maxwell transmission, as fitted to two of the London Country VRs, and a number of this batch also later received all over advertisements.

During 1981 the Secretary of State, Norman Fowler, referred the operations of the Bristol company to the Monopolies and Mergers Commission, together with fellow National Bus Company subsidiary Trent from the Midlands, the municipal Cardiff Corporation Transport and the West Midlands Passenger Transport Executive, to

> ascertain whether any of the undertakings were abusing any monopoly situation existing in their favour or whether any of the undertakings were pursuing a course of conduct which operated against the public interest.

Perhaps to the disappointment of the Secretary of State, whose Government had in mind to deregulate and privatise the National Bus Company in order to introduce competition into the operation of local bus services, the MMC generally found that no abuse of monopoly power existed within the Bristol and Trent companies, and of the 43 recommendations it made, only three were specific to the National Bus Company. Indeed, the Commission found that the Bristol and Trent companies' relationship with the National Bus Company was both relevant and beneficial to their efficiency. Despite this, however, by 1984, and after successful re-election the previous year, the Conservative Government was to publish the White Paper 'Buses', which proposed the break up of the National Bus Company into smaller units and the transfer of these units to the private sector, together with wholesale bus deregulation outside of London.

Commenting on the Market Analysis Project undertaken by Bristol, along with other National Bus Company subsidiaries, the Monopolies and Mergers Commission took the view that the project had the aim of improving the financial viability of the services, given the existing pattern of demand, and, as a corollary, it also provided a firm database from which to begin negotiations with local authorities on the level of support required. It continued that the Bristol company, as a result of the MAP schemes introduced between 1980 and 1982, had seen a 30.4% reduction in peak vehicle requirement and 24.4% reduction in mileage. All areas in NBC had shown an improved operating ratio of revenue to operating costs, that in Bristol City from 74.1% to 88.9% and in Gloucester from 79.8% to 90.8%.

The MAP studies usually resulted in better vehicle utilisation and reduced the availability of buses between the peaks. A consequence of this was that the maintenance team found it more difficult to carry out repairs, whilst the increased annual vehicle mileages necessary to make better use of the vehicle assets meant that there was a more frequent requirement for the vehicles to be serviced. Coincidentally, there was a reduction in the percentage of spare vehicles that were made available to each depot, and it was very difficult to implement around the clock maintenance where this did not exist, especially as skilled fitters were proving difficult to come by and very few were prepared to work night shifts. This combination of circumstances therefore resulted in an increase in maintenance difficulties within the company.

In addition, the reduction in fleet size led to a requirement for a commensurate reduction in overheads, with the closure of, amongst others, the Trowbridge, Highbridge and Wotton-under-Edge depots and the Trowbridge and Wells bus stations, although outstations were established where depots were closed so as to capitalise on local employment opportunities, retain loyal staff and, of course, reduce empty running.

Towards the very end of the year, and in partnership with the company, Avon County Council introduced their 'Avonfare' scheme, which was based on, and replaced, the Woodspring maximum off-peak fare scheme, but which now meant that a local authority supported maximum off-peak fare existed over the entire County of Avon.

1982

Deliveries this year were once more entirely double-deckers, but this time consisted of the Bristol VR's replacement, the 'Olympian'. This new model had been developed at Bristol Commercial Vehicles in Brislington as the B45, and was to become NBC's new standard double-decker. Not only was it to succeed the VR however, it was also intended that this model would replace the Atlantean and Fleetline from Leyland's range and was to be badged as a 'Leyland'. BCV nevertheless remained only half owned by Leyland and confusingly, many early Olympians, among them Bristol Omnibus examples, were in any case licensed as 'Bristols'.

The Olympians for Bristol Omnibus were powered by Gardner 6LXB engines and the chassis design included a number of established 'Bristol' features such as dropped-centre rear axle, perimeter framing and front-mounted radiator, while air suspension was standard.

The new buses took the fleet numbers 9500 to 9529. To relieve pressure on ECW, Bristol Omnibus was persuaded to take Olympians with bodywork by Charles H. Roe (C.H. Roe by now having joined BCV, ECW and Leyland National as a jointly owned NBC/Leyland company through Bus Manufacturers [Holdings] Ltd) to become the only NBC customer for Roe Olympians other than London Country. As a consequence, these buses were rather taller than might otherwise have been the case, with an intermediate height of 14 feet 2 inches.

(*left*) A leaflet promoting the Avonfare scheme.

(*right*) This family of caricatures was launched in late summer 1979 to promote the company's ticket offers and ran for several years. It was one of the largest advertising campaigns ever undertaken by Bristol Omnibus and included not only press but TV coverage (the latter was then not common). Five MCW Metrobuses introduced in Bath from 1980 each carried advertising for one of the characters and ticket types. Many other buses had every poster position filled with red and yellow ads to support the campaign. The characters included 'Freddie Fare Card', 'Reggie Rovercard' and the 'Weekenders'.

(*left*) 1982 Leyland Olympian 9512 (JHU 911X) was one of the batch that was delivered in National green. The 'Transign' electronic destination equipment has already started to fail in this October 1983 view, as it seems to be showing 'BURNHAM-OZ-SEA'. (*M.S.Curtis*)

(*below*) 9504 (JHU 903X) was one of the company's first Leyland Olympians, although the chassis was actually built at Bristol: the 76-seat bodywork was built by Roe. This bus was one of eight delivered in all-over white for the Bristol Clipper service, but in this July 1982 view it is at Weston-super-Mare and in use for driver familiarisation. (*M.Walker*)

Other features of the bodywork included a single front door and seats for 76 passengers, together with Transign destination equipment with a rear route number box, which of course could now be operated from the driver's cab.

A number of the batch were delivered to the company in an all-over white livery, the intention being to use them on a specially dedicated limited stop network in Bristol to be marketed under the 'City Clipper' brand, but problems were being experienced within the city in getting an agreement with the trade unions to accept these buses for one-person operation, since for the previous 12 years full-sized bus deliveries to the city had employed separate entrances and exits. Agreement was eventually reached to operate the Olympians without a conductor in the city but the white buses found a ready use at Marlborough Street bus and coach station where, because of a national rail strike, National Express long-distance coach services were suffering severe overloads. Whilst intended for operation in the city, the Olympians' first weeks of service were as duplicate 'coaches', principally operating between Bristol and Birmingham, and despite their bus seats and bus speeds, at least their colour was correct! Most of the white Olympians were eventually repainted green, while others adopted white (with turquoise) 'Clipper' livery once negotiations with the staff had been concluded.

Further VRTs did, however, enter service during 1982, but these, again, were secondhand examples. Southdown Motor Services supplied WUF 527-530K, and WUF 532-537K, 70-seat dual-doorway, flat-screened buses from the same batch as Bristol's own 5002-5009: in fact the chassis numbers of the first four fitted nicely in the gap between the chassis numbers of Bristol's own batch, and their body numbers were in the sequence a little before the Bristol ones. They did however have a slightly different destination display layout and green moquette seating – and in any case were regarded as stop-gaps before more new buses arrived. Most were withdrawn within four years.

For country services, JNU 136-139N, 1975 Gardner-engined, 74-seat, single-doorway VRTs came from East Midland Motor Services of Chesterfield, which received fleet numbers 5600-5603, and were almost identical to the company's 5500-5503.

(*below*) The ten two-doorway Bristol VRTs that were acquired from Southdown Motor Services in 1982 were very similar to Bristol's own 1972 VRTs. 5207 (WUF 535K) in central Bristol in September 1983. (*M.S.Curtis*)

Secondhand single-deckers arrived in the shape of HHA 197/8L, 44-seat Plaxton-bodied Leyland Leopard coaches that came from Midland Red (Express), Birmingham and were sent to Swindon to provide additional capacity on the National Express services passing through that town. They took fleet numbers 2102 and 2103. Two additional coaches were used to supplement busy National Express services, these being NNN 2/3M, 49-seat, Duple Dominant-bodied Leyland Leopards that were borrowed from the East Midland company, and which worked from Marlborough Street, Bristol, during the Christmas period.

1983

More Bristol-built Leyland Olympians entered the fleet during 1983. Twenty-five such vehicles, in all respects to the same specification as those delivered the previous year, formed the intake of new double-deckers. The final member of this batch, 9554, was also to be the last of over 4,000 Bristol-built buses delivered to the company, thus ending an association that had commenced 75 years earlier, in 1908. In future, Olympian chassis would be built elsewhere.

The 1983 Olympians were joined by a batch of 11 Leyland 'Tiger' coaches, the Tiger being Leyland's heavier and more powerful replacement for the Leopard, featuring the new TL11 engine as successor to the popular 0.680 unit, and semi-automatic gearboxes, operated by means of a small binnacle to the driver's right, in a similar style to the Leyland National & Olympian. The Bristol Omnibus Tigers were fitted with Plaxton's new 'Paramount 3200 Express' (3200 signifying a coach that was 3.2 metres high; a taller version, the 3500, was available at 3.5 metres high) most with seats for 53 passengers and featuring a folding entrance door. Significantly, these were the company's first 12 metre-long vehicles (39ft 4ins), although this length had been permissible for some years. By the time they entered service towards the latter half of the year, significant changes were taking place in the structure and management of the company.

In the summer of 1983 the National Bus Company had announced that the Bristol Omnibus Company was to be broken up into four smaller units (in advance of the white paper). Indeed, throughout the country NBC companies were being divided into smaller units, intended to allow a more local style of management. The NBC explained that subdividing companies created 'natural market units' which latterly were 'appropriate for a deregulated environment and privatisation'.

The Bristol company was broken into three operating units, one for Bristol City (which was again to isolate the city's operations from the rest of the network), another for the country area (equivalent to the then Southern Area of the company, including Bristol's Marlborough Street bus and coach station), and a third to encompass the operations at Cheltenham, Gloucester, Stroud and Swindon. Once again, greater prominence was given to local fleetnames throughout the fleet, with the retention of 'Gloucester', while resurrecting 'Bath' and 'Cheltenham' and introducing new titles such as 'Swindon & District' and 'Bristol Country'. The Swindon & District name was perhaps the cleverest, since it exploited the use of the Borough name which had been lost to the former Swindon Corporation Transport (the only municipal bus undertaking in the entire Bristol Omnibus area) when it was renamed 'Thamesdown Transport' in 1974, with local government reorganisation.

The intention was that the first two units of the Bristol company (covering the Bristol and Southern areas) should form the basis of a new, smaller Bristol Omnibus Company, each unit having a separate manger, with Graeme Varley taking over Bristol City and Trevor Smallwood in charge of Bristol Country.

The Northern Division of the company, with 165 vehicles, was effectively hived-off as a new, self-contained company from September 1983 and from that point, ceased to have a part to play in this story.

A further section of the Bristol Omnibus Company, its Central Repair Works (CRW) at Lawrence Hill, was also to be split off as Bristol Engineering Limited, with all operating companies now being able to buy in their engineering services from Bristol Engineering or from other companies as they saw fit.

As each of the new sections of the company set about establishing their own identities, it was many of the 1983 new vehicle deliveries that showed in which direction each was heading. Tiger coaches, that might have been expected to carry small 'Bristol' fleetnames as a part of their National Express livery, instead took to the streets with one of four local names, with 2200-2202 bearing 'Swindon and District', 2203/4/7/8 'Bristol Country', 2205 and 2206 'Weston and Wells' and 2209/10 carrying the 'Bath' name.

New Olympians for Bristol city services displayed the almost meaningless fleetname 'Citybus', while it was left to Marlborough Street's allocation of service buses to have the honour of another new fleetname, 'Bristol Country Bus', which henceforth became the only depot to retain mention of 'Bristol' – despite this remaining the company title of which the smaller units were components. Completion of this round of new fleetnames for vehicles – there were more to follow – became fully effective from November 1983.

Meanwhile, as the new unit managers got to grips with the changed structure, Bristol Omnibus also had a new Managing Director, Mike Wadsworth (who had earlier succeeded Ken Wellman in the post of General Manager during 1981). He had the unenviable task of overseeing a further break-up of the company that would eventually lead to himself being out of a job!

And the influx of more secondhand buses also continued. No fewer than 15 secondhand Bristol VRT double-deckers joined the fleet during the year. 5604-5608 were a batch of N-registered Gardner-engined 74-seaters that were built in 1975, supplied by United Automobile Services of Darlington, whilst 5609-5616 came from the West Riding Automobile Company (who had themselves acquired a number of the company's FLF double-deckers some 15 years earlier).

The two remaining VRs to be transferred from other companies had been built as convertible open-toppers, and came from Southern Vectis on the Isle of Wight, although originally purchased by the Hants & Dorset company. These two 1977 buses were among the batch of 50 convertible VRTs built for NBC – in which Bristol

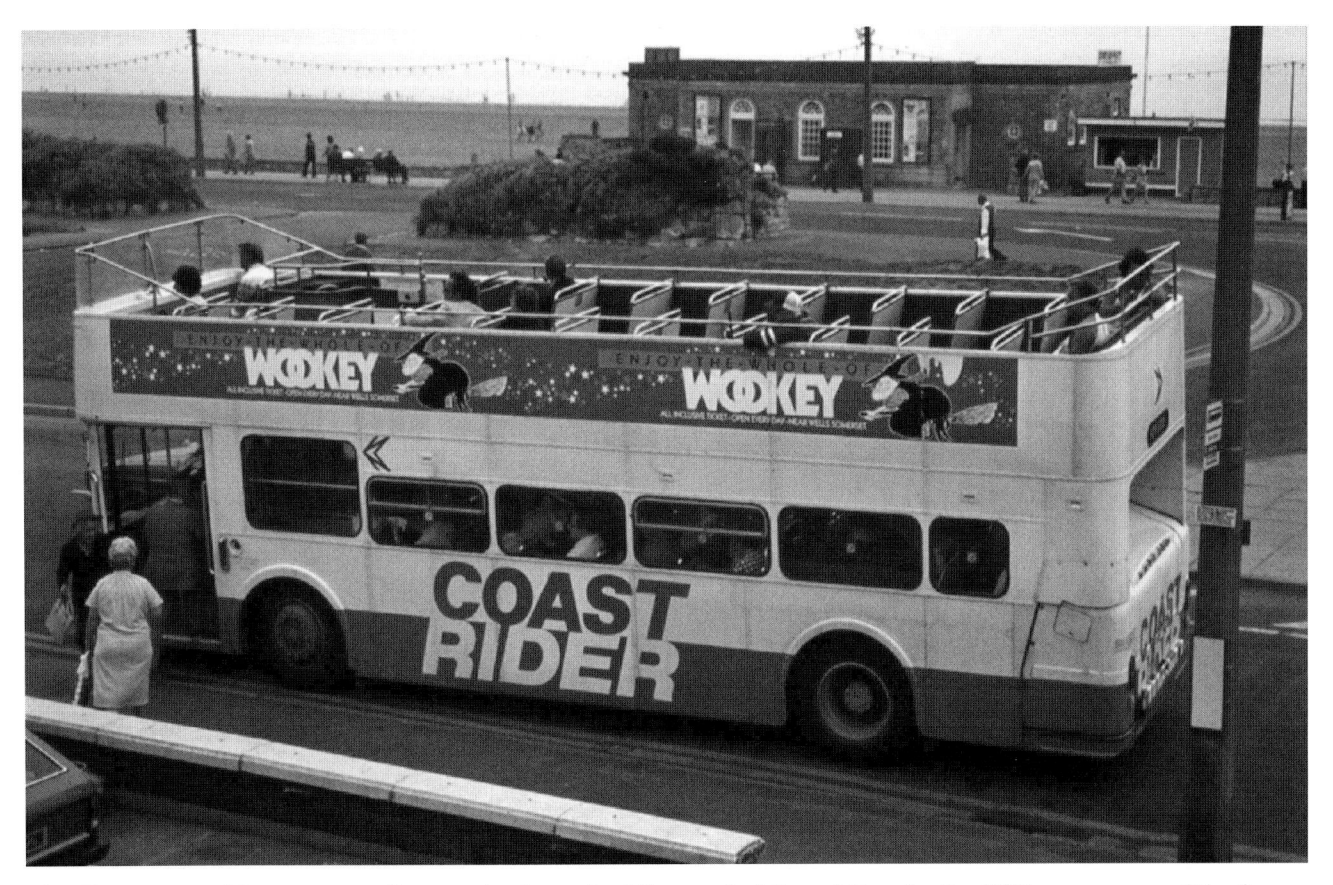

The Weston-super-Mare open-top fleet received a revised livery of white and blue for the 1982 season: one of the former King Alfred Motor Services, Roe-bodied Leyland Atlanteans shows off the new scheme in July 1983, outside the bus station and depot. (*M.Walker*)

expressed no interest at the time of their construction. They were exchanged for two equivalent closed-top buses, to allow yet another increase in the open-top bus fleet operating out of Weston-super-Mare, where the Weston seafront service, and the Weston-Brean-Burnham operations had been revised and combined, resulting in open-top buses running every 30 minutes from Sand Bay (to the north of Weston) to Burnham (in Somerset), a journey of almost one and a half hours. These two VRTs entered service at Weston in their Southern Vectis livery of green lower deck with white upper panels (with the remainder of Weston's open-top fleet by this time painted in white and light blue). The convertible VRTs were to stay just one summer at the seaside, however, before being transferred inland to Bath.

As may be expected with a leisure service, the open-top vehicles at Weston-super-Mare did not need to run out of the depot until after the morning peak, to be 'on service' along the seafront just as the local hotels and guest houses finished serving breakfast and the holiday-makers came out to enjoy the day. This meant that open-top buses were often 'spare' during the morning peak period, and for some time a one-man operated open-top bus was allocated to operate a local school bus in Weston, albeit only carrying a small number of school children so that it was not necessary to use the top deck. In addition, when the Radio One Road Show made its annual visit to Weston beach for its live broadcast of pop music, open-top buses operated a shuttle service from the railway station to the seafront (appropriately numbered 275, the Radio One frequency!), one year taking over £100 in 10p fares before they were required to take up their regular route.

Further 'acquired' vehicles to arrive during 1983 were two Plaxton-bodied coaches. Former National Travel (South West) Leyland Leopard WFH 169S joined the Bath fleet as 2104, painted into the company's new 'local coach' livery of white and kingfisher blue, whilst XOO 871L, an ex-Eastern National Bristol RELH6G adopted the fleet number 2091 and was sent to Swindon, where, although still in National Express livery, it carried the Swindon and District fleetname.

Finally, three secondhand Bristol RE buses came to the fleet from Cumberland Motor Services. These were broadly similar to those already operated by the company, with Leyland 0.680 power units. They entered service on country routes early in the following year, taking fleet numbers 1260-1262.

What became a highly successful open-top tour of Bath started rather tentatively for the 1983 season with one Leyland Atlantean but soon additional buses were required. During 1984 the two former Southern Vectis convertible open-top Bristol VRTs joined the tour, although in a revised livery of cream and green and with Bath fleetnames. (*M.S.Curtis*)

In May 1983 an open-top bus tour was introduced in Bath to link the important tourist sites, using one of the ex-King Alfred Leyland Atlanteans released from Weston-super-Mare by the arrival of the two convertibles. As explained previously, a tour had existed for many years, as befits a tourist city of Bath's calibre, principally a 'closed door' tour provided by Bristol Greyhound coaches, although supplemented from 1963 by the Special Bus Service operated with the little Trojan and then the Ford Transit. The new service, was launched by the Mayor of Bath, Councillor Elgar Jenkins, on an extremely wet Bank Holiday Monday. The tour operated at hourly intervals, and offered a hop-on, hop-off facility as well as a full hour tour. Demand for the service soon outstripped supply, so the company hired a convertible open-top VRT similar to the ones recently acquired from Southern Vectis, in the shape of Devon General VDV 135S, and the frequency of operation was doubled. A former Bristol Joint Services twin doorway VR of a similar age was sent to Devon General in exchange and was used in Exeter.

At this time, the concept of open-top city tours was in its infancy, with most open-top buses still performing coastal runs, as at Weston. The popularity of city tours of this kind grew enormously however, becoming among the company's most lucrative services, as Bristol Omnibus rapidly discovered. In Bath, 25,000 passengers were carried during the summer of 1983, its first season.

Incidentally, the introduction of the open-top tourist service was not the first time during the Green Years that open-top buses had appeared in Bath. K-type open-topper 3613 had been used there for driver training in the summer of 1961. Indeed, this practice was continued as members of the new Weston open-top bus fleet were similarly used for driver training during the winter months.

As a result of changes to vehicle requirements brought about by the MAP service revisions, a number of former Joint Services dual-door buses had migrated to country fleet depots, and indeed at Weston-super-Mare a batch was used to convert the remaining crew-operated buses on town service 105 to OPO, although there was often a disagreement between management and staff at country depots about the use of the centre door, especially when these buses operated on rural services where there was often only a small section of hard standing for passengers at bus stops. Drivers naturally lined this up with their front door, occasionally leaving alighting passengers to step onto muddy grass. In due course, many of the two-doorway buses allocated to country depots were converted to single-doorway to overcome this problem.

A month before the introduction of Bath's open-top tours, another new service was introduced, connecting Bristol and Bath with Trowbridge, Warminster and Salisbury – with the Trowbridge to Salisbury section having its origins in service 241 that had been operated by the Bristol company following the takeover of Western National's Trowbridge operations. The 241 had been a joint operation with the Salisbury depot of the neighbouring Hants & Dorset company, although the Salisbury operation had previously been part of the Wilts & Dorset company, the two having been merged together some years earlier. The new, larger Hants & Dorset company carried a red livery previously associated with Wilts & Dorset, although changed to the, by now, familiar National red shade. At the time of the introduction of this new service, numbered X41, between Bristol and Salisbury, Hants & Dorset was split in a similar manner to the Bristol company – with the revival of the Wilts & Dorset name for its Salisbury operation!

The new service operated hourly between Bristol, Bath and Warminster (a new direct link for Bristol) and at two-hourly intervals through to Salisbury, a journey time of around two and a half hours; for operation on this new service Bristol sent five of their Leyland National 2 buses away to the bodybuilder Willowbrook at Loughborough, to be equipped with coach seats, the buses entering service on this new limited stop route in the dual-purpose livery of the top half white and the lower half green. The new service and the new joint working arrangements now regularly brought red Wilts & Dorset vehicles into Bath and Bristol bus stations.

Among other niche markets to be identified were limited stop or 'X' buses which were introduced during the late seventies and early eighties to exploit the leisure market, operating from major centres of population to recreational or seaside resorts.

Another important source of extra revenue occurred in June, with the staging of the famous Glastonbury Festival, based at Worthy Farm in Pilton, about five miles to the east of Glastonbury and 30 miles south of Bristol and Bath. This event saw thousands of festival goers descend upon Marlborough Street and Bath bus and coach stations, and Bristol's Temple Meads railway station. Frequent double-deck shuttle buses were provided between Bath and Bristol to the festival site, operating late into the nights before the event, whilst connecting services were operated from Glastonbury, Wells and the nearby Castle Cary rail station, which is situated on the main London to south-west England railway line. Close liaison with the festival organisers and the local police saw shuttle buses given priority over local traffic, and a temporary 'bus station' was instituted, either in a nearby field or road junction. Return traffic started to leave the festival site by late on the Sunday evening as the musical events wound down, but the greatest movement of revellers took place on the Monday after the event when bus after bus was despatched from the site to Bristol or Bath, completely full with passengers, their luggage and tents. If the weather had been unkind, buses often had to be hosed down inside to remove the worst of the mud before being sent back to the festival for another load. Any available bus was pressed into service, including buses borrowed from neighbouring independents, and, on at least one occasion, open-top Leyland Atlantean 8604 that, in the words of the driver, 'took one look at the hill out of Wells and cried'. On that occasion the passengers left the festival site in high spirits but before they had reached Bristol the heavens opened and they were soaked through, in a manner reminiscent of the delivery of the first open-top buses to Weston some 30 years earlier. Wet weather provided the one occasion when the brown plastic seating in some of the VR double-deckers really came into its own, as the application of a water jet from a hosepipe soon cleared the accumulated mud. In due course, however, it became common practice to cover all seats with black plastic sacks to make the cleaning of the bus much easier.

In July 1983, single-door double-deckers were finally accepted for one-person operation within the city of Bristol itself, with the removal of conductors from busy cross-city service 87 from Warmley to Southmead. Complementary service 88, with which it ran alternately, became the last bastion of regular all day operation of two-person operated FLF 70-seaters in the country, with the service finally being converted to one-person operation in the summer of 1984, although the few remaining conductors and crew drivers were kept on until their retirement.

One of the results of the new management structure, particularly within the country sector, was that more autonomy was given to the District Managers, allowing them to search out fresh markets and experiment with new services. One such experiment was the open-top 'Christmas Lights Tour' introduced for the 1983 Christmas period by Bristol Country Bus, using an ex-King Alfred Motor Services Leyland Atlantean that was especially licenced for the purpose. It operated a purely Bristol City service from the city centre through the shopping areas of Park Street and Whiteladies Road to the Downs, a round trip time of one hour, over almost

1983 Roe-bodied, 76-seat Leyland Olympian 9542 (NTC 141Y), pictured operating from Bristol to Clevedon in September of that year. (*M.S.Curtis*)

the same route as the service 600 open-top route of ten years earlier and taking in the city's Christmas lights. It lasted just one season and operated at just below a break-even level, but served as a foretaste of the experimental services that the new country service operation was keen to try in order to tap new revenue sources.

1984

Technological developments continued during 1984, with the Bristol company chosen for trials of 'ELSIE', the Electronic Speech Information Equipment, which was designed to help the blind and visually handicapped by enabling bus stops to 'talk' to passengers. The Government and NBC financially supported the experiment which was launched in Weston-super-Mare by the Minister of State for Transport, Mrs Linda Chalker MP (who, incidentally, travelled to Weston by a special National Express coach).

Designed by the Department of Transport, nine 'talking bus stops' were involved in the trial, each consisting of an interactive loop buried beneath the roadway, which transmitted a signal to an on-bus transponder which, it turn, relayed information to a device mounted on the bus stop. When activated by depressing a button, an announcement gave the time, the route numbers served by the stop and when the next bus was due; this was repeated as the bus approached. Correct operation of the system relied upon the driver entering his running card details when starting duty or changing buses, whilst the system had to be easily amended to keep up with service changes. The Government funded the scheme for two years, but when it ended Avon County Council felt unable to continue with a grant, and the experiment came to an end.

For the fourth consecutive year, no new single-deck service buses were taken into stock during 1984. However, 20 further Olympians joined the double-deck fleet, which differed very slightly from earlier examples. Their chassis, of course, were no longer built in Bristol, Olympian assembly having by now been transferred to the Leyland National factory in Workington, Cumbria, which had plenty of spare capacity. Like earlier deliveries, these carried Roe bodywork, 14 of which seated 76 passengers and were for Bristol city services; whilst six, although similar, were delivered with convertible open-tops and painted in a new style of white and blue seafront livery for use at Weston-super-Mare. These were to carry names chosen in a competition among local school children, and their arrival at Weston, together with the later conversion of a number of dual-door VRTs to single entrance, permanent open-top configuration, saw the demise of most of the secondhand Atlanteans and Fleetlines. The open-top VRTs were shared between Weston and Bath, although the continuing growth in passenger numbers on the Bath Tour also saw the hire of another convertible open-top Bristol VRT, this time from Southdown Motor Services of Brighton. The Brighton bus stayed in Bath for three months while a similar but permanent closed top VRT was loaned to Southdown in exchange.

In 1983 the company acquired a number of secondhand ECW-bodied Bristol VRT double-deckers: 5615 (MUA 874P) was a 1975 example and is seen in Bath in March 1984. By this time the Bath City services had been renumbered by removing the initial '2', as part of the company's process of re-establishing local identity. (*M.S.Curtis*)

More Tiger coaches also arrived during 1984. These consisted of seven Duple Laser-bodied examples, four of which seated 51, while the remaining three seated 47 and also incorporated demountable toilets, the first Bristol Omnibus vehicles to be delivered with this facility. There was to have been an eighth coach but this was instead sent to Wessex National, the Bristol-based National Express operator that had grown out of the well-known Bristol independent coach company which had previously worked closely with Bristol Omnibus in coordinating its tours and providing Greyhound express service duplication. In exchange for this last coach, Bristol Omnibus received a very special secondhand vehicle for the country service fleet, of which more later.

As with the previous years' delivery of Plaxton-bodied Leyland Tigers, the Duple Laser coaches were put to work on National Express work, and although they were very stylish in their design, their low build and small boot capacity often meant that duplicates had to be provided due to insufficient luggage accommodation. Although not operated by the Bristol company, a Duple Laser-bodied Leyland Tiger of the National Welsh company usually operated the overnight Cardiff to Gatwick Airport service which called into Bristol bus and coach station in the very late hours of the night, and similar overloading problems often caused a headache for the Bristol night maintenance staff, who were the only company employees on duty at that time.

All of the 1984 Laser coaches had 'Transdot' electronically operated destination displays, the latest version of the system that worked by means of employing a large number of very small round panels in the destination display that were black on one side and white on the other (the 'dots'), and which were activated to change their display by means of electric impulses in response to a pre-programmed set of instructions – in much the same way as the Transign equipment, but employing the benefit of many fewer moving parts.

The last new coaches delivered to the Bristol Omnibus Company, and for the Green Years, were seven Duple Laser 2-bodied Leyland Tigers in National Express livery. 2222 (B222 WEU) rests at Vauxhall, London, between National Express trips, after the Green Years had ended. The 'Transdot' electronic destination display reads 'Happy Christmas'! (*M.Walker*)

More secondhand coaches came to the fleet from East Yorkshire Motor Services of Hull, comprising five 14-year old Plaxton-bodied Leyland Leopards. These entered service in National Express livery as fleet numbers 2105-2109, although three of them lasted barely one season before being withdrawn. Two further coaches were sent from the National Bus Company dealer, Amalgamated Passenger Transport of Lincoln, but were returned within the day as being unsuitable. The Bristol company was seeing a further increase in its requirement for coaches, particularly as the new country area management team were keen to develop coaching activities in order to broaden its operational base, especially as the future of so many loss-making rural services lay in the hands of local authorities with limited budgets for socially necessary services.

As a result, and in addition to the secondhand coaches acquired, the company also borrowed three 1981 Plaxton-bodied Leyland Leopards from United Automobile Services of Darlington, which were operated from Bristol and Bath depots; together with some spectacular double-deck coaches from National Travel (West), Manchester, for use during the busy month of June on National Express services. The double-deck coaches were 74-seat, toilet-equipped, tri-axle MCW 'Metroliners' and also worked from Bath and Bristol.

The Bristol City operating unit was also anxious to acquire suitable secondhand buses, and purchased three dual-doorway Leyland Nationals: two came from Hampshire Bus (a new name for part of the former Hants & Dorset company) which were new in 1972, having originated with London Country Bus Services Ltd, although never having actually worked for that company. These entered service in a new style of red and yellow striped livery where they joined similarly-coloured buses on the important service linking Bristol's Temple Meads Railway Station, the Centre and Clifton. This service had been re-branded 'City B Line', a name similar to that used earlier for the ill-fated Marconi bus location system in the early 1970s.

The third Leyland National (which like the Hampshire buses seated 46) came from Midland Red (North) of Cannock, but entered service in the standard green colour scheme.

The Bristol City operation also exchanged a double-deck Bristol VRT with the South Wales Transport Company for a period of a month during the early part of the year, the borrowed vehicle having been fitted with an anti-vandal screen in the cab, and was used to evaluate this fitting. As this bus had only one door, it was used as a two-person vehicle during the day, but without a conductor during the evenings.

The final secondhand vehicle to be acquired was a very special one from Wessex National. Built only two years earlier, ADD 50Y was a long wheelbase Olympian, powered by a Leyland TL11 engine, and supporting an ECW 65-seat coach body. It was very much an experimental vehicle, reflecting Leyland's attempt to break into the market dominated by the three-axle Metroliner, although production versions would only ever be developed for use on long-distance commuter runs (or for export). Although built in late 1982 (and originally allocated registration SND 50X) this coach was not licenced until mid 1984, being acquired by Bristol in December. At that point it was returned to Eastern Coach Works to be modified, with a reduction in size of its large rear luggage locker and the addition of four further seats. It entered service during April of

Late in 1984 the Bristol City operation and Avon County Council re-launched the service that linked Clifton and the city centre with Temple Meads railway station, using a fleet of red and yellow striped Leyland Nationals and the marketing name 'The B Line' – similar to the name that had previously been used for the Marconi bus location system – although this time also using a caricature of a bee. Second from left at this official launch is Graeme Varley, manager of the city operation. (*Bristol Evening Post*)

the following year on an all day limited stop service X1 operating between Bristol and Weston-super-Mare; and was the first vehicle in the fleet to wear a completely new livery for country services.

Despite the introduction of further new and secondhand vehicles, withdrawals far outstripped new arrivals causing a dramatic reduction in vehicle numbers during the early eighties. The combined operations of Bristol City (with 259 buses), Bristol Country (269) and Cheltenham & Gloucester (165) had witnessed a reduction in fleet strength of almost a third between 1980 and 1984 This trend was about to change, however, with the introduction of much higher frequency urban minibus services which replaced many conventional buses in each of the operating sectors.

As 1984 unfolded, it transpired that this would be the last year in which conventionally liveried green vehicles would be delivered to the company. Having been 'green' for 40 years, things were about to change. During the following year completely new company names and colour schemes were applied to Bristol's buses, followed by a further split of the company. Country services were completely separated from what remained of the Bristol Omnibus Company, with the formation of another new company. For everyone involved with Bristol Omnibus Services, whether as management, staff or as a passenger, the 'Green Years' had nearly come to an end.

***

215

(*above*) The company entered the 1980s as a National green fleet – this is the busy Marlborough Street bus and coach station in Bristol. National express coaches departed from the higher numbered platforms to the right of this picture. (*M.S.Curtis*)

(*below*) 1971 Plaxton-bodied Leyland Leopard, former Bristol Greyhound coach 2157, the 1970 Commercial Motor Show exhibit. It was repainted and renumbered to be local coach liveried 2085 in 1979, but was withdrawn in 1980. (*M.S.Curtis*)

(*left*) Former London Country Bus Services 35-seat ECW-bodied Bristol LHS number 304 (RPH 105L) dating from 1973, has just entered service on the Windmill Hill Community Bus service in this September 1980 view at Bristol's Centre.
(*M.S. Curtis*)

(*right*) Delivered as coach 2186 in 1976, and after carrying fleet number 2309 for a short while, Plaxton-bodied Leyland Leopard 2096 carries route branding for the limited stop service linking Bristol with Gloucester and is seen inside Bristol bus and coach station in August 1981. (*M.Walker*)

(*left*) Former Gloucester City bus G1153, a twin-door Bristol RELL of 1970, was converted to become an immobile office and staff restroom. It was initially sited at Devizes, although it is seen here at Lawrence Hill depot in October 1982. In this condition the bus needed to be towed to wherever it was required. (*M.Walker*)

(*above*) Some Bristol FLF double-deckers remained on Bristol city services into the 1980s, and 1967 bus 7312 (KHW 304E), shown here in late 1978 crossing traffic lanes at Bristol's Centre, was amongst the last to be withdrawn. (*M.S.Curtis*)

(*below*) People walk 'under the clock' past the company's mock Tudor office buildings at the Centre; despite the growing problem of traffic congestion faced by the company during the late 1970s and early 1980s, traffic is very light in this March 1980 view. Compare this photograph with that on p.10. (*M.S.Curtis*)

(*right*) 1976 two-doorway Bristol VRT 5079 (NFB 115R) shows no signs of its previous Joint Services ownership in this 1980 view outside the company's Bristol Centre offices. (*M.S.Curtis*)

(*left*) Following service revisions in Bristol, a number of former BJS twin-doorway Bristol VRTs were re-allocated to country depots. 1976 bus 5049 (LEU 257P) works on Weston town services in August 1981, before it was fitted with an appropriate destination linen. The sticker on the windscreen declares 'to and from Cricket Ground'; Somerset County Cricket Club were playing a match in the town at the time. (M.Walker)

(*right*) Further white, Roe-bodied Leyland Olympians were delivered in 1984, although this time the chassis had been built in Lancashire and the bodies had removable roofs. 8609 (A809 THW) loads at Weston's Old Pier in this August 1984 view, before operating along the seafront and out into the Somerset countryside towards Brean, near Burnham-on-Sea. (*M.S.Curtis*)

219

Although the design of vehicles changed over the Green Years, the operational problems they faced did not. Two-door Leyland National 1437 (GAE 299N) battles through the snow in Hungerford Road, Bristol, in January 1982. (*M.S.Curtis*)

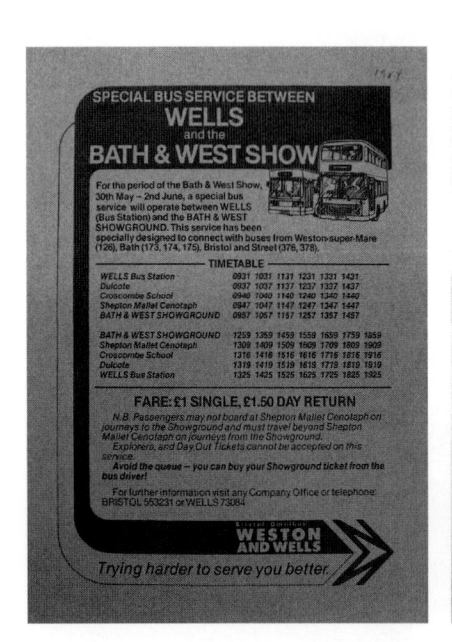

7. Moving Away From Green

Although public transport usage in Britain had been gradually declining after its peak in the 1950s – and Bristol and the surrounding areas had followed these trends – the structure of the bus industry had remained largely unchanged following nationalisation of the Tilling group in 1948.

Buses formed an important and indeed essential part of almost every British family's life throughout most of the postwar period and so prominent were the bus fleets in British towns and cities, that the colours they wore often intrinsically characterised the very location. That's why, to most citizens of the time, it actually mattered what colour their buses were as often it represented a significant feature of their daily lives. Outside London, this situation has largely disappeared today.

Nevertheless, public transport was often criticised. As passenger losses increased, services were cut or required financial support from local government while fares inevitably increased too, resulting in a generally less attractive service overall.

The 1985 Transport Act was to change the framework in which bus services were operated – at first instilling new life into the bus industry, although in the long term the results have been very mixed. Already, there had been a relaxation in licensing requirements for express coach services as a result of the 1980 Transport Act.

From 26th October 1986 all local bus services outside London were deregulated while in addition, each of the 72 subsidiaries of the state-owned National Bus Company was, one-by-one, privatised over the period from July 1986 to March 1988. Deregulation and privatisation became the order of the day. Initially, the return of brighter liveries and improved promotion of services resulted. A great many companies – including those throughout the former Bristol Omnibus territory – commenced operation of high-frequency minibus services in urban areas; while elsewhere the return of crew operation attempted to win back passengers.

However, the bus industry was to change constantly. The government had a vision of lots of competing operators reacting to offer high standards of service but over the next decade a process of consolidation and expansion was to follow, so that by the 1990s a handful of major groups once again controlled most of the country's bus services, which were now back in private ownership. Local authority influence over services varied considerably from area to area, but to a large extent public coordination of services had been lost. Inevitably, operators at first competed over the most profitable routes while many poorly patronised services, particularly in rural areas, were lost forever.

Even before the full effects of the 1985 Act were known, orders for new, full-sized buses fell dramatically which had a catastrophic effect on bus manufacturing in Britain. Bristol Commercial Vehicles had closed by the end of 1983 while Eastern Coach Works followed early in 1987. Their products continued to be made elsewhere under the 'Leyland' name, but even this once mighty manufacturer was to fall victim to falling orders and was rapidly engulfed by overseas producers.

Although the National Bus Company had, generally, merged operators together, with smaller fleets often completely absorbed by larger companies in an attempt to reduce overheads, this situation was reversed prior to privatisation, with a number of previously disused company names being revived in the process. In addition, engineering and accountancy units were created to continue to serve the operating companies, but few lasted very long – each new company preferring instead to deal directly with these functions, especially where rival concerns were created from former components of the same company.

As already described, in the case of the Bristol Omnibus Company Ltd, its operations were divided into three. The Cheltenham & Gloucester Omni-bus Company was formed in September 1983 to take over the operations centred on Cheltenham (whose buses became red once more, reviving the Cheltenham District name); Gloucester (with blue buses carrying a City of Gloucester fleetname); Stroud (retaining green but with the Bristol name replaced by Stroud Valleys) and Swindon (which shared Cheltenham's red livery, with a Swindon and District fleetname). For the time being, these liveries continued to be applied in NBC house-style.

Just over three years later, in October 1986, Cheltenham & Gloucester was sold to its management as part of the privatisation process, with the individual area identities strengthened by revising the shades and fleetnames employed. The company thrived for several more years before finally being absorbed, late in 1993, by Stagecoach, one of the country's largest and most acquisitive group of bus companies. Corporate Stagecoach livery soon appeared on vehicles throughout the Cheltenham & Gloucester territory, initially comprising white with orange, red and blue stripes and later white with the relief colours arranged in segments.

The country bus section of Bristol Omnibus became Badgerline, with vehicles finished in a bright green and yellow livery. Olympian doubles were built by Leyland after the closure of BCV and ECW. Here, at Bath bus station on their first day in service during October 1989, are Leyland Olympians 9005 & 9010, with bus and coach fronts respectively. (*M.S.Curtis*)

Whilst buses with similar livery could be found throughout the length and breadth of Britain, thereby removing the local identities, many former Bristol Omnibus staff continued to be employed and some high-quality services were established throughout the region, under the Stagecoach brand.

From April 1985, the remainder of the Bristol Omnibus fleet started to appear in two guises, carrying new names and colours. The Bristol country services fleet was henceforth re-branded as 'Badgerline' – a bold departure from the previous company image although the main depot names of Bristol, Bath, Wells or Weston remained displayed on vehicle sides, even when the new fleet colours of bright green and deep yellow were applied in an unconventional diagonal fashion. A new company, Badgerline Ltd, was formed in time for all 'country' vehicles, staff and operations to be taken under its control from the beginning of 1986. During September that year, the management successfully purchased the company, to become only the second NBC operating subsidiary to be sold. This gave Badgerline a considerable advantage as the opportunity arose to bid for further NBC companies as they became available. As a result, and through further acquisition, Badgerline expanded into a group which, from its Weston-super-Mare base, controlled not only the former Bristol country services but later, other bus companies providing services in many parts of England and Wales.

Finally, city services in and around Bristol itself remained as the 'Bristol Omnibus Company' but trading under the title of 'City Line'. At the same time as Badgerline's new image was launched, City Line vehicles began to appear in liveries comprising red, blue and yellow in various styles. Fleetnames included 'City Rider', 'City Clipper' and 'City Dart' but despite the BOC title being retained, and with all services centred on this important West Country conurbation, no other mention was made of 'Bristol' in the livery – which was perhaps extraordinary, especially since Bristolians have long held a certain pride in their home city.

In contrast to Badgerline, City Line was among the later NBC operating companies to be sold. This occurred during September 1987, when the company was acquired by Midland Red West, another former NBC operating company purchased by its management the year before. However, in April 1988 Midland Red West became part of the growing Badgerline group, which brought City Line and Badgerline back under common ownership.

These were innovative years when the Badgerline organisation was rarely out of the headlines,

In the colours of City Line, as the Bristol city section of Bristol Omnibus became, Olympian 9554, the last bus ever built by Bristol Commercial Vehicles for the Bristol Omnibus fleet, takes a corner at speed at Longwell Green. (*M.S.Curtis*)

management and staff morale was extremely high and the group as a whole was viewed as one of the leading companies in the transport industry. After several years of growth, the Badgerline group merged with the GRT bus group in June 1995, to create FirstBus.

Like several other emerging transport groups, FirstBus gradually adopted a corporate livery style but unlike others, decided to drop references to local areas on its vehicles, and even the group title was shortened to simply 'First' during ensuing years. It is therefore First who became largely, but not entirely, responsible for bus services in the former Badgerline and City Line areas, with some buses finished in a predominantly dark blue and white livery application, reminiscent of pre-war Bristol Tramways livery! As part of the inevitable rationalisation that occurs with the formation of large organisations, a considerable number of former Bristol Omnibus managers and staff did not stay with FirstBus, leaving an unusually severe break in the chain of experienced personnel to carry forward operations.

Even the title 'Bristol Omnibus Company' was itself removed from 1st March 1999, when the local company was renamed 'First Bristol Buses Ltd', finally severing the link with its historic past.

The only other NBC sale of a Bristol-related company occurred in March 1987, with the disposal of Bristol Engineering Ltd. This was formed largely from the company's Central Repair Works which had previously undertaken major chassis, engine and body overhaul work and hoped to serve the newly privatised bus companies, as well as attracting new customers. Much of the former CRW premises then became a Leyland service centre which survived for a few years as a servicing and repair facility, and parts supplier, but was progressively merged with the local Volvo Truck & Bus agency, eventually vacating the Lawrence Hill workshops.

Bristol's Green Years had reached a conclusion therefore with the arrival of deregulation and the privatisation of the former Bristol Omnibus Company. However, a little of the old company survives to remind us and future generations of when green buses, usually built in Bristol, provided the principal means of transport for the inhabitants of the city and surrounding areas.

In early 1972, when Tilling green and cream buses still dominated many of the local streets, a group of three enthusiasts formed the Bristol Vintage Bus Group, dedicated to the restoration and preservation of former Bristol Tramways and Bristol Omnibus vehicles. Their work proved to be an inspiration to other preservationists and has resulted in various Bristol vehicles being saved and regularly run.

First now dominates the former operating areas of City Line and Badgerline, having inherited their services. Their predominantly dark blue and white livery is almost a return to Bristol Tramways' pre-war colours of 70 years earlier. This Wright-bodied Volvo is operating through Saltford, on a section of route that was among the first to see motor buses 100 years ago. (*M.S.Curtis*)

Other Bristol vehicles also survive in private ownership, including the Bristol Road Transport Collection which is closely associated with the Bristol Aero Collection; and the Bristol Omnibus Vehicle Collection. The latter was formed in recent years with the authors of this book closely involved. This growing collection is now approaching 20 vehicles and includes the first underfloor-engined Bristol bus, NHU 2, the prototype LSX, together with A954 SAE, an Olympian double-decker which was the last Bristol-built vehicle supplied to the Bristol operating company.

Finally, the company titles, 'Bristol Tramways & Carriage Co Ltd' and 'Bristol Omnibus Company Ltd' which fell into disuse for a short time, were acquired in December 2003 by the authors of this book, for possible re-activation in connection with the archiving and preservation of the company history.

These preservation activities, together with the huge photographic archive which remains of the company's activities, should ensure that Bristol Omnibus Services – the Green Years will be remembered for generations to come.

The Green Years are recalled by many preserved vehicles from the former Bristol fleet. This early Bristol MW followed by the original LS, form part of the Bristol Omnibus Vehicle Collection. (*M.S.Curtis*)

(*above*) A delightful postcard portraying Bristol City Centre in the early 1960s, showing Bristol KSW and FLF double-deckers together with one solitary Bristol L-type saloon. The KSW furthest from the camera is at the stop outside of the company's mock Tudor head offices and 'under the clock'; other traffic is scarce. It is difficult to believe that the central area has been built over the river, and would at one time have been alive with shipping – hence the name of the road to the right of the picture, Broad Quay. (*Photographic Greeting Card Company*)

(*below*) Most Duple-bodied Bedford OBs carried the Vista coach body; the bus body was much less common. Bristol 215 (MHU 54) of 1950 is pictured leaving Stroud bus station, the last home of these buses with the company. By the time of their withdrawal in 1962, the simple yet dignified block capital BRISTOL had replaced the Bristol crest as the fleetname. (*Ken Jubb*)

(*above*)1942 Bristol K-type 3629 (HHU 890) with a 1938 Bristol-built body, at Bristol Tramways Centre in 1952. 3629 was built with a Park Royal body, but in common with many of Bristol's wartime buses, received a second body in 1951. The livery of 3629 is of the brighter 'Festival of Britain' style; what was to become the standard green and cream layout is shown on the double-decker behind, with black mudguards replacing green. (*C. Carter*)

(*below*) Resting outside Bath Abbey is 1936 Bristol GO5G 3814 (DKN 31), acquired by the company from Maidstone & District Motor Services in 1939, in exchange for a new Bristol K-type, and allocated to the Bath Electric Tramways fleet. The bus was re-bodied with a new 59-seat ECW body in 1950, and carries the 'Festival of Britain' livery in this 1952 view. (*C. Carter*)

(*above*) Bristol Joint Services C3105, a 1938 Bristol K5G, had its tall radiator and high bonnet line replaced with the more modern look when it was re-bodied by Bristol's own body works in 1949. The livery is 'Festival of Britain' style, although this time with black wheels and wings. (*M. Mogridge*)

(*below*) In the mid 1960s, the wings and wheels of Bristol's buses were again painted dark Brunswick green, as depicted on Joint Services Bristol KSW C8233 of 1955, climbing out of Sea Mills en route to central Bristol and Lockleaze. (*M. Walker*)

(*above*) New to Bath Electric Tramways in September 1956, L8382 (WHY 937), an LD Lodekka, is in standard Tilling green and cream with black wings, with the 'Bath Services' fleetname. (*Ken Jubb*)

(*below*) The prototype Bristol FLF (995 EHW), after renumbering from LC8540 to LC7000, and with a modification to the front Cave Browne Cave radiator grilles that remained unique to this vehicle, but still with the hopper ventilators that were replaced with sliding ones by 1964. The red paint on the radiator header tank pressure cap indicates that the bus has been treated with antifreeze. The livery represents the company's standard double-deck livery of the late 1950s and very early 1960s. (*Bristol Vintage Bus Group*)

(*above*) Country services 7117 is a 1963 Bristol FLF Lodekka in Tilling green and cream, but still with black wings, and the Bristol scroll fleetname. It is seen at Stroud bus station, operating the Chalford-Stroud-Stonehouse service 421, the depot's busiest and most frequent route. (*Ken Jubb*)

(*below*) Bristol FLF C7135 (828 SHW) of the Bristol Joint Services fleet, exhibits a hybrid livery in this September 1973 view. Painted in National green and white, the bus still has Brunswick green wings and, of course, the Bristol scroll fleetname with the small city coat of arms. It is at Lawrence Hill depot, dressed for the service to Fry's chocolate factory at Somerdale near Keynsham. (*M.S. Curtis*)

229

(*above*) LHY 989 was delivered in 1950 as 33-seat, twin-doorway Joint Services bus numbered C2749, but became country services 2488 when it was converted to a 35-seater, one-man bus in 1959. In this form it is shown at Weston-super-Mare railway station, waiting to depart on the South Road circular service, one of the earliest routes in the town to be operated without a conductor. The livery style, together with the Bristol coat of arms, represents the 1950s standard for L-type buses. Note also the folded radiator blind: drivers would be advised each day of 'today's screen position', dependent upon the ambient temperature, and the degree of engine cooling required. The destination display has been rebuilt from the former 36 by 18 inches standard to the new 36 by 12 inches. (*M. Mogridge*)

(*left*) 2041 (KHW 310E) was the first of a new generation of dual-purpose vehicles; it was a Bristol RELH model with 47 semi-coach seats in its ECW body, and entered service in May 1967. Looking resplendent in its green and cream colour scheme, with shining brightwork and wheel discs, it is seen in Shepherd's Bush, London, when only three months old. (*M. Walker*)

(*above*) Bristol MW 45-seat service bus 2622, new in July 1965, represents the standard National green and white livery applied to the fleet, a scheme which contrasts with Ledbury' 17th-century, black and white Market Hall. (*Ken Jubb*)

(*below*) 1968 Bristol RELL 1088 illustrates the last version of the traditional Tilling green and cream livery for one-man operated buses, and the sloping 'Bath Services' fleetname that was applied to Bath's single-deckers of the period. Delivered to Bath Electric Tramways as a 53-seat, single-door bus, it was converted to a dual-door, 44-seater when only a year old for operating without a conductor on Bath City services, where it is pictured in September 1973. (*M.S. Curtis*)

(*above*) Bristol's first batch of eight Bristol VRT dual-door, 70-seaters were the only ones to receive the brighter livery. Three of them pass close to their operating base, Muller Road depot, in this 1972 view, the two facing the camera being outbound from the city to Lockleaze. Only six of this batch of K-registered VRs were scheduled for service at any one time, and the two closest to the camera should have been at least ten minutes apart. The white and magenta Bristol Greyhound MW coach ascending the hill in the traffic queue is almost certainly two-man operated and running on a works service from the aircraft factories at Filton or Patchway. (*M. Walker*)

(*left*) A non-standard version of NBC white and green livery adorns semi-coach 2078 (GHY 140K), the last of the 1969 Bristol RELH 49-seat, dual-purpose buses, seen here at Cheltenham whilst operating an express service. (*Ken Jubb*)

232

(*right*) This postcard view captures a typically British seaside scene at Weston-super-Mare in the early 1960s. One of the four convertible open-top Bristol FS buses based in the town stands at the Old Pier (Birnbeck) terminus ready to return to Uphill on seafront service 152. The bus would have made a three-point turn to reach this position on the bus stop. The crew, in their lightweight summer jackets, are upstairs, looking over to the pier where one of P. & A. Campbell's steamers is docked. At busy times during the 1950s the pier approach car park would have been full of buses awaiting the steamer's arrival. (© *J. Salmon Ltd, Sevenoaks, Kent*)

(*below*) The Weston-super-Mare open-top fleet was repainted from the traditional cream for the 1976 season, and carried liveries that represented the tramway systems within the company's operating area, together with a unique name for each bus. In this company publicity photograph, which was sold as a postcard, the unique Bristol FLF open-topper, 7900 (841 SHW), stands beside one of the two former Crosville Bristol LD convertible open-toppers, and two of the convertible open-top Bristol FS buses. The liveries represent, from left to right, Bristol (with Concorde on the side panels), Weston-super-Mare (Grand Pier), Bath (Royal Crescent) and Swindon (the steam locomotive City of Truro). (*Bristol Omnibus*)

(*above*) The final, colour version of the National logo is worn by Cheltenham's 3505, a 1980 Leyland National 2 52-seat bus, seen leaving the town's Royal Well bus station for Tewkesbury, at the northern edge of the company's operating territory. (*Ken Jubb*)

(*below*) 1953 Bristol LS coach 2863, along with some others of the batch of 10, was delivered in a non-standard livery of cream and black, but was shortly repainted into the standard cream and green coach livery. In this view the only clue to ownership is the Greyhound symbol on the side panels. (*Bristol Vintage Bus Group*)

(*left*) The 'Berni bus', C7109, a 1963 Joint Services Bristol FLF, received the company's first over-all advertisement livery in November 1971 and is seen here at Southmead on service 87. It was later returned to fleet livery, but was the first of many to carry over-all advertisements. (*M. Walker*)

(*right*) Bristol-built, Roe-bodied Olympian 9529 (LWS 45Y), of 1982, passes through the Haymarket area of the city's shopping centre, wearing the 'City Clipper' livery applied to the network of limited stop services introduced in 1985, at the very end of the Green Years. (*Ken Jubb*)

(*right*) Bristol Greyhound's second Plaxton-bodied Leyland Leopard coach, 2158 (YHU 522J), represents the white and magenta coach livery; subsequent deliveries of Leyland Leopards would have the silhouette Greyhound represented in full colour. (*Bristol Omnibus*)

(*left*) In the opinion of the authors the 1968 ECW-bodied, 45-seat Bristol RELH coaches were the best ever operated by Bristol Greyhound, being dressed in the then current cream and signal red livery and with a bold script fleetname. Seven of the eight coaches can be seen in what was a ten coach private hire in connection with the opening of the new National Smelting Works by the then Prime Minister at Avonmouth on 10th May 1968. (*Bristol Omnibus*)

(*right*) Coach 2104, the 1978 Plaxton Supreme-bodied Leyland Leopard acquired from National Travel (South West), photographed in Bristol's Marlborough Street bus and coach station in March 1983, and wearing the Kingfisher blue and white 'local coach' livery. The depot offices and staff canteen are behind the coach. (*Ken Jubb*)

(*above*) The diminutive Trojan that came from the Wilts & Dorset company, who had in turn acquired it with the business of Silver Star Motor Services, 2049 (367 BAA). Whilst with Bristol it spent most of its life providing a link between the Pump Room and the Assembly Rooms at Bath, and is pictured here outside Bath Abbey, on a wet day in the city. (*Ken Jubb*)

(*below*) As recorded, over the twelve months of 1975 the Cheltenham District fleet was transformed from red to green. The company's two 1965 Bristol FLF buses are seen here during the changeover period in June of that year. 7184 (BHY 715C), in red, pulls past 7185 (BHY 716C), in green, in Cheltenham town centre. (*M.S. Curtis*)

(*left*) Cheltenham District's 84 (OHY 954), a sixty-seat, open-platform Bristol KSW of 1953, in Cheltenham's red and cream livery and with the town's crest in the middle of the fleetname. (*Bristol Vintage Bus Group*)

(*right*) Cheltenham District's 7075, a 70-seat Bristol FLF that entered service at the end of 1962. The yellow fleet number plate behind the open door indicates that this bus is allocated to the northern division. (*Bristol Vintage Bus Group*)

(*left*) Only two Bristol KSWs were ever painted into National red livery, both from the Cheltenham District fleet. Bus number 8562 (previously 91), of 1955, still looks good in June 1975 despite its 20 years of age. The bus carries the Cheltenham arms, the Cheltenham fleetname, and the National logo. It was withdrawn from service later the same year. (*M.S. Curtis*)

(*left*) Two of the three 3-seat Morris Marina cars hired by the company from Godfrey Davies vehicle rentals for the Dial-a-Ride scheme operated in partnership with British Rail, seen here at the new Bristol Parkway railway station in April 1972. Note the standard company legal lettering on the front door of LKG 579K. (*M. Walker*)

(*right*) In this January 1973 view at Bristol's Lawrence Hill depot, tuition bus NAE 30, formerly C3475, one of the 1951 batch of 7'6" wide Bristol KS types, wears the old training bus colours of fleet livery with an orange stripe. This colour scheme was, at the time, being replaced by the cream and orange colour scheme of the unidentified tuition bus behind. (*M. Walker*)

(*left*) The second generation mobile Inspector's 'BRUIN' cars for Joint Services never did have the same appeal as the Morris Minor saloons. Morris Marina van LHY 803L in National green with the National logo on the side panel and the scroll on the roof sign, is pictured at Bristol's Lawrence Hill depot in September 1974. The Transit van in front wears the older colour scheme. (*M.S. Curtis*)

(*right*) 'Jumbo' recovers Joint Services LC8443 (YHT 936), a 1957 Bristol LD, at Lawrence Weston, a large postwar estate to the west of the city in August 1969. Bristol's Central Repair Works built the bodies of three Jumbos on 4-wheel drive A.E.C. Matador chassis in 1964/1965. The orange colour scheme is highly visible. (*M. Walker*)

Acknowledgments

We would like to express our thanks to everyone who has assisted in the preparation of this book. As is often the case in works of this kind, a great many people generously supply material which is thoroughly examined to form the basis of the final text, but which often cannot be fully included owing to space restrictions.

A number of individuals assisted us with our research and particular thanks go to those former staff (and others) who allowed themselves to be interviewed about their recollections: Chris Blick, Dave Bubier, Dave Clarke, Brian Ede, Geoff Gould, Geoff Lusher, Clive Norman, Harold Ottway, Tony Peacey, Alan Peters, Barbara Rex and Fred Spencer.

Geoff Bruce and Allan Macfarlane, fellow 'Bristol' enthusiasts, together with Barbara Rex, read through and checked the draft, making many helpful suggestions. Kate Moon typed the interviews with former Bath staff.

The photographic selection is drawn from a wide range of sources, including those commissioned by the company itself, and these are individually acknowledged in the picture captions. However, the following should also be taken into account:

Those credited 'R.R. Bowler' were supplied by Brian Jackson of Weymouth, who found them among a large collection of transport photographs depicting a range of subjects.

'ECW' indicates Eastern Coach Works. Many from the pre-1960 era are now privately owned by Simon Butler, who has enabled them to remain available and has produced copies to superb printing standards. Later versions have in some cases been obtained from Brian Ollington Photographers.

Bristol Tramways/Bristol Omnibus photographs are acknowledged accordingly. Many of the street scenes commissioned by the company are now held by Bristol Record Office as part of the company archive. BRO has been of enormous assistance in making items available to view or copy. Mike Colson has enabled us to include other early street scenes and company pictures.

In addition, valuable assistance has been provided by Dave Withers, Phil Sposito, Alan Neal and the team from Bristol Vintage Bus Group. Thanks go also to the Bristol Interest Circle, Bristol Reference Library, Peter Davey, Madge Dresser, John England, Allan Field, John Hambley, Brian Hussey, Ian Allan Library, Allen Janes, Ken Jubb, Kevin McCormack, Mike Mogridge, Malcolm Morgan, Tony Peacey, The PSV Circle and The Omnibus Society.

Words to the 'Bristol Buses' song are reproduced by kind permission of Keith Christmas.

It has been a pleasure and privilege to prepare this account of *Bristol Omnibus Services – The Green Years*. We hope that those interested in transport history together with former staff and 'Bristol' bus passengers – of whom there are many thousands – find something of interest within its pages.

Bibliography

Bristol Joint Services Committee minutes
Bristol Tramways & Carriage Company minutes
Bristol Omnibus Company minutes
ABC Bristol, Ian Allan, London, 1949 to 1966
Buses Illustrated and *Buses* magazines,
   Ian Allan, London, 1949 to date
MCW Gazette and *BCV Magazine*, staff magazines of
   Bristol bus manufacturing works, 1946 to 1971
Omnibus, staff magazine of Bristol Tramways/Bristol
   Omnibus, 1954 to 1972
The People's Carriage, Bristol Omnibus Company, 1974
The War that went on Wheels, The Tilling Group, London,
   1946
Appleby, John B., *Cheltenham's Trams & Buses Remembered*,
   Transport Publishing Company, Glossop, 1973
Batten, John, various unpublished articles
Birks, John A., *The National Bus Company, 1968-1989*,
   Transport Publishing Company, Glossop, 1990
Chislett, Steve, *Buses and Trams of Bath*,
   Millstream Books, Bath, 1986
Curtis, Martin S., *Bristol – A Century on the Road*,
   Glasney Press, Falmouth, 1978
Curtis, Martin S., *Bristol Buses in Camera*,
   Ian Allan, London, 1984
Daniels, N.P., *Stroud's Buses*,
   Matador Publishing, Market Harborough, 2003
Davey, Peter, *My First 44 Photographs* series,
   privately published, 1990s and 2000s
Dresser, Madge, *Black and White on the Buses*,
   Bristol Broadsides (Co-op) Limited, Bristol, 1986
Jones, Geoffrey, *75 Years of The Traffic Commissioners*,
   Roads and Road Transport History Association, 2006
Jones, Graham & Macfarlane, Allan, *The Bristol KSW*,
   Oxford Publishing Company, Oxford, 1985
Macfarlane, Allan, *A Pictorial Tribute to The Bristol
   Omnibus Company, 1936-1983*,
   Oxford Publishing Company, Oxford, 1985
Martin, Colin, *Cheltenham's Buses, 1939-1980*,
   Tempus Publishing, Stroud, 2001
PSV Circle/Omnibus Society, various publications

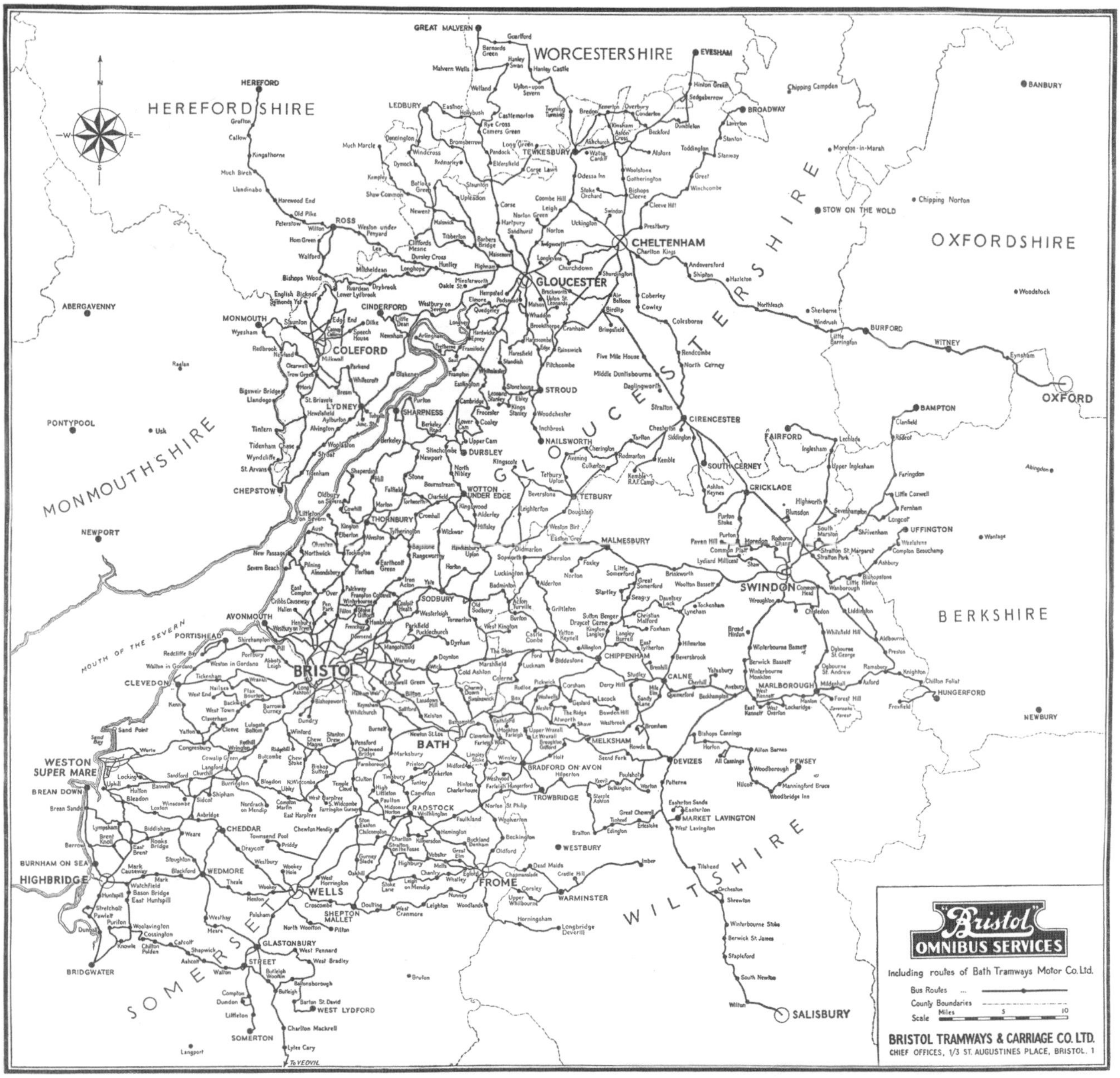
"Bristol"
OMNIBUS SERVICES
Including routes of Bath Tramways Motor Co. Ltd.
Bus Routes ...
County Boundaries
Scale Miles 5 10
BRISTOL TRAMWAYS & CARRIAGE CO. LTD.
CHIEF OFFICES, 1/3 ST. AUGUSTINES PLACE, BRISTOL. 1
WORCESTERSHIRE
HEREFORDSHIRE
GLOUCESTERSHIRE
OXFORDSHIRE
MONMOUTHSHIRE
BERKSHIRE
WILTSHIRE
SOMERSET
MOUTH OF THE SEVERN
GREAT MALVERN
EVESHAM
HEREFORD
BROADWAY
TEWKESBURY
CHELTENHAM
GLOUCESTER
ROSS
CINDERFORD
COLEFORD
MONMOUTH
LYDNEY
SHARPNESS
STROUD
NAILSWORTH
DURSLEY
WOTTON UNDER EDGE
TETBURY
CIRENCESTER
FAIRFORD
SOUTH CERNEY
CRICKLADE
BAMPTON
BURFORD
WITNEY
OXFORD
STOW ON THE WOLD
BANBURY
CHEPSTOW
NEWPORT
ABERGAVENNY
PONTYPOOL
THORNBURY
MALMESBURY
SWINDON
UFFINGTON
SODBURY
AVONMOUTH
PORTISHEAD
CLEVEDON
BRISTOL
CHIPPENHAM
CALNE
MARLBOROUGH
HUNGERFORD
NEWBURY
MELKSHAM
DEVIZES
PEWSEY
BATH
BRADFORD ON AVON
TROWBRIDGE
WESTBURY
WARMINSTER
MARKET LAVINGTON
RADSTOCK
FROME
WESTON SUPER MARE
BREAN DOWN
BURNHAM ON SEA
HIGHBRIDGE
CHEDDAR
WEDMORE
WELLS
SHEPTON MALLET
GLASTONBURY
STREET
BRIDGWATER
SOMERTON
WEST LYDFORD
SALISBURY
To YEOVIL